MUDLARK'S GHOSTS

AND THE RESTORATION
OF A HERRESHOFF
MEADOW LARK

Ian Scott

MUDLARK'S GHOSTS

and the restoration of a Herreshoff Meadow Lark

SEAFARER BOOKS

SHERIDAN HOUSE

For Glynis, Carey, Caitlin, Catriona, Cameron
and the next sailing generation – Matilda, Felix, Isabella ...
and those to come

© Ian Scott 2006

Published in the UK by
Seafarer Books • 102 Redwald Road • Rendlesham • Suffolk IP12 2TE • England
www.seafarerbooks.com
ISBN-10 0-9550243-1-5
ISBN-13 978-0-9550243-1-3

Published in the USA by
Sheridan House • 145 Palisade Street • Dobbs Ferry NY 10522 • USA
www.sheridanhouse.com
ISBN-10 1-57409-245-6
ISBN-13 978-1-57409-245-5

A CIP record for this book in the UK is available from the British Library
A CIP record for this book in the USA is available from the Library of Congress

Photographs and illustrations © Ian Scott unless otherwise credited.

Boat fittings illustrations on pages 65, 91, 154, 155, 164 and 165 © Davey & Company, London, Ltd

Frontispiece; maps on pages 15, 34, 36, 67, 104, 105, 158 and 163;
and structural diagrams on pages 61, 73, 113, 168 and169: Louis Mackay, © Ian Scott

Copy-editing: Hugh Brazier

Design and typesetting: Louis Mackay
Text set digitally in Proforma

Printed in China, on behalf of Compass Press Ltd,
via MBC Print Consultancy

Contents

7 Foreword

9 Thanks

11 Introduction

18 **1 PASSIONS**

18 A passion for boats

25 A passion for wood

32 **2 MUDLARK AND ME**

32 Sharpies

33 Twelve Square Metres

40 A proper boat

44 L Francis Herreshoff

47 Meadow Lark

55 *Mudlark*'s Ghosts

57 Fenwick C Williams

58 Dr Horvath's request

59 Mr Williams's response

67 The builder

68 Why Mr Smith did what Mr Smith did

75 Ownership

83 3 THE FIRST SEVEN YEARS

88 First draft: what not to do

92 Second draft: the return of the bumbler

99 Third draft: the chequebook years

111 4 REMAKING MUDLARK

111 2000: the deconstruction story

114 From hard ...

116 To harder ...

117 And harder ...

118 The game plan

124 The hardest job I've ever done

126 Time out

128 2001: Deconstruction (continued)

132 2002: The frame's the thing

139 Boarding school

143 Fair thee well

145 Back to the bottom

146 But this is where I came in!

150 Back to work

162 January to July 2005

164 August to December 2005

165 Last act

168 Some technical terms

170 Bibliography

172 Ian Scott

Foreword

Into this world of mass production comes this one-off book by a one-off author about a one-off boat.

There have been several boating books in which the author describes rebuilding an old wooden boat – but invariably the rebuild is the preamble to some boating odyssey. Yet here there is no epic voyage: the rebuild is the amble. And amble not only conveys the pace of Ian Scott's restoration, it also hints at his willingness to pause for reflection – practical, historical and philosophical – along the way.

By one-off author, I don't mean one-book author; I mean Ian Scott is not your typical writer of boating books, nor indeed your typical boat owner. By my reckoning, he now has eleven boats: six at Wells-next-the-Sea in Norfolk, England; five at Oxford, Maryland, in the USA. That's eleven more boats than most people own and, I'd guess, nine more boats than most boat owners own. But once you get over any pang of envy for someone who has not one whole fleet of boats but two, the voice of boating experience tells you that eleven is a lot of boats to look after, especially when, at any one time, around half of them are on the wrong side of the Atlantic.

Mudlark, the one-off boat, is a kind of Meadow Lark. The Meadow Lark design was a svelte interpretation by the renowned yacht designer L Francis Herreshoff of the classic American sharpie, a long thin vessel with a shallow box-like mid-section. An easy-to-build shape but not a strong one – and certainly not in Meadow Lark's case because LFH had sacrificed strength of construction to simplicity of construction. Unfortunately, *Mudlark*, a modification of Meadow Lark by another famous designer, Fenwick C Williams, did not feature a stronger hull amongst any of his modifications. He did give her a bigger rig, however. And she had the small cabin and twin cockpits requested by her commissioning owner, Dr Horvath. And she was built by a semi-pro boatbuilder who used a great deal of walnut; not a marine timber. *Mudlark* is most definitely a one-off.

Restore an old car or motorbike and, though the original manufacturer may be long gone, chances are you can get hold of a workshop manual to tell you how it all went together. It's not like that when you're rebuilding an old wooden boat. Even when new, there wasn't a workshop manual. Instead, there was an individual craftsman who personally fabricated individual components to fit other individual components made by other individual craftsmen. While they were not always making it up as they went along, from this distance in time and technology it can seem as if they were. And while they were not by any means always making mistakes, sometimes – and the real devotees find this very hard to accept – they were. Yes, back then in the golden age of custom boatbuilding, reputable designers and craftsmen sometimes made cock-ups. Just like you and me. For this reason if for no other – and this book merits reading for many reasons – this book should be required reading for anyone contemplating doing up an old wooden boat.

Pete Greenfield

www.watercraft-magazine.com

Thanks

Authors' thanks to spouses sometimes seem like afterthoughts at the end of Oscar-like lists of everybody associated with the book. I know they're not. I know most authors know that without spouse support their books might have stayed unwritten. And I know spouses tend to understand. Nonetheless, I want to start with love and gratitude to Glynis, without whom there would have been no *Mudlark*, no restoration and no book. This is for her. That is to say the book; I'll hang on to the boat.

Love and thanks to my son Cameron, who spent many teen weekends on board when he might have had more fun at home and later, in university vacations, helped deconstruct and reconstruct the boat. The place I told him to put his hand when I drilled through the stem into the cutwater is permanently recorded (under the paint) as 'Cam's Hole'. And to Catriona, who didn't touch *Mudlark* but paid her dues when she helped with *Moonfleet.*

Thanks (because it seems least invidious, in rough order of appearance) to the American crew: Pete Dunbar, who sold *Mudlark* to me in 1993; Bob Bauernfeind, who has been an invaluable and unflappable mentor since the start of my ownership; Tim McManus, Bob's former business partner; Georgiana Frost, who allowed me to stay on and on at Easton Point Marina and was kindness itself throughout my stay, as was Larry Russ who ran the marina yard; David Van Ness of Van Ness Engineering, who rebuilt my ancient engine – twice; Jack and Sharon Morrison, who welcomed me to Gateway Marina; Vicky, Jackie and Diane, who made it a cheerful place, and John Hummer and Rick Kayhoe for all their help; Maurice Ellison, who sorted out my sails; Steve at Oxford Boatyard, who renewed my running rigging; Skip Aldikan, who polished my bronze; Jane McCarthy, who took the launch picture; and, posthumously, Ted Squier, who never saw *Mudlark* but whose bequest of nautical literature aided her restoration.

Thanks (in no particular order) to my friends in Norfolk: Richard Cracknell, who on two visits to America with his wife Alison helped me understand what was wrong with my boat and gave me all sorts of advice; James Case, who told me about English boatbuilding techniques; Charlie Ward (whose barge yacht *Juno* is an inspiration to everyone), who shared his formidable wisdom on classic boats; Andrew Wolstenholme, who explained (to me) arcane aspects of yacht design and made a vital suggestion; John Crook, who sold me two other boats and lots of bits for this one; and posthumously, William Cracknell, who gave me hours of priceless advice and looked after my English boats with exquisite skill.

And thanks to those who made this book possible: Pete Greenfield, who published an article on the project in *Water Craft* in 2003 and wrote a thoughtful foreword for this book; Louis Mackay, who did a superb job of design; Hugh Brazier, who was a patient and sympathetic editor; the staff at Wells Public Library, who borrowed copies of books I owned in America but needed in England when I was writing this one; and above all Patricia Eve of Seafarer Books, whose encouragement, enthusiasm and patience literally made it happen.

None of the above is accountable for anything that might be wrong with either the boat – or the book.

Ian Scott
Wells-next-the-Sea, Norfolk
Oxford, Maryland
September 2006

Introduction

This book tells three interwoven stories. The first is the story of why I spent twelve years of a diminishing lifespan restoring a curiously modified and in some ways badly built interpretation of L Francis Herreshoff's leeboard sharpie ketch, Meadow Lark. The second is the story of how that experience shaped my appreciation of wooden boats, the timbers they are made of, the designers and craftsmen who make and repair them, the tools they use, the boatyards they work in, the towns and villages around the boatyards, the sailors who sail the boats and not least, my outlook on life. The third is the story of my efforts to understand decisions made by four dead men – designer L Francis Herreshoff, naval architect Fenwick C Williams, commissioning owner Dr Peter Horvath and builder U W Smith (collectively known as *Mudlark*'s Ghosts) – that affected the durability and performance of my boat and the challenges and frustrations I faced in restoring her. All three stories are told from the perspective of someone who works, lives and sails on both sides of the Atlantic and writes regularly about two nations divided by a common language – and reversed channel markers.

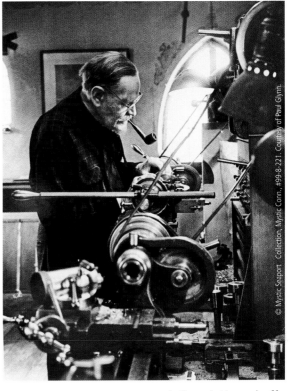

L. Francis Herreshoff at his lathe.

My Meadow Lark was originally named *Rozinante*, but for most of her 53 years she has been *Mudlark*. A more suitable name, I've always thought, because the image of London urchins scavenging in the muddy nineteenth-century margins of the River Thames – the original mudlarks – seems far closer to my creekcrawling, gunkholing, sail-in-a-heavy-dew *Mudlark* than James Baldwin's image of Don Quixote's 'ill-shaped, long-haired, short-maned, big-hoofed, knock-kneed, sway-backed, broad-eared, watery-eyed, slow-paced, awkward' mule (Baldwin 1905).

I also like the fact that *Mudlark*'s etymology rings transatlantic bells – although the bells are louder one side than the other.

I can rejoice that *Mudlark* is an all-American boat; that her designer was an all-American genius; that his Meadow Lark was an evolution of an all-American workboat; and that the modifications that make *Mudlark* different from every other Meadow Lark were dictated by the all-American environment of the Chesapeake Bay. Built on the Western Shore of the Bay in 1953, *Mudlark* has spent most of her

MY BOATS

Mudlark is the star of this book. But she was neither my first nor my last boat, and all the others have at least walk-on parts in what someone called my nautobiography. In order of appearance my boats are:

Shalom – a wood and canvas kayak, built 1962/3 (Wells) (sold 1965)

Tinqua – an International 12 Square Metre Sharpie, built 1947 (Wells) (sold 2003)

Pocahontas – a Twinkle Twelve dinghy, built c.1960 (Wells)

C4 – an 18-foot Old Town canoe (Oxford)

Mudlark – a Herreshoff Meadow Lark, modified by Fenwick C Williams, built 1953 (Oxford)

Lesser Mudlark – a Cabin Boy skiff, tender to Mudlark, built c.1985 (Oxford)

Moonfleet – a Lone Gull II, designed by Maurice Griffiths, built 1975 (Wells)

Metalark – an aluminium speedboat, built c.1947 (Oxford)

Outje Boutje – a Clinker pram dinghy, tender to Moonfleet, built c.1985 (Wells)

Matilda – a Dutch Tjotter, built c.1975 (Wells)

Meadowlark – a Columbia 21 daysailer, built c.1965 (Oxford)

Felix – a sea kayak, built 2002 (Wells)

Bubbles – a Baby Boat by Nanni Diesel, built 2004 (Wells)

life on the Eastern Shore and has never left the sheltered waters of America's largest estuary. Which is probably just as well – because neither the original (Meadow Lark) nor the modified *Mudlark* think much of big seas or heavy air, although I know at least one Meadow Lark made it from Florida to the Bahamas – and back.

I am more tentative about the Thames. I was born far too late to have seen mudlarks; my direct associations with the river have been limited to day trips from Richmond in the late 1940s and early '50s, departures from Westminster, a dunking at Oxford when I fell off a punt (the pole got stuck) and twice-daily commutes across the Vauxhall, Albert or Chelsea bridges (I varied my route) from central London to Wimbledon in the early '70s. I doubt my working-class London forebears foraged in low-tide ooze – though I suppose the odd mudlark might have hitched rides on my maternal great-grandfather's horse-drawn bus or, a generation later, filched drinks from the wine-house where my grandmother served them. Nor can I make much of my dim memories of fire-reddened skies as Thames-side docks burned after air-raids in the early 1940s. I can however claim I was born in London, lived there for 25 years and since moving to America in 1972 have visited more times than I can count, nowadays drawn by the irresistible pull of daughters and grandchildren on either side of the river.

For all that, we – *Mudlark* and I – have lived roughly parallel lives. True, I am twelve years older, but the gap gets proportionately smaller. In a marriage, a gap in age that seems big in the early days seems (and relatively is) smaller after a few decades – and so it is in this case, with one partner now 65 and the other 53.

When *Mudlark* was being built in 1953 Eisenhower was in the White House, the Korean War was winding down, sweets (a.k.a. candies) were still rationed in England, and boatbuilding materials were still scarce both there and in America (which explains why *Mudlark*'s bill of materials included exotic oddities).

When *Mudlark* was launched on Cuckold Creek off the Patuxent River in

April 1954 I was bicycling to school in short trousers, learning to play rugby, coping with early adolescence and beginning to acquire a vicarious knowledge of wooden boats by reading and re-reading Arthur Ransome's epic tales of small craft and small boys and girls on the English Lakes, the Norfolk Broads, the Suffolk marshes, the North Sea and the Hebrides. Although I didn't know it, and it was to be a long time before I set foot on one, my lasting affinity with wooden boats had taken root.

Glynis and I moved to Washington with our then small family in 1972 when I joined the World Bank. Over the next 25 years (except when we went to Martha's Vineyard) we returned every summer to north Norfolk, where we acquired a converted barn before barn conversions became popular, and began to acquire a small fleet of mostly wooden boats. It was not until the early '90s that time and circumstances allowed me to begin the acquisition of another small fleet of mostly not-wooden boats on the Chesapeake Bay, chief among them *Mudlark*. I retired in 1996 as a Director of the Bank to return to academia, write, consult, give speeches – and play with my boats on the left and right banks of the Atlantic Ocean.

The project to restore *Mudlark* was one of several new ventures that began with the new Millennium, and their parallel existence helps explain why it took so long to finish. *Mudlark* could certainly have been remade in less than five years if I had not got hung up on what

Mudlark under sail on the Tred Avon River, October 1993.

economists call intervening opportunities and other people call distractions, driven two long-distance motor rallies, re-engaged with academia, coordinated a couple of other long-term projects, given and sold advice, listened to myself talk, edited a book on Norfolk and proselytised for the *Eastern Daily Press* and the BBC.

Things would also have gone faster if *Mudlark* had been the only boat on my agenda but no, in the middle of the project I was seduced by an antique aluminium speedboat and bought a Columbia 21 for what I thought was a song only to discover – too late – that the main bulkhead was rotten and that I would have to spend months rebuilding it before I could sail her to my dock. And while *Mudlark* languished in America I used some of my time in Norfolk to build a sea kayak from an imported American kit and name it *Felix* for our grandson; buy and restore a Dutch Tjotter already named for our first granddaughter *Matilda*; buy and restore a Maurice Griffiths Lone Gull II called *Moonfleet* and a tender called *Outje Boutje*; buy a French sailboat advertised as the smallest vessel ever designed by a naval architect and call her *Bubbles* in honour of our second granddaughter; and maintain three other wooden boats I already had there.

It would also have helped if I had made more realistic allowances for the fact that each time I got back to *Mudlark* after my times-out I could not simply continue where I had left off. It took time, sometimes a long time, to find my tools, remember where I was in the process and regain my rhythm. It was particularly frustrating when I had barely re-started before it was time to take off again.

But the distractions had two positive sides. First, because almost all of them involved transatlantic travel, I was able to poke around chandleries in England, Denmark, Holland and Sweden for maritime objects not available in the USA. The name badges on the bow, the mainsheet winch, the main-hatch runners, some of the cabin lights and oil lamps, the engine hatch doors, two of the new portlights, a clutch of Tufnol blocks and two Walker logs come to mind.

Second, while my approach to the job was initially anchored in Chesapeake practices, customs and traditions passed on by friendly advisers, my irregular but frequent visits to England and conversations with English boatbuilders and restorers gave me other ideas. At times I was confused. Who should I trust? Whose method was best? Could I try both? The result was a hybrid that, to my mind at least, married if not the best of each, then an array of alternatives, including at least one that turned out to be crucial.

This is neither a 'how to' nor a 'how not to' book, although there is practical stuff – much of it in the 'how not to' category – that someone like myself with more commitment, enthusiasm and time than experience, skill or knowledge might find useful. Indeed one reason for writing this book was to demonstrate that anybody can take on projects like this if they really want to, that old boats, if not too far gone, are not for burning, and (truly) that if I can do it anybody can do it.

The second reason for writing the book was to demonstrate that the returns on a project like this far exceed the obvious ones of saving a piece of maritime heritage, saving a lot of money, assembling a formidable set of tools, and acquiring the skills to use them reasonably safely and more or less effectively. I did not anticipate how this project would change the way I thought about work, craftsmanship and risk. Still less did I think it would change the way I look at workers, craftsmen and risk-takers. I am not a better person for having done it, but I believe I am a more appreciative one.

This is almost as much a book of pictures as it is a book of words, or as a publisher friend said of another volume, as much a 'looking book' as a 'reading book'. There are pictures and drawings that describe Herreshoff's original Meadow Lark as published in *Rudder* in 1947; the modified design for *Mudlark* (derived from a set of nicely aged blueprints) drawn by Fenwick C Williams in 1952; pictures of the workshops where the action occurred, taken with whatever camera came to hand; pictures that record the restoration process from start to finish, including images of rotten wood, good fifty-year-old cedar, new mahogany and a marine engine that should probably be in a museum but is actually powering *Mudlark* into her second half-century; pictures of the cast of characters, dead and alive, who move like shadows through this book playing large parts in a small drama; and pictures of some of my other boats.

I have divided the text into four unequal parts. The first, which covers the background to the others, describes my passion for wooden boats; my views on the wooden boat revival; my particular fascination with *old* wooden boats (the 'wooden boats' in question being *recreational wooden sailing boats*, not wooden boats in general or wooden motor boats); my reflections on the wooden boat as a metaphor for durability, utility and continuity in a throwaway world (in which the American lawnmower engine manufacturer Briggs and Stratton has invented a disposable outboard); my conviction that because a wooden boat is an assembly of bits and pieces of wood with (keels apart) few straight lines, it is a source of endless inspiration; my belief that because carvel construction has not changed much in several centuries it is a precious link with the past; my (quizzical) reactions to people who go overboard on all this; and why I reject the notions that a cold-moulded hull is not a wooden boat, that trunnel fastenings are better than stainless ones and that hemp is superior to synthetic rope.

The Chesapeake Bay region, showing the position of Oxford, Maryland, in relation to Washington DC, the Delmarva (Delaware, Maryland, Virginia) peninsula and the Atlantic seaboard.

The second part describes my evolution (over many years) as a boat owner, my acquisition of two small collections of mostly wooden boats at Wells-next-the-Sea in Norfolk, England, and at Oxford, Maryland, USA, and my efforts to maintain, restore and sail them; my views on sharpies; and the 1993 purchase and initial restoration of *Mudlark*.

The third part covers the first seven years of my ownership of *Mudlark*, from 1993 to 2000, culminating in what I have called a moment of truth (in fact an extended moment) when I came to terms with the fact that without urgent surgery she would die – and my decision to save her with what (improbably) turned out to be my own hands.

The fourth and longest part of the book describes a three-month process that somehow stretched to more than six years and ended when she finally re-entered the waters of the Chesapeake Bay in 2006.

Having decided (in October 1999) that the boat would sink if she was not quickly restored, and that I must restore her myself, I describe my search for premises that culminated in the discovery of a heated boatshop at Easton Point, just a few miles up the Tred Avon River from Oxford; how with help from my son I removed the chineboards and found bad planks, bad bottom boards and a bad stem and asked anybody who would listen why this boat was not on the bottom of the Chesapeake Bay; why, for the first of many times, I wondered if I should quit before getting further down a Quixote-like path; and why I continued.

The story of deconstruction (2000–2003) traces the removal of the stem, parts of the bottom and sides, the fuel, water and electrical systems, the engine and peripherals, the cockpit, head, galley and interior until I had a bare hull. It is the story of what happens when you say to yourself, 'While I'm at it why don't I ...?', 'I might as well do that too', 'I'm never going to do this again so I must do it right', 'Why does everything take so much longer than expected?' and 'Thank God I'm not paying someone else to do this'. But it is also what happens when you conclude it would be absurd to do some of it right and some of it half-right and decide to spend as much time and money as it takes to do a proper job because this is probably the last time you will ever do something like this.

The story of reconstructing the hull (2003–2005) traces the rebuilding of the bow section (new stem, cutwater and bottom planking), replacing or sistering every frame in the boat, re-planking parts of the sides and bottom, refastening everything, filling every exterior seam with epoxy, battening the bottom seams, laminating double-layered chineboards on the sides and bottom, coating the hull inside and out with epoxy, refinishing the deck, replacing the portlights, rebuilding the coachroof and deck trim, and moving the boat from Easton Point to Gateway Marina on the Choptank River and installing her in splendid isolation on the ex-car-deck of a beached ferry boat that used to carry passengers across the mouth of the Chesapeake Bay, where I painted the hull, coachroof and deck with two-part polyurethane and varnished the brightwork. The book ends in 2006 with *Mudlark* not just restored but improved, back at her dock in Oxford, Maryland, after an absence that was meant to last three months and lasted more than six years.

The substantive themes interwoven with the chronologies of deconstruction and reconstruction range from reflections on tools, epoxy and paint, to reflections on boatyard communities and the people who live, work and hang round in them, to reflections on the distinctive culture of the Eastern Shore (and the in-some-ways superficially similar yet profoundly different culture of my English home in north Norfolk), to reflections on the workmanship of risk and the meaning of wooden boats.

The 'hands on' reflections tell how I became familiar with tools I had never heard of when I started; how I learnt, with the help of mostly minor operator errors (and only a handful of Emergency Room visits), to respect them; how I learnt that anything on a wooden boat can be fixed if you're willing to take the trouble to fix it; my gradual mastery of the WEST System, with extraordinary support from the technical staff at Gougeon Brothers in Bay City, Michigan, and less intensive but critical advice from Wessex Resins and Adhesives Ltd in England; and the advice I got from Bob Bauernfeind – without the promise of which I would never have started – and Dave Van Ness in Ridgewood, New Jersey – who spends his life restoring Graymarine engines and persuaded me mine could be made as good as new even though it is as old as the boat.

The reflections on boatyards contrast my dealings with the traditional, even venerable, up-market yards of Oxford, Maryland, with the middle-class yards and the rough-and-ready environment of Gateway Marina at Trappe, Maryland, where the process ended, as well as the marina at Easton Point, where most of the work was done. I also contrast my experiences at Eastern Shore yards with my experiences in Eastern England, pointing to similarities and contrasts in attitudes, values, workmanship and techniques.

My reflections on the Eastern Shore of the Chesapeake Bay are about the historic area of Talbot County and neighbouring Dorchester County (the settings for Michener's *Chesapeake*), focusing on genteel Oxford (first port of entry in Colonial Maryland), diverse Easton (seat of Talbot County government) and gritty Cambridge (in Dorchester), and the palpable contrasts between them.

My reflections on craftsmanship focus on how I balanced the trade-offs between time, money, technology and skill; how I learnt to appreciate the wisdom of David Pye's thoughts on the 'workmanship of risk' and how it applies to me as well as to such masters as Gannon and Benjamin in Vineyard Haven, Massachusetts; how I learnt to be humble; how my slow results became a source of growing pride and satisfaction; why I (and everyone I know) have stopped believing anything I say as to when (or if) I will finish – although except in quick-passing moments I never doubt I will; why I sometimes felt guilty because the monthly rent of the boatshop was more than some families could afford to spend on housing; and my deep and abiding gratitude to my wife, who put up with the bills as well as my frequent absences.

The Herreshoff yard, at Bristol, Rhode Island, where L Francis Herreshoff, son of the famous 'Captain Nat' Herreshoff, grew up and learned his craft before setting himself up independently as a yacht designer.

Ultimately, however, the most important reflections are based on my imaginary conversations with *Mudlark*'s Ghosts – the four men whose decisions about the original design and the modifications to it that, for better or worse, made *Mudlark* unlike any other Meadow Lark. Why did L Francis Herreshoff draw the chine log so small? Why did Dr Horvath insist on a smaller cabin and two cockpits when he knew that would change the sail plan? Why did Mr Williams change the sail plan but not the position of the leeboards, thereby creating lee helm? Why did Mr Smith butt planks on single frames and make the frames of walnut? Some of the questions – there were many others – were relatively inconsequential. Others went to the heart of *Mudlark*'s performance, durability, seaworthiness and safety.

My interpretations of their objectives, ambitions, values, habits, practices, norms, prejudices and constraints seem reasonable to me but may be right or wrong. There is no way to know if they would also have seemed reasonable to the Ghosts.

What wouldn't I give for just five minutes alone with each of them?

I
Passions

A passion for boats

Copacabana Beach, Rio de Janeiro, January 1983

● My flight to New York has been delayed. Annoying. But at least Varig told me about the delay before I left for the airport and I'd rather be in this hotel than in their lounge, which has too many chairs crammed into it.

My colleagues have already left so the delay means I have some hours to kill. I've seen much of what there is to see in Rio on previous visits and anyway I'm a lousy lone tourist. I'm not really hungry so I won't have an early dinner and although I know 38,000 feet is a stupid altitude to eat and drink I've always enjoyed Varig's food and wine even if I regret them later, so I'll wait anyway. Meanwhile I need something to read and economic reports aside there are just two options.

———◆———

● I'm sitting on the balcony overlooking the South Atlantic with Arthur Ransome's *Coot Club* in my hand and *Teasel, Titmouse, Death and Glory* and *Margoletta* in my imagination, re-reading, for the umpteenth time, the adventures of Tom Dudgeon, the twins, the odious George Owden, plodding PC Tedder and the Hullabaloos. And remembering this was the book that got me hooked on wooden boats.

I'm sure I'm neither the first nor last sailor whose passion for boats was prompted by Arthur Ransome. I know from the small library of books about Ransome that he was an oddball, as deeply flawed as the rest of us and, even, at times, quite unpleasant. But he certainly knew his boats, how to sail them and how to write about them. No one else, in my experience, has captured the feel of wooden boats as well as he did.

He writes about boats so evocatively you can not only see them, you can also hear and even smell them. No wonder he struck a chord that has resonated in me for nearly fifty years, though that does not explain why the chord was there. After all, lots of children must have read Ransome's books without falling in love with wooden boats. And most children who have fallen in love with wooden boats have never heard of Ransome. I suspect the boat-struck children of Port Townsend,

Washington and Annapolis, Maryland, not to mention the boat-struck children of Douarnenez, France, and Sydney, Australia, were incurably afflicted with boats in complete ignorance of *Swallows and Amazons*, *Secret Water* and *The Big Six*.

So where did the chord come from? Could it be genetic? It seems far-fetched particularly because, to the best of my knowledge, none of my relatives were boatbuilders or sailors. True, my father's wartime job was repairing motor torpedo boats and motor gun boats at Lowestoft. But that did not make him a boatbuilder any more than other fathers who became temporary soldiers, sailors and airmen became professional soldiers, sailors and airmen. At the end of the war they all went back to their regular jobs, just as in 1945 my father went back to carpentering houses and offices. So the answer is I don't know. I suppose few of us know where our obsessions came from, and have to settle for the fact that they exist.

Material matters

The purpose of a boat is to let you explore all or part of the two-thirds of the earth's surface not covered by land. Every wood, ferro-cement, fibreglass, aluminium or composite hull powered by oars, paddles or sails and/or petrol, diesel or electric motors is a magic device that, depending on its size, design and build can take you across a river, a pond, a lake, an estuary, a sea or an ocean.

Aircraft and wheeled vehicles are also magic devices and their magic, like that of boats, is a function of the fact they enable us to travel farther, faster, higher than we can travel without them (or in the air, at all). It has nothing to do with how they look or what they are made of. From a functional viewpoint – as a means of transport – the magic properties of a mass-produced fibreglass boat without aesthetic value that can cross the English Channel or the Chesapeake Bay quickly, safely and comfortably are equal to those of a handbuilt wooden boat that can do the same things. Just as, from a strictly functional viewpoint, the Volkswagen Corporation's $1,300,000 Bugatti Veyron is equal to its prosaic New Beetle. Both will get you from London to Brighton or from New York City to Chicago. The Beetle will just take a bit longer – although with traffic and speed traps, who knows?

It's at least theoretically possible that passions about fibreglass, aluminium or ferro-cement boats are rooted in affection for those materials. It's far more likely they are driven by an informed understanding of their physical and economic attributes, notably their strength-to-weight ratios, formability, initial costs, ease of repair and maintenance and their derived abilities to keep the sea, take the ground and withstand external shocks. America's Cup contenders have long been built of exotic materials, not because their designers were passionate about carbon fibre or Kevlar but because they were passionate about performance. Functionally speaking, the best boat is the boat that works best.

It is not then surprising that many of the world's most functional boats are built not of wood but of other materials. Raising my head about 30 degrees from its eyes-down position (I never learned to touch-type) I look nor'-nor'-west down the harbour channel to the yellow-walled red-roofed building that houses the Wells Lifeboat. Now I swivel about 20 degrees west to look across the quay at the memorial to the crew of the rowing-sailing lifeboat *Eliza Adams*, lost with all hands in 1881. Like many later boats she had a wood hull, but the hull of the *Doris Mann of Ampthill*, down there under the red roof, has a fibreglass hull because a heavily laid-up fibreglass is now the best material for the job.

In similar vein, Nansen's *Fram* had a massively reinforced wood hull with a rounded bottom that helped release her from the lateral grip of converging pack ice and was, for her time, a very capable vessel. But modern arctic exploration vessels have steel hulls because steel is now the best material for those extreme conditions.

Yet *Fram* was by no means the last boat to have a wood hull because wood was deemed best. Even in the 1960s, when it became increasingly fashionable to say wood hulls were too costly to build and maintain and the fibreglass revolution gathered momentum, a few builders continued to argue that for certain purposes, notably yachts up to about 70 feet LOA, wood was still the best option – and a few buyers continued to buy. Not because wood looked better but because a well-built wooden hull was stronger, more infinitely repairable, warmer and, when cold-moulded, lighter than any other material. Nonetheless, the common opinion was – and to a degree still is – that wooden boats, like astrolabes, were history, and that those who clung to them, like those who continued to light their cabins with oil lamps, heat them with coal-burning stoves and rely solely on manual bilge pumps were hopeless romantics.

In one of the best-written books on wooden boats I've ever read (Ruhlman 2001) non-sailor, non-boatman American author Michael Ruhlman points out it is only since the 1970s, when wooden boats became increasingly rare, that people have said things like 'Look at that wooden boat', because until then, most of the boats in most of the developed world's harbours and marinas had wood hulls. To have said 'Look at that wooden boat' would have been like saying 'look at that yellow banana.'

If, in the early 1970s, those who said 'Look at that wooden boat' had stopped to consider the future of wooden boats they might have assumed it would be a future in which all wooden boats, like the one they were looking at, would be *old* wooden boats and that once they had rotted out, it would be a world *without* wooden boats. All new boats would have hulls of fibreglass or other industrial materials. After all, many other things once made of wood – furniture, baskets, toys, dashboards – were now made of plastic. Wood came from trees and the supply of the trees that yielded boatbuilding timber – teak, mahogany, white cedar, white oak – was shrinking and would surely shrink further.

We now know that the mid-1970s saw a turn in the tide that just a few years earlier had promised to overwhelm the few remaining builders of wooden boats in wealthy countries (the tide never turned against them in poorer countries where much of the hardwood for wooden boats comes from because most of those countries lacked access to industrialised alternatives). At first a trickle, then a steady trickle, but never a flood, the new tide brought two changes.

The first was that attitudes to *old* wooden boats began to change. Boats that could not be given away a few years earlier found buyers, often young buyers who could not afford boats with industrialised hulls. And some of them seemed to be searching for something that had nothing to do with functionality but was related to the natural beauty of wood, and for something else besides, that seemed related to ... what wooden boats *meant*.

There were other buyers too, because by the early 1970s some of the recreational fibreglass sailing boats built in the '60s had begun to age. There was growing evidence that fibreglass hulls were neither indestructible nor, depending on the damage in question, easily repaired, and that they were not, after all, maintenance-free. Some fibreglass hulls began to delaminate, others developed osmosis, stress fractures emerged around bulkheads and hardware mountings and the seductive sheen that had attracted many new buyers began to wear off. The result was that some better-off boat owners, including some who had previously owned and abandoned wooden boats, began to reconsider their options and to look for wooden boats in restorable condition. This did not drive brokerage prices through the coachroof or even much above the cabin sole but it signalled a shift in the market for recreational boats. And owners of wooden boats who had never contemplated getting rid of their wooden boats began to feel less isolated.

The second change in Europe and America in the mid-'70s was that owners and would-be owners began to consider the possibility of commissioning *new* recreational wooden boats as alternatives to restoring older ones. On both sides of the Atlantic, and in a few other places like Australia and New Zealand, what is now casually called 'the Wooden Boat Revival' began.

It is sometimes claimed that Brooklin, Maine, was the birthplace of the resurgence of wooden boat building and restoration, because it was there, in 1974, that Jon Wilson published the first issue of *WoodenBoat*. It is also sometimes said that 'the rest is history'. But it never is just 'history', is it?

The first reason it's not just 'history' is that the statement is only partially true. I did not start subscribing to *WoodenBoat* until 1978, when I was living a thousand miles from the sea in Santa Fé de Bogotá, Colombia, and thus missed issues 1 to 23. It is a publishing marvel that within ten years *WoodenBoat's* circulation went from zero to around 100,000. It was and is an outstanding magazine and Jon Wilson and his associates deserve huge recognition for navigating a shipload of aspirations across a sea of uncertainty. But I think the popular myth overstates the magazine's contribution.

Second, it not just 'history' because, concomitantly, it understates the contributions of others who became readers of and in some cases contributors to *WoodenBoat* and played important roles in their own right. The journal was the catalyst of a resurgence that might not have happened had Jon Wilson not dreamed. But if the industry had not been kept alive through the early '70s by a diminishing number of craftsmen who clung to wood as new materials threatened to drive them out of business, the catalyst would have had nothing to catalyse. *WoodenBoat* struck a nerve and found a remarkably large niche in the marketplace for ideas, dreams and lifestyles. It helped give shape, form and bulk to that marketplace. But *WoodenBoat* would not have succeeded as well as it did had it not been for latent interest in wooden boats and the values they represent.

What were those values and why did they matter?

To each, his (or her) own boat

Michael Ruhlman suggests parallels between the resurgence of wooden boats and the growing popularity of eating organic food, wearing natural fibres and exposing wooden floorboards in old houses. He seeks to explain the disproportionately large circulation of *WoodenBoat* by positing that some of its readers must have been attracted by the wholesome *nature* of wooden boats, the culture around them and the journalistic excellence of the magazine rather than by fascination with wooden boats *per se*. It has even been suggested (not by Ruhlman) that the resurgence of wooden boats has something in common (patience, endurance, tradition, an antidote to instant gratification) with renewed interest in five-day international cricket.

A lot of guff has been written on the subject of the wooden boat as an icon of continuity in a throwaway world that is fed up with plastic and is searching for, among other things, natural beauty, integrity and endurance. Assuming a spectrum from stern prose to romantic poetry, it seems to me that guff lies somewhere beyond the poetic end of the spectrum. My own passion for wooden boats certainly doesn't end with rational functionality measured by such objective criteria as seakeeping, comfort, strength, speed and ease of handling, or even such subjective criteria as beauty, exhilaration, excitement and integrity.

Good wooden boats are fit for purpose. A punky, leaky wooden boat, no matter how fine her lines, how bright her brightwork or how striking her paint job, is not a good boat. A badly built version of a good wooden boat design is not a good boat. A tatty, ratty, neglected wooden boat is not a good boat.

To evoke passion, a wooden boat must *be* right and *look* right. It must make sense and stir the senses. It must appeal to mind and heart, reason and emotion, thought and feeling. And if we – owners, builders, restorers, sailors, boatmen and boatwomen – are to achieve an acceptable equilibrium in terms of demands on our time, our purses (measured in initial and current costs) and not least our patience, it must be a balanced proposition.

Our emotional responses to wooden boats are responses to the *Gestalt* (why don't we have an English word for that?) of form and function; to the aesthetics of hull forms, rigs and rigging, sailcloth, bronze and stainless fittings, wooden blocks and carvings, finishes and colour schemes. They are responses to beauty derived from the forms of wooden boats and their accoutrements. A wood hull with scruffy paintwork, dull brightwork and cheap aluminium fittings will also evoke responses. But they will be responses of regret, sorrow and pity among those who cannot bear to see our, no *their*, maritime heritage mistreated.

Some wooden hulls are so perfectly fair and so smoothly finished they resemble plastic. Put the refinished wooden hull that provided the plug for a run of fibreglass hulls beside a replica and you might, at first, find it hard to tell the difference, particularly if both have identical wood trim and wooden spars. But look harder and you will see a slightly wavy surface on the port side of the wooden boat where a sander dug too deep, nicks and dents that were not smoothly filled, and (on the replica) a wood transom that lacks depth because it is made of half-inch veneered plywood while the original has inch-and-a-half mahogany.

Step aboard and the game's up. You can see the frames and probably the seams in the wood hull. Then drop a winch handle or a screwdriver and hear a high C6 from the replica and a booming C3 from the original, the difference between 'ping' and 'boing', 'clink' and 'thunk', and the contrasting resonances of manufactured and natural materials. It's things like that make people swoon over wooden boats and say they just *love* the way they sound as well the way they look and that they seem so real it's as though they have souls of their own. And overlook the fact that a plank-on-frame hull offers significantly less space than a fibreglass hull of the same size because frames, stringers, knees, carlins, breasthooks and shelves take up space.

Yet besides the passions aroused by being fully functional and beautiful, beyond the happy marriage of reason and emotion, a good wooden boat offers the additional and infinite pleasure of a third passion. As any writer will tell you, intellectual passion is not the oxymoron it seems and in its way is every bit as satisfying as – although not a substitute for – emotional experiences more often associated with passion.

In fact many of the most passionate advocates of wooden boats will say their most exciting passions are rooted in knowledge, including the knowledge that a wooden boat, besides being a functional and beautiful artefact, is a physical expression of the truly amazing *idea* that hundreds or thousands of flat board feet of timber can be crafted to form the complex curves required of animate and inanimate objects that move efficiently through water; that while some wooden boats embody state-of-the-art chemistry, others (give or take a trunnel here, a silicon bronze screw there) are built today in essentially the same way they have been built for centuries; that while some of the tools we routinely use to build wooden boats – band saws, table saws, mitre saws, reciprocating saws, sabre saws, planers, jointers, power planers, routers, drills, sanders – are so reliably predictable they will cut and finish wood to the finest engineering tolerances, we can, if we dare, use tools identical to those used by previous generations of boatbuilders and repairers; and that by using traditional tools we can vicariously share the satisfactions, disappointments and risks of countless predecessors.

Breathes there the man or woman with soul so dead s/he does not thrill to the experience of treading on castle battlements, climbing cathedral steps or pacing stone quays where millions of feet have trodden over a thousand years? Breathes there the man or woman with soul so dead s/he does not thrill to the knowledge s/he is walking in the footsteps of giants who, over a thousand years, produced wonderful boats with – by today's standards – primitive tools?

When pushed beyond their limits, the three dimensions of passion – function, emotion and intellect – take you to the land of guff and muddled thinking and the hopeless romanticism sometimes diagnosed as boat-sickness that leads people to buy rotten boats and pretend they can save them and spend all their time and often their money trying to make them look right, ignoring the fact that those boats should never return to the sea because they are dangerous, and it's too late to save them, and the best place for them (having removed the fittings and anything else of value) is a bonfire. All the while gushing guff.

You don't want to go there. But I believe those who can balance conflicting arguments, master self-destructive impulses, retain a realistic perspective, know when to walk away and learn how to make ultimately sound choices (despite flaky impulses) can combine the ownership of a seaworthy vessel with a higher degree of aesthetic pleasure and intellectual satisfaction than they can enjoy with any other kind of boat.

———◆———

I have often noticed that, at boat shows, such as the 'World's Largest In The Water Boat Show' held in Annapolis, Maryland, each October, most of the people climbing on and off yachts go up and down the companionway with nary a look at what's on deck.

Accommodation is the focus of interest. How many berths, how many burners; how much storage space; what are the colour choices? The engineering of the through-hull fittings, the size of the self-draining scuppers, what sort of backing plates hold the hardware to the deck, and the quality of the hardware itself are taken for granted. Or at least seem to be.

Perhaps it's just a peculiar form of behaviour that affects people at boat shows. Perhaps people do look thoughtfully at the important things as well as the less important things before they actually buy. And maybe they don't. In an age when production boats are bought and sold in much the same way as production automobiles, I suspect there's a tendency to leave 'technical stuff' to the manufacturer's judgment and integrity.

There are, of course, industry standards. And companies that hope to stay in the boatbuilding business more than a few months comply with and exceed them. But it's odd how most of the boats that populate boatyards and marinas across the USA are thought about in terms like those used to describe cars. What, after all, is the difference between saying 'I've got an 04 BMW 325' and saying 'I've got an 05 Hunter 30'? And if there's a hint of disdain in that it's because I'm critical of sailors who neither know nor care about yacht design and construction and because it seems irresponsible to go to sea in a boat about which you are ignorant – although people do it all the time and every so often they drown.

But having said that I must also say I am sick of the pointless and endless debate over the relative merits of wood and what wooden-boat snobs whimsically call 'the other stuff', and that I have a very poor opinion of those who equate fibreglass with frozen snot and declaim that a boat with a cold-moulded wooden hull is not a wooden boat. I probably feel much as they do about wooden boats but I find those attitudes unacceptably dismissive and would even suggest a parallel between recognising the value of alternative boatbuilding materials and recognising alternative forms of genius.

Old-fashioned views of intelligence tended to confine genius to intellectual achievement, but we now know there may be genius in a Shane Warne leg break, a David Beckham free kick, a Magic Johnson jump shot, Yo Yo Ma's bow work, Van Gogh's brushwork or Zakharova's footwork. Analogously, who is to say a mass-produced boat is an inferior form of transport? Or that boats made of fibreglass, aluminium, ferro-cement, steel and complex composites are intrinsically inferior just because I and others think good wooden boats are the stuff of magic?

This book is about a wooden boat and I would be dishonest if I failed to say I hope it might persuade people who might not otherwise have done so to consider restoring other wooden boats. It would also be dishonest if I failed to say I also have an aluminium boat and two fibreglass boats (only one of which has wooden spars and wood trim) and that I cherish their diversity. Not as a matter of convenience (no matter what I think and say, wooden boats will continue to be a minority preference) but as a matter of principle.

So to each his (or her) own boat.

A passion for wood

What is it about wood, other than its natural beauty, that makes it a preferred material not just for hulls but for furniture, house siding, roofs, lamp-posts, bowls, picture frames, garden pergolas and cross-country skis? How often is something advertised as made of 'real wood' rather than a poor plastic facsimile – like the simulated wooden sheets glued on the side panels of the Mercury Colony Park wagon we owned in Washington DC in the early 1980s that looked tackier and tackier as it got scratched and scuffed and even worse when the 'wood' began to peel off.

Why we want wood

Wood has achieved premium status as a boatbuilding material because there is *demand* for wooden hulls, spars, decks, cabin sides and doors, hatches, grabrails, toerails, rubrails, blocks, bitts and Samson posts as well as interiors that, except in the cheapest mass-production boats, are invariably fitted out with at least a modicum of wood. Most boat buyers want a bit of wood, even those who would never dream of a buying a boat with a wood hull (either because they think they can't afford one or because they have bought in to the notion that wooden hulls demand endless maintenance). But what is it about wood that makes them want some – and others want nothing else?

The most common factor is the most obvious: that people like the way wood looks, the infinite contrasts in colour, texture and grain that gives varnished, oiled or polished wood a timeless, intuitive appeal. Most buyers of boats with industrial hulls (except a wooden boat owner manqué) will probably have no more to say because the appeal of wood begins and ends with cosmetics, eye candy and relief from gelcoated monotony.

Those who favour wood hulls will usually start by saying that when suited to the job at hand, wood is stronger and more durable than any other material, although not necessarily more workable. They will tell you that a properly selected, prepared, jointed, protected and fitted (though hard to work) angelique keel will last forever. They will tell you that a well-laid teak or wana deck will last longer than a moulded deck and much longer than one laid with Treadmaster or other proprietary materials. They will point to the Viking longships, the *Mary Rose* and the Norfolk Wherry *Albion*, built in 1893 and still going strong, as evidence that the physical properties of wood make it good, better, best.

Then there is a minority who (choosing their words carefully because they don't want to be taken for New Age tree-huggers) will say they want wood in or on their boats because everything made from wood is unique, because every piece of wood has a distinct character and because wood is a living, breathing substance that demands and repays constant care and attention. They may (or if worried about being taken for tree-huggers may not) add that the organic nature of wood means wooden boats are good for the souls of those who build, own and sail them, and they may even whisper that wooden boats have souls of their own.

The woodworkers ...

Such goodness would not of course be accessible to buyers if demand for the construction, maintenance and repair of wooden boats were not met by a *supply* of skilled craftsmen (and increasingly craftswomen) willing and able to make it accessible. These craftsmen (shorthand for both sexes) are a remarkable breed, not least because in the 1960s they almost died out. Having survived, they march to the beat of a different drummer. They come in all shapes and sizes and from more diverse backgrounds than you will find in most workplaces. Where but in a wooden boatyard do you find artisans with no knowledge of anything but boatbuilding, working alongside ex-lawyers, ex-teachers, ex-doctors, ex-business executives, ex-almost everything you can think of, who would not dream of doing any other kind of manual labour?

Most wooden-boat craftsmen live and work in small towns and villages beside rivers, lakes and oceans, and occasionally at the end of muddy tracks in sheds in their own backyards or (in at least two cases I know) in the corner of a field.

Some have been formally trained and qualified in apprenticeships or on courses run by one of the several boatbuilding schools that have been established since the 1970s in Europe and North America, or on other courses offered by mainstream colleges. Some, self-taught, have spent years acquiring basic skills and the rest of their lives refining them. They work in unheated workshops and in the open air, often in conditions that would not be tolerated in unionised industries. And most earn incomes that other people might laugh at until they hear the craftsmen laughing back and begin to wonder who, after all, made the best career choice.

And here's the most quirky thing of all: these craftsmen, particularly in America but also in Britain, occupy a special place in the hierarchy of those who work with their hands. Not because their craftsmen-peers have concluded that wooden boatbuilders are superior to other woodworkers. Not because they are paid more. But because their clients include more than a few who, notably successful in their chosen fields, now treat wooden-boat craftsmen with respect that amounts to awe and write and talk about them in such a way that in watery communities in Maine and Massachusetts, and on the east coast of England and the west coast of Scotland, some wooden boatbuilders have achieved iconic status.

MUDLARK'S WOOD

Teak Tropical Asian hardwood. Mid brown, oily, extremely resistant to marine borers and impervious to salt water. Used for some trim pieces in earlier repairs to *Mudlark* but not in final restoration.

American white oak Strong, heavy, rot-resistant. Creamy white. Used for bulwarks and other structural pieces in original build of *Mudlark* and for all frame repairs and other structural applications such as backing for butt blocks in restoration.

Honduran mahogany Red-brown, fine-grained, stable and even-textured. Strong and easy to work. Not used in original build of *Mudlark* but used extensively in reconstruction for replacement planking, new stem and cutwater, and cabin and coaming trim.

American black walnut Rarely used in boats except for cabin furniture but strong and resilient as well as good-looking with dark brown-purple colours and complex figuring. Extensively used in original build of *Mudlark* for frames and leeboards. Used in reconstruction to strengthen leeboards.

American white cedar Not especially strong but stable and very rot-resistant. Light brown and fragrant. Used in original build of *Mudlark* for all planking including bottom and for some trim pieces. Not used in reconstruction.

Yellow cypress Grows in swamps in southern USA. Stable and rot-resistant. Creamy yellow. Not used in original build but used in reconstruction to replace rotten cedar planking in bottom because cedar of required dimensions was not available.

Sitka spruce Native to North America, where it grows up to 90 metres tall. Pale brown. Very strong for weight. Used in original build of *Mudlark* for all masts and spars and still sound.

So what is it about wooden boats that makes people want to spend their lives building and repairing them, and why (most of them having learned to work with other materials) do those people strongly prefer to work with wood?

An elemental part of the answer is given by Jim Trefethen in an almost lyrical passage in his lively 'how to' book *Wooden Boat Renovation: New Life for Old Boats Using Modern Methods* (1993). Describing what he does to find peace under pressure, Trefethen explains he goes to his shop, sharpens the blade of a smoothing plane (in itself a soothing action), secures a block of wood on his bench and starts to remove thin aromatic shavings in a rhythmic motion. He's right. We've all done it and we all know exactly what he means when he says that half an hour later most of the things that were wrong with the world when he started are, after all, right.

In an introduction to George Nakashima's *The Soul of a Tree* (1981), George Wald, Harvard biochemist and 1967 Nobel Laureate wrote: 'One can gain knowledge from words, but wisdom only from things ... one cannot teach wisdom. Nakashima has wisdom. He is probably the wisest person I know.'

George Nakashima was an American craftsman and artist of Japanese ancestry whose furniture is prized around the world. He was also a superb exponent of what makes woodworkers tick, and in *The Soul of a Tree* wrote what seems to me a fine credo for woodworkers and, with a few minor amendments, wooden boatbuilders:

> When trees mature it is fair and moral that they are cut for man's use, as they would soon decay and return to earth. Trees have a yearning to live again, perhaps to provide the beauty, strength and utility to serve man. Even to become an object of great artistic worth ...
>
> Each tree, every part of each tree, has only one perfect use. The long, taut grains of the true cypress, so well adapted to the making of thin, elegant grilles, the joyous dance of the figuring in certain species, the richness of graining where two large branches reach out – these can all be released and fulfilled in a worthy object for man's use ...
>
> We must make things with great hope and faith, for there is joy and fulfilment in creation. We must try to recapture a close relationship with nature ...
>
> It is a stirring moment when out of an inert mass drawn from nature we set out to produce an object never before seen, an object to enhance man's world; above all a tree will live again ...
>
> Gradually a form evolves, much as nature produced the tree in the first place. The object created can live forever. The tree lives on in its new form ...
>
> We must each make as perfect an object as we know how ...
>
> Like all true craftsmen, a woodworker is completely dedicated, with a strong sense of vocation. Often his craft has been handed down from generation to generation. A woodworker's hands develop in a special way with intense and concentrated use. The flesh becomes stronger and heavier in certain areas, better fitted to grasp and use the tools ... He has a special intensity, a striving for perfection, a conviction that any task must be executed with all his skill. Basically the woodworker is not driven by commerce, but by a need to create the best object he is capable of creating ...
>
> The reality of the age brings up the question of machinery. As much as man controls the end product, there is no disadvantage in the use of modern machinery and there is no need for embarrassment. Gandhi and his spinning wheel were more quixotic than realistic.

A power plane can do in a few minutes what might require a day or more by hand. In a creative craft, it becomes a question of responsibility, whether it is man or the machine that controls the work's progress.

Again, if in doubt, find your nearest wooden boatbuilder, sit him or her down and listen. You probably won't hear Nakashima's words, but some of their thoughts, feelings, ideas and values will echo his. And because people who work with their hands generally don't spend a lot of time on philosophy, and because conversations are voyages of self-discovery, even the boatbuilder may hear and understand for the first time.

... and their work

Wood can be worked with muscle-powered hand tools, electric power tools and industrial machinery. Notwithstanding knots, whirls and irregularities that distinguish wood from industrial materials and give it character, personality and uniquity, *automated* machines (in which human operators do not affect performance) can fashion wood into essentially interchangeable objects. Given sufficient demand to justify the costs of designing, constructing and operating the machinery and an adequate supply of the right wood for making such things as prefabricated houses and furniture, wood can be an industrial material.

Yet it is impossible to envisage an automated process for building a wooden hull of any kind – plank-on-frame, clinker, cold-moulded or strip-planked – because the processes, though different in each case, are in all cases complicated, involve many steps and demand continuous human intervention. And because humans are fallible, and although the blend varies from one type of hull to another, the end result is a joint product of art and science. It is also a joint product of what David Pye, a British architect, industrial designer and craftsman (with more than a passing interest in ships and boatbuilding) called the workmanship of risk and the workmanship of certainty, the former a function of a fallible craftsman, the latter of infallible machinery.

Pye was no friend of guff and *The Nature and Art of Workmanship* (1968) is a forceful, thoughtful riposte to a century of fuzzy thinking about craftsmanship – which he defines as workmanship in which the quality of the result is not predetermined but depends on the judgment, dexterity and above all the care of the workman.

Pye saw that the workmanship of risk may yield poor results, that poor workmanship produces poor quality and that when a fine piece of wood is ruined by carelessness it may yield negative value. And he rejected the notion that craftsmanship and mechanical tools are incompatible, believing that the use of power tools increased productivity but did not eliminate risk. Indeed, as anyone who has misjudged the gouging potential of a belt sander knows all too well, the power of a power tool may substantially increase the risks. So for Pye, the distinction had far less to do with whether a tool was muscle powered or electric powered than with the *process* used to produce results.

Pye was thus at odds with proponents of the Arts and Crafts movement who believed the only way to mimic the integrity of the medieval craftsmen for whom electric power was not an option was to use the *same* tools and techniques they used, in the mistaken belief the key to integrity lay in replicating their processes. Pye would also have been at odds with Colonial Willamsburg – briefly the eighteenth-century capital of Virginia – where authentic craftsmanship is today interpreted to require the use of eighteenth-century tools, including pedal-powered lathes.

Pye thought those who take that approach to craftsmanship misunderstood William Morris, a leading exponent of Arts and Crafts. At Oxford, Morris was strongly influenced by John Ruskin's view that medieval craftsmen had been free to enjoy creative individualism and, with Oxford contemporaries and fellow members of the 'Brotherhood', Edward Burne-Jones and Dante Gabriel Rossetti, toyed with 'a crusade and holy warfare against the art and culture of their own time'. But, said Pye, Morris came to see that the essence of handicraft was 'work without division of labour' and to recognise that 'handicraft did not exclude the use of machines'.

Everyone with more than superficial knowledge of the resurgence of wooden boatbuilding and repair will see the implications for those who argue for and against the use of modern materials and techniques in the restoration of old wooden boats. There may be amateur (i.e. not doing it for a living) boatbuilders who use nothing but hand tools and light their shops with tallow candles and would feel at home in Colonial Williamsburg. And there are professional (i.e. for profit) boatbuilders for whom an epoxy-saturated wooden hull is not a wooden hull.

But I cannot envisage a contemporary professional shop without a complement of perhaps old but nonetheless serviceable stationary tools, a reliable supply of electricity and one or more craftsmen who understand that the enduring value of the workmanship of risk resides in 'care, judgment and dexterity' and not in the kind of tools they use or the power that drives them, and who also understand that the workmanship of risk continues to thrive in a world where almost everything we use is produced with the workmanship of certainty. Because, in Pye's words,

> it can produce a range of specific aesthetic qualities which the workmanship of certainty, always ruled by price, will never achieve. The British Museum, or any other like it, gives convincing evidence of that. And one need not copy the past in order to perpetuate those qualities. People still use oil-paint, but they do not copy Titian.

During World War I, the United States Navy, impatient at the slow speed of building wood-hulled submarine chasers, turned to Henry Ford for a fast answer. Assuming what worked for cars would work for boats, Ford committed to build a hundred 200-foot steel hulled 'Eagle Boats' at the rate of one a day. But:

> His first boats leaked oil out and water in. Ford's workers hadn't mastered ship riveting. They got into trouble using ladders so they wouldn't have to erect scaffolds. Ford simply

didn't realize how much specific craftsmanship was involved in shipbuilding. The Navy cut his contract to 60 boats, and Ford delivered them over a year after the war ended. They needed fitting and retrofitting, and then they functioned no better than alright. They were awkward at sea. Within five years, three were lost in accidents. When WW-II began, only eight of the 60 were still in use, and then only in American coastal waters. A German torpedo took one of them. (Hounshell 1987)

Ford (and the US Navy) learned the hard way that what worked for cars did not work for boats. And in the near-century since he tried and failed nobody has found a way to build boats using the workmanship of certainty.

One reason is that all the materials that have so far been used to produce complete boats depend, in some measure, on the workmanship of risk. Fibreglass hulls are now mass-produced from computer-designed moulds based on computer-aided designs. But the mould must be finished and fitted out and no boatbuilder has yet found a way to finish boats – except very small boats driven by oars, outboards or sails, canoes and kayaks that require virtually no finishing – using automated processes.

The other (compelling) reason is that boat economics don't allow for mass production. Cars are mass-produced because they are sold in volume. Horse-drawn coaches and carriages would have been mass-produced too had there been mass markets. But there were small markets, as indeed there were once small markets for the most expensive motor cars, which is why, until the late 1960s, firms like Park Ward, Mulliner and Thrupp and Maberly continued to build bodies for Rolls Royce and Bentley. There are still anomalies, notably the wonderful cars produced at Malvern Link, Worcestershire, by the Morgan Motor Company using essentially the same designs and production techniques – cars are still pushed from shop to shop by hand – it has been using for sixty years.

The corresponding anomaly in the boatyard world would be an automated production line. But pictures of rows of wooden Chris Craft power boats being built in what in the 1950s was termed a 'mass production' facility are misleading. Although relatively large volume production and standardised parts made it possible to achieve long runs of certain boats, they were all built with the workmanship of risk, which is to say with skill, dexterity and judgment. And even in yards where today fibreglass hulls are popped out of moulds at what, by wooden boatyard standards, are astonishing speeds, all but the smallest and simplest must be finished by hand. Bulkheads must be bonded; decks must be bolted to hulls; interiors must be fitted out; decks must be furnished. Indeed the real anomaly is that many of these boats are built in high-volume yards whose not-very-well-paid workers have limited skill, dexterity and judgment. As a result the real risk is the risk of ownership – which is of course borne by the buyer rather than the worker.

2

Mudlark and me

Sharpies

Endearing though it is I cannot say that a catboat reminds me of a cat, that a Bermudian (or Marconi) rig makes me think of Bermuda (or a modern radio aerial), or that I associate jollyboats with a good time. To be sure, all those terms are intriguing but none is even vaguely anthropomorphic. The term *sharpie* – evocative, descriptive, simple – is another matter. Ask a landsman what sort of boat he thinks a sharpie might be and most of the time he'll say 'narrow', 'pointed', 'sharp-ended' or words to that effect, and he'd be right. A sharpie is 'a precision instrument for cutting water' (Scott 1999).

Mention sharpies in America and many sailors with knowledge of traditional yacht design will think of Captain Monroe's *Egret* and her nineteenth-century Florida siblings that, so well adapted to the thin Florida flats, skimmed shallows where other boats could not follow. Others might think of fast, shallow-draft, low-freeboard New England workboats that evolved a unique fitness for purpose in the inshore fisheries of Massachusetts, Connecticut and Rhode Island. Yet others might mention sharpie workboats in coastal Louisiana and Mississippi. Most will be categorically certain that the sharpie is a uniquely American invention and will agree with Reuel Parker that 'The sharpie weaves an essential motif in the fabric of American history ... is exemplary of Yankee ingenuity ... (and is) truly an American invention' (Parker 1993).

And they may be wrong. Because if, like most hull forms, the sharpie was conceived as a response to the need for working vessels that could cope with specific conditions – in this case shallow water – those conditions were by no means specifically American. Indeed they exist in many places in Europe and other parts of the world as well as what is now the United States. And it seems to me likely, although I cannot prove it – partly because crudely built boats (and early sharpies must have been crudely built boats) sink or rot without trace – that the *idea* of the sharpie must have occurred independently to many boatbuilders in many parts of the world who built boats using little but their eyes long before yacht designers were a known species. There are, after all, just so many ways you can make a hull and it seems to me sharpie hulls must have been conceived at different times in different places to meet demand for boats that could sail in thin water and had other specific attributes.

The most distinctive features of a sharpie – most of which were designed to harvest shellfish, deliver mail or board and unboard pilots in shallow tidal flats, estuaries and inshore banks – are hulls with shallow drafts, low freeboard, hard chines, high length-to-beam ratios, flat, flared midsections, flat, vee'd or slightly rounded bottoms, moderate rocker, sharp entries with at most slight bow overhangs, flat, often vertical transoms, no more than moderate sheer, and centreboards or leeboards.

To keep them upright sharpies have internal or external ballast (or none at all). They also tend to have sail plans with low centres of gravity, which usually means low aspect and gaff rigs (big sharpies – over, say, 25 feet – invariably have divided, usually ketch, rigs). To be efficient and competitive workboats and to get out of harm's way in a hurry they must also be fast, which means their slippery hulls cannot be too heavy. To be easy to build and repair they are simply constructed. To be affordable most are built of readily obtained materials. When the wind dies, they can be moved with oars (on bigger boats sweeps), quants, poles and inboard or outboard engines.

The sharpie evolved as a boat for specific conditions. And what we now call its design parameters – a concept unknown to generations of builders whose only concern was to build boats that worked – have probably changed little in the several centuries that have elapsed since the first plank-on-frame, flat-bottomed sharpie floated somewhere in the then known world.

Twelve Square Metres

My affinity with sharpies was the result of an accident. In 1962, soon after I met my wife Glynis, I spent the Easter vacation at her parents' home in north Norfolk, where I fell in love with her and the physical and cultural landscapes in which she had grown up. Wells-next-the-Sea, recorded as Guella in the Domesday Book, was a small but thriving commercial port serving an arable farming hinterland and about a dozen villages. Yet it was probably less well known outside its immediate area than it had been in 1580 when, with 19 vessels of more than 16 tons, it had been a nationally significant port.

As a port and service centre for local agriculture the Wells I met in 1962 was a gritty, down-to-earth sort of place where people were valued less for *what* they were than for *who* they were; less for what they owned than for what they had done with their lives; and less for their pedigrees than for what they could be relied on to do in an emergency. I had been nowhere like it before and have been to few places like it since.

But even then Wells was not all work and when it played it sometimes sailed. A sailing club had been founded in the 1930s after clubs had been established at Brancaster Staithe and Blakeney. But unlike those clubs, which even in their

The north Norfolk coast.

early days had attracted weekend and holiday members from London, some of whom had become flag officers, Wells Sailing Club always had and has retained a distinctive social and economic profile. Although some of the early officers were doctors and other local worthies its diversified membership included farmers, fishermen, mill, maltings and granary workers, shopkeepers, tradesmen, policemen and local government workers including, from the outset, more than a few women.

In the pre-war years Wells sailors raced in heavy, clinker-built sixteen-foot jollyboats with a crew of three. They were slow but seaworthy and many members who were not seamen during the week learned to sail in them and sail well. Meanwhile, the better-off sailors in Kings Lynn and Brancaster Staithe were among the first in Britain to get their hands on a new design, a carvel-built 19' 8" sloop almost too big to be called a dinghy yet too small to be called a yacht.

The new boat, designed by naval architect D H Wustrau for a design competition run by the Deutscher Segler-Verband in 1930, was initially known as a *Scharpiejolle* – a sharpie-hulled jollyboat. It soon became better known as the 12 Square Metre Sharpie, as the first examples were quickly put to their intended purpose of racing and day-cruising on the inland lakes of north Germany. But the German Navy soon saw other uses for the new design and by the mid-1930s it had become a sail training platform for cadet officers at the German Navy base near the Baltic port of Rostock.

Two famed German yards, Abeking & Rasmussen in Hamburg and Kroger's in Warnemünde, soon began producing sharpies in volume. Some went to Holland, others to England, and by the late 1930s the International Yacht Racing Union had accepted the 12 Square Metre Sharpie as an international class, initially accommodating both gaff and Bermudian rigs. However, the disadvantages of the taller rig (sharpies kept on moorings at Kings Lynn in Norfolk in the 1930s had a disconcerting tendency to blow over) led to a gaff-only rule that, like other class rules, was strictly enforced.

When Hitler invaded Poland in 1939 every sharpie in Europe, all but a few of them Kroger-built, had essentially identical rigs, hulls, spars, centreplates, washboards, rudders and distinctive wishbone tillers, the peculiar virtue of which is that the helmsman goes about facing forward, sliding one hand across the bar of the wishbone while moving across the boat. You can still see them. Not on boats but hanging on walls and suspended from beamed ceilings in the homes, boatsheds, garages and businesses of current and former sharpie sailors in north Norfolk and elsewhere. There were a few non-Kroger hulls, including several from a budget-minded (some said murderous) builder operating in a field near Horsham, Sussex.

Costing half as much as Krogers, they became known as 'Horsham Coffins'. None has survived.

Post-war international competition did not resume until the 1950s, by which time local experiments and innovations – some born of necessity in the absence of materials in the post-war environment – had drawn some boats out of class rules. But in 1955 the International 12 Square Metre Sharpie was chosen as the two-man centreboard class for the Melbourne Olympics the following year. The UK entry *Chuckles*, sailed by Jasper Blackall and Terrence Smith, took the bronze medal and the sharpie achieved a new status.

Uffa Fox, who had crewed a sharpie at Burnham Week in the early 1930s, considered building one and decided against it, but some Brancaster sailors ordered new ones from Lester Southerland who, with his father, had built several before the war. Others sought out German-built boats brought to Britain as war reparations by the Royal Navy, and half-a-dozen others built in Malta by German prisoners of war, all with 'wing' suffixes (*Redwing, Lapwing*). The sharpie was, for a while, the height of Brancaster fashion.

Although, from the outset, class rules mandated construction methods and materials, some variations were accepted. Whereas the pre-war Kroger boats had two butt-jointed planks per side, Abeking & Rasmussen had opted for one. And when post-war scarcities meant gaboonwood of the specified dimensions was unavailable in Europe, substitute mahoganies were used for side planking, mahogany was used instead of oak for frames, and spruce, not mahogany, went into bottoms. Measurements were another matter: keels, frames, deck-beams, battens, floors, stretchers, strakes and planks – whatever they were made of – had maximum dimensions. So were weights, although the use of substitute woods meant a given part on one boat might weigh more or less than the same part on another. When hull, spars, centreboard, rudder and wishbone tiller were put together a dry sharpie (a wet one was naturally heavier) weighed in at 650 lb (300 kg). Not a boat with which to dispute right of way in a strong breeze (as more than one skipper of a fibreglass cruiser who has chosen not to give way to racing sharpies has found to his cost).

International 12 Square Metre Sharpie.
(Illustration by permission of *Classic Boat*)

Fashions change, and by the early 1960s Brancaster sailors had been dazzled by the possibilities of Fireballs and 505s with early fibreglass hulls. It was not long before their sharpies were going cheap, many going less than ten miles to less affluent owners at Wells. Before they tired of them some Brancaster owners, perhaps not trusting themselves (or thinking of competitive advantage) had chosen to crew local watermen. At Wells, some of the new owners were themselves working seamen and the club quickly established itself as a centre of excellence for sharpie sailing.

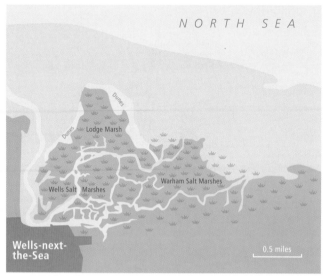

The salt marshes at Wells-next-the-Sea.

My first outing on a sharpie was in K68, named *Sea Thrift* (for the compact, salt-loving plant that each spring pinkly suffuses the salt marshes that dominate this part of the north Norfolk coast). She was owned by Billy Neale, who ran the fish and chip shop on the Northfield estate. Our ride was wet, wild and wonderful. The rig groaned, the sea gurgled, the hull throbbed as we picked up speed, my arms ached (no winches, no blocks) and I was thrilled as we rode a following sea with the forward half of the hull poised above the water and slowed until we were picked up by the next wave and shot forward.

Quite a boat, I thought. One day I'd like to have one – but meanwhile it would be wonderful to have almost anything that floated. At Christmas I asked for a kayak. Not a ready-made one but a kit.

———◆———

In mid-December 1961 a huge, crude, sacking package resembling a large sausage arrives at Wells railway station from Granta Canoes in Cambridge. It contains lengths of pine, plywood, canvas and paper plans for a sixteen-foot two-person kayak with a wood frame and painted canvas hull. On vacations over the next year I take my first tentative steps at boatbuilding. I steam the pine frames in a copper boiler in Glynis's grandmother's scullery, breaking several. Glynis's grandmother, a one time fire-breathing Salvationist, says they broke because I worked on the boat on Sundays. I privately question her judgment but don't say so. She says the same thing when I break yet another ⅛" drill bit, something I do so often the man at Pope's hardware store at the top of Standard Road knows what I want without me having to ask.

It takes a long time to finish the skeleton, and between university vacations I store it in a garage just long enough to house my work-in-progress. The hull is held together with glue and cheap (non-stainless) screws. The ends are particularly crude because I am nervous about fairing the stringers where they land on the stem and stern pieces.

Eventually, the canvas goes on and I paint it with red household paint and add a name. We call her *Shalom* because by the time I finish the project it's a year and a half later and Glynis and I have spent most of the previous summer working on a kibbutz in Upper Galilee. I'm not sure what people made of the fact that the name was in English on one side and Hebrew on the other. But she floats. We explore the creeks, pick her up and carry her when we run out of water, take her a mile or so off the beach, struggle against wind and tide and have a wonderful time. When we go to South America in 1964 we leave *Shalom* in a shed and eventually someone sells her in our absence for £16 – by which time I suspect the screws had rusted and the frame was falling apart.

Tinqua

Fast-forward fifteen years. We're living in McLean, Virginia, a close-in suburb of Washington DC. I'm making my way in the World Bank. We have just bought a summer home in the village of Binham overlooking the ruins of a Benedictine priory created through the combined efforts of Henry VIII, who dissolved the monastery, and Oliver Cromwell, whose men defaced the font in the half of the nave that had been left standing by Henry to serve as a parish church. I want a boat to sail when we're in Norfolk, even if it is only for a few weeks a year.

Tinqua, built in 1947 at Brancaster, being launched at Wells.

I learn that a sharpie named *Yvonne* is for sale. She is a local boat, built by Lester Southerland at Brancaster in 1947. I buy her, going half-shares with my brother-in-law. We rename her *Tinqua* after one of the lesser known China Clippers, many of whose names (*Cassiopeia*, *Southern Cross*, *Aurora*, *Northern Lights*, *Flying Cloud*, *Taeping*, *Thermopylae*) are favoured by sharpie owners. We sail her – he helms, I crew – in weekend races at Wells and sometimes at Brancaster Staithe and Burnham Overy Staithe, a few miles west. On one never-to-be-forgotten afternoon we sail to Brancaster in long tacks against the tide and a dying breeze, arriving well after the ebb has set, and are deeply grateful to Mervyn Nudds, the harbourmaster who tows us in to the hard. I can still taste the first beer.

Tinqua, though beautiful, is a racing machine, the more so as, within the rules, we add the go-fast gear without which, in the 1970s, a sharpie is uncompetitive. She is not a boat for a family picnic on the East Hills that lie beyond the Wells salt marshes. Nor a boat for exploring the creeks, although I know Dutch sailors who claim they routinely use 12 Square Metre Sharpies for family cruising and even camping.

But then there is no such thing as a boat for all seasons, times, places, moods and fancies. The 12 Square Metre Sharpie was built for a purpose, and even though the original purpose included day-sailing and cruising in north Germany I know there is not a chance my family will ever go to sea in her. The odd race perhaps, preferably with someone else at the helm (OK, so I raise my voice sometimes), but not an overnight to Blakeney or a quick thrash to Overy Staithe and inside Scolt Head Island through the shallows (and I mean shallows) of Norton Creek to Brancaster Staithe.

So we need another boat. I ask Robin Golding to find me a clinker dinghy, well behaved, predictable, about twelve feet, seats, headroom under the boom, good for an outboard if we don't want to sail, more or less easily rowed. And he comes up with a Twinkle Twelve and tells me it's a right built boat. An unusual formulation of words, I think, but this is Norfolk and people can use words as they please and I know what he means. It turns out I don't. He means it was built by Wright and Co. of Ipswich, and when I buy her in 1974 she's about fifteen years old, give or take a few years.

Robin sells her to me for £100. He's a genius. So was the designer. So was Mr Wright. The Twinkle Twelve is one of the best family boats of all time. A varnished hull, half-decked, dry, stable (I've never seen one go over) and very comfortable. Our family of four fits easily with picnic gear, oars and other bits and bobs and everyone thinks she's the bee's knees. I just think she's a lovely, very fit-for-purpose little boat and know from the day I buy her I shall keep her for ever. She has no name and we call her *Pocahontas* after the Native American princess who, like Carey and Caitlin, had roots in both Virginia and Norfolk.

So now we have not one, but one and a half old wooden boats in England, and I can use both of them for four or five weeks a year and the rest of the year I can think about them – and that's not at all bad because I have learned that part of the pleasure of owning old boats is just thinking about them even when they are an ocean away. But most of the time I am in America and although the psychic thrills of ownership are wonderful I'm beginning to think it would be really nice if we had a boat on the other side of the Atlantic too. This seems a bit greedy until I tell myself lots of people own more than two boats and that it would be great to take my family for sailing weekends on the Chesapeake Bay, which is after all one of the world's great cruising grounds and a lot less demanding than the North Sea and only an hour and a half from McLean.

In March 1976 we move to Bogotá, Colombia, where I am the World Bank's Resident Representative. A couple of years later, with an eventual return to Washington in the offing, I start thinking about a boat for the Bay. It occurs to me one option would be to have a wooden cruiser built in Britain and ship it out.

In the late 1970s very few British boatbuilders are still building wooden boats. But I come across a 24-footer built in Essex by Alan Platt. He sends details. The price seems very reasonable – less than £7,000 with sails and engine – and I tell him that when I am in England on leave that summer I will visit to see the Finesse 24 for myself.

Glynis – perhaps to humour me, perhaps because she fears I might do something stupid like write a cheque for a downpayment – comes too. We drive across Norfolk and Suffolk through lovely places like Lavenham (where, fifteen years later, my first book on Norfolk will be published) and then Essex which (at least in parts) is lovely too, despite the jokes. After lunch we find Alan's boatyard behind his house about a mile from the sea at Thundersley near Leigh-on-Sea.

The 24 is a clever design (there is a Finesse 21 and a larger 27) with sound compromises between freeboard and coachroof and length and beam. The choices visibly intended to put sailing and seaworthiness ahead of accommodation but there are still four berths, an enclosed head, a galley and even 5 feet 8 inches of headroom in the main cabin. Even Glynis is impressed.

Built like the proverbial brick privy, the boat's integrity bespeaks his integrity.

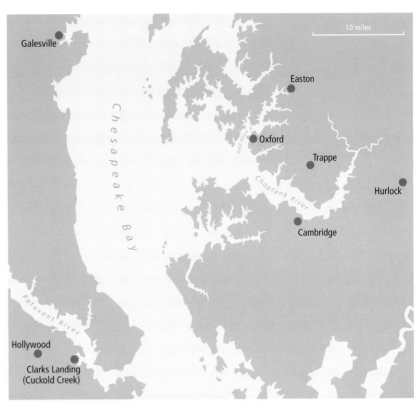

The middle reach of Chesapeake Bay.

The clear blue eyes, the straight-grained stringers, the calm voice, the tight joints, the firm handshake, the carefully eased edges, the understated language, the excellent paint-job are all of a piece. I learn more about craftsmanship in a two-hour visit that includes a trip to board a seven-year-old version with dry dust in the bilge lying to a swinging mooring at Leigh-on-Sea than from all the books I've been devouring a thousand miles from the sea in Bogotá, where my sailing is done in a Lightning on a reservoir the Bank had helped finance in the 1960s.

I am thrilled. I want a Finesse. I want to ship one to the USA and sail her on the Bay. I convince Glynis it's a good idea. Then I start checking how much I would have to pay for transport. I think there must be a mistake and call around but the sums continue to make nonsense. It will cost as much to get her there as to buy her. Sadly I tell Alan Platt it's not on. But I don't forget the boat and put a large photograph of a 24 on a wall in my Bogotá office and tell people who ask it's the boat I didn't buy.

We return to Washington and in December 1980 my fortieth birthday comes and goes. I have a secret and ridiculous dream that Glynis will buy me (us) a boat big enough for weekends on the Bay. Of course it doesn't happen. Years later I will decide it was a really stupid idea and am glad she didn't share or even know about my dream. But a few weeks later we go to the Washington International Boat Show at the Washington Convention Center, where we find a stand selling timeshares in sailboats on the Chesapeake from a base at Galesville on the West River. We buy a share, and subject to passing an on-the-water test of seamanship, we are afloat.

I pass the test and as soon as the weather warms we start sailing. The timeshare company has a mixed fleet of fibreglass cruisers between 27 and 36 feet. Most of the time we get a bulbous bathtub of a boat with a brown boot-top in which all the design compromises have been weighted towards accommodation. She sails like a pig but we're out on the water and Carey and Caitlin love it. The experience teaches me two things.

One is that the choice between getting out on the water in a poorly designed plastic boat and not getting out at all is a no-brainer: you get out on the water.

The other is that once you have seen the difference between a well-found wooden boat that makes the right sounds and looks right and feels right and smells right, and a fibreglass tub, you make up your mind that as soon as ever you can you will buy a wooden boat. But mine will have to be built in America because an English one is just impractical unless she can come on her own bottom and that, quite simply, is not an option. Partly because I'm not nearly a good enough sailor to sail the Atlantic. Partly because I find the open ocean less interesting than water from which you can make landfalls as and when you want.

A proper boat

Fast-forward again to the early 1990s. We are still in Washington. The timeshare arrangement came to an end several years ago, mainly, we think, because it allowed members to cancel bookings at any time without penalty, which meant you could get up on Saturday morning, decide it was blowing too hard or not enough and/or was raining, call the timeshare company and cancel. Just like that. So apart from an 18-foot Old Town canoe which displaced 1,000 pounds and would take all six of us (Cameron having arrived in 1982), we were, on the American side of the Atlantic, boatless. But through the '80s I was very busy at the Bank, the house and garden took a lot of what spare time I had, and I realised it would be hard to justify boat ownership for another year or so ...

Then, in January 1992, came 'Barely Born in March'.

In the preceding twenty-odd years we had shared our home with a variety of four-legged things, mostly, thank God, for brief periods. Many of their bones now lie in graves around the garden of our former house in McLean, Virginia. The graves once had markers that long ago succumbed to the forces that destroy untreated wood in that part of Virginia. Three – no, four – gerbils, a hamster, a rabbit. Carey called them rodents, even the rabbit – which was going a bit far although, ears apart, rabbits do resemble big gerbils. Our dog Chiquita was another matter.

It's said that life begins neither at conception nor at birth, but when the family dog dies and the children leave home. Well the dog was dead and two of the children had, more or less, left home, Carey to work in Moscow as a journalist and Caitlin to Edinburgh to study anthropology. But Catriona and Cameron were still very much with us. Which is why we had a horse.

Glynis was entirely to blame for the fact that Catriona, like a lot of girls her age, was into horses. About five years earlier she had thought Catriona might like to ride. So she took her on a mystery expedition to a nearby stables and Catriona was hooked. Or rather I was. Because I had to pay. Until now that had meant leasing a horse and paying for lessons.

Both of them swore they had told me what they were doing, and I confess recalling wisps of conversation at dinner after the Christmas holidays about going to look at horses and asking Denise (she was Catriona's riding coach) for her opinion. But I was shocked rigid when, one evening towards the end of January, they announced they would buy the horse tomorrow. Actually, I had sensed trouble before dinner. I always sensed trouble when one of my daughters began a sentence, 'Daddy dearest', or something like that.

'Of course you knew about the horse,' they said. 'Anyway it's a very good price for a thoroughbred.' The wrong word to use on me. I knew about thoroughbreds. We had a thoroughbred once. A male West Highland White Terrier called Camiade Claymore Muckle Flugga the Fourth. We called him Muck. We liked short names for dogs. His predecessor, a sweet-tempered poodle, had been left behind in the Caribbean in 1968 when we had moved back to England because of the quarantine arrangements then in force. He was called Gruts. 'Muck' seemed a suitable name for his successor.

In London, I had asked people what sort of dog to get. It had to be good with babies, because Carey was then a very new baby. And somebody, who I afterwards realised must have had something against me, told me to get a 'Westie'. So we paid a ridiculous sum of money to a lady who lived as far from civilisation as you can get in Essex for a vicious, malevolent, foul-tempered, unpredictable, bloody-minded dog.

I sometimes took him for walks on Wimbledon Common. And not until we were walking home, usually near one of the discrete signs that spelled out the penalty for fouling the pavement, would he evacuate his bowels. When we left London after two years to go to Washington, we gave him back to the breeder we got him from. She seemed absurdly grateful considering we were grateful to her. Actually, it was the dog that should have been grateful because I had been muttering about deep-sixing him off the Albert Bridge late one night. But as Glynis pointed out, if I had done that, two things would have happened. I would been seen and arrested for trying to eliminate a dog with what the CIA calls 'extreme prejudice'. Worse, he would have survived.

But back to the cheap thoroughbred horse that was just right for Catriona. A quick dash across the thin ice of all the things that must be added to the purchase price of a horse. Like food, stable charges, more food, vet bills, yet more food, farriers' bills and even more food. Oh, and don't forget insurance. As if I would.

It seemed to me a lot of money for a totally unreliable mass of quivering horseflesh poised on spindly legs that might – if the gerbils were anything to go by – keel over and present me with an undertaker's bill at any moment. But what could I say? I eventually lapsed into silence.

So the horse came. Or rather we went to it, which meant going to a different stable than the one where Catriona had been leasing a horse. Not an improvement. At least the other road had been fun to drive if there wasn't much traffic. Twisty and turny and lots of ups and downs. The new stable was at the other end of an eight-lane freeway. With tolls.

But with the horse came an idea. If, I thought, we can afford to buy and keep a horse, surely we can also afford to buy and keep a boat. The logic was dreadful but it was worth a try so I put it to Glynis, who to my great surprise said 'why don't you look for one?'

———◆———

My collection of *WoodenBoat* magazines sat in an honoured place in gold-tooled binders in the library of our McLean house. I built the shelves and cupboards that covered every wall soon after we moved in and later looked at them with embarrassment. 'You did it all?' asked visitors, pretending to be impressed or disguising their contempt for my workmanship, and I told them not to look too closely because the joints were awful and the finish was rubbish, although I didn't go on to blame my lack of experience at the time or the fact I had few tools and was not sure how to use them, because I had learned as a child a good workman never blames his tools.

I began to collect *WoodenBoat* long before we even thought about names for a third daughter and, as it turned out, even longer before we started to think about names for a third boat (counting the two in England). I had read every copy from cover to cover and had always read it backwards, which is to say, starting at the back. As a matter of fact I read most magazines that way, but there was a special reason for doing that with *WoodenBoat*. All the advertisements were there.

In earlier years, even though I knew it was unrealistic, I had yielded to an uncontrollable (OK, uncontrolled) urge to call owners or brokers selling wooden boats. You never knew. Someone might offer to give me one. Or I might take leave of my senses and buy a boat before I realised what I'd done. But it hadn't happened. Long before the point of no return – actually, well before the point of even going to look – although in one instance I had got as far as asking for photographs – I had withdrawn. But my mind's eye had seen half-formed images of wonderful old wooden boats covered in cobwebs lit by slanting sunbeams in boatyards in Maine, Massachusetts and Maryland.

Now, however, I had a licence to look with an intent to buy. It was no longer a case of pressing my nose against the shop window until it fogged over but of marching through the door, chequebook in mind if not in hand. A legitimate customer. A serious prospector. So the March–April 1993 edition of *WoodenBoat* was not read, but gobbled. I read and re-read every word. Especially the brokerage pages and the classified advertisements. I called three brokers, all in New England.

And reconfirmed what I'd long since known: that the people who build, buy, sell, sail and repair wooden boats were a breed apart, an extraordinarily civilised, considerate, sensitive, reasonable breed.

And by express mail, the brokers had sent me friendly notes and details of boats that more or less fitted my requirements: about thirty feet overall; shallow draft to make it suitable for the Chesapeake Bay; a divided rig to accommodate a range of conditions and several sizes of crew; adequate auxiliary power for getting into and out of narrow slips with a crosswind; and four berths because that seemed a realistic maximum for a family of six that had already begun to spread its wings; and, oh yes, it should be somewhere on the Mid-Atlantic seaboard, or at a stretch New England, because this was a big country. It was one thing to bring a boat from Devon or Scotland to Norfolk, another to buy one in Seattle or Florida and get it to the Chesapeake.

When it came down to it, there was just one boat in the classified advertisements that looked like a possibility. No, I couldn't have a Baltic Trader. For one thing it was in San Francisco. More important, it was so deep it wouldn't be able to stray far from the underwater canyon that allows ocean-going ships to navigate to the head of the Chesapeake at Baltimore. And though the fifty-year-old catboat was only in New Jersey – America's answer to Essex – it was obviously in museum condition and financially out of sight. Anyway I wanted a divided rig.

———◆———

Even the one that looks like a possibility may be a long shot. It's a Meadow Lark, built to a very well-known design by L Francis Herreshoff. It so happens that the boat I pursued most intently in the years I was responding to the odd advertisement even though I had little or no hope of buying anything was also a Meadow Lark. And in Herreshoff's compendium of *Sensible Cruising Designs*, it was the Meadow Lark, along with the Rozinante and H-28, that most captured my imagination.

The Meadow Lark in question is lying (as they say in England) in Oxford, Maryland, on the far side of the Chesapeake Bay. It's obvious, even from the one-paragraph advertisement, that this is not your typical Meadow Lark:

> 35' HERRESHOFF MEAOWLARK [a misprint]. 1953 mahogany/cedar over walnut. Cedar masts, walnut leeboards, huge double cockpit, documented.

35 feet? Walnut? Cedar masts? Double cockpit? I've checked the design in Herreshoff's book (Herreshoff 1973). Nothing about walnut. In fact I've never heard of walnut on a boat, but that, no doubt is my ignorance. The masts are supposed to be Sitka spruce, not cedar. What is a double cockpit doing on a Meadow Lark? There's only one in the design. And why is this one two feet longer than the design specifications?

I am however intrigued and decide to call the owner about three o'clock on Friday afternoon. He isn't there. His wife gives me his office number. He isn't there either. I get anxious and call again. Still out. I go home and call from there. I get him. The boat is still for sale. Surely there's something wrong with it at the price – $6,000. But Pete Dunbar says no, she's basically sound. Just needs cosmetic work.

Of course I didn't say so but I thought there had to be more to it than that. After all, I have details of three other Meadow Larks in brokerage, two in New England, one in North Carolina, all priced between $17,000 and $20,000. Yet Mr Dunbar sounds like a man I would trust. So we'll go to see her. Not tomorrow. But on Sunday, which as it happens will be Easter Sunday.

L Francis Herreshoff

L Francis Herreshoff (LFH) was what we sometimes call in Norfolk, England, a 'rum bugger'. This term describes personality rather than sexuality and means he was an eccentric, a bit of a curmudgeon and a man of very specific opinions he was increasingly apt to express with a blend of didacticism and avuncularity. It has also been suggested by people better qualified to judge than I am that he was a genius: an artist of form, a poet of purpose and an engineer of rare practicality and functionality.

A lifelong bachelor with a goatee beard, LFH did not follow his famous father, Captain Nat Herreshoff, into the then thriving Herreshoff Manufacturing Company in Bristol, Rhode Island, partly because Captain Nat thought his mildly dyslexic son would be better off managing the family farm. But LFH soon tired of farming and in 1925, after five years as chief draftsman at the Boston yacht design firm of Burgess, Swasey & Paine, where his talents quickly marked him as the best designer of R Class boats on Massachusetts Bay, he set up his own design business at 20 Lee Street, Marblehead, Massachusetts. He died in Marblehead in 1972 aged 82 having produced 131 designs 'taken to the point that a boat could be built from the drawings' (Herreshoff 1973).

Phil Bolger (1983) says LFH thought himself a lesser man than his father yet felt no compulsion to be either like or unlike him. Instead he developed a style and a perspective on boats, yachts and life that was distinctively, even uniquely, his own. He was, in every sense that mattered, his own man, and his fiercely independent spirit was one of his most defining characteristics.

Another was a passion for speed that initially led him to design a series of successful six-, eight- and twelve-metre yachts, to introduce the 30 Square Metre class to America and to develop the ultimately unsuccessful *Whirlwind* for the 1930 America's Cup challenge. But LFH grew increasingly impatient with the rules that governed the metre and other racing classes because, in his view, they militated against speed. After 1930 he had little to do with competition, prompting Bolger to say he was 'temperamentally unsuited to hang on long as a race boat designer' and to speculate that his frustration with rules led him to adopt the reactionary and often dismissive views for which he was later famous (Bolger 1983). But after he hung up his rule books he continued to design fast boats that raced successfully;

some of his most successful designs, including *Tioga*, *Ticonderoga*, *Mitena*, *Persephone* – all designed to win races – were drawn in the 1930s.

His passion for speed was also reflected in the Ferrari and Gullwing Mercedes in which he tooled around Marblehead. Not, I think, to display his wealth or flaunt his capacity to spend it but because he thought fine cars, like fine boats, were magnificent blends of form and function whose engineering and craftsmanship were worthy of his admiration. Just as Enzo Ferrari might have admired such Herreshoff achievements as the beautiful and powerful *Ticonderoga*, LFH, while rejecting the notion that human beings can ever make perfect things, had a better eye for a near miss than the rest of us.

Had he not changed course, had he continued his search for performance within the constraining parameters of racing class rules, it is unlikely that, in the 1930s, '40s and '50s, he would have turned much of his attention to the cruising designs for which he was best known. Which means Meadow Lark among other designs would not have been conceived. His lifetime output – measured in numbers of designs – was modest by comparison with those of some contemporaries. But because he broadened his focus, it was remarkably diverse.

Some designers – then as now – stayed with the big stuff: large yachts and fat commissions. But Captain Nat had produced small boats as well as a succession of America's Cup legends. The *oeuvre* of LFH was even more eclectic and included canoes, rowing boats and dinghies as well as schooners, sloops, ketches and three-masters. It was his later work on a startlingly varied range of boats – on which, free of restrictions and unbound by rules, he could conflate his passion for innovation with his obsession with simplicity – that ultimately defined him.

LFH pushed envelopes and tested boundaries and in the process created new knowledge. But it was never knowledge for its own sake, experimentation for the sake of experimentation or change for the sake of change. His innovations always had an intended purpose: to go faster, to work better, to save time and money, to be stronger, safer and almost invariably simpler, because, as he showed time and again, simpler was better. And his quest for simplicity explains why he eventually tired of designing yachts to fixed parameters – especially when he thought the parameters in question were constraints to progress.

He was neither a conventional nor an inverted snob. His well-known enthusiasm for cedar buckets as sea toilets was a perfect metaphor for his attitude to life in general. Keep it simple. If it works, use it. If it doesn't, build something better. Cedar buckets provided as much amenity as he felt was needed. So he urged sailors to use them. He was on to something, although he wouldn't get away with it now.

LFH was a notable writer. Commenting on a series of articles he wrote for *Rudder* magazine during World War II, W Starling Burgess, for whom LFH had worked in the 1920s and who, like him, was the son of another famous designer, wrote in a letter to the editor of *Rudder* (cited by Taylor 1973):

Mr Herreshoff's is the sort of writing which many people long for and seldom find. Personally, I consider it may well prove to be of lasting literary value. Has it occurred to you that he writes as Thoreau would have written had he been a sailor.

A naturalist with no known interest in the sea, Henry David Thoreau's *Walden* (1854) is a seminal work, partly because it celebrates the natural world, more because it is a compelling statement that few words are better than more words, short ones better than long ones and simple ones better than complex ones. Burgess could have used no higher praise for Herreshoff's writing, which, like his boats, has strong lines, exquisite details, solid craftsmanship, enduring appeal and a serene balance between art and technique.

LFH became progressively more irritated, opinionated, conservative and at times iconoclastic about boats, designs, designers and life in general. Interviewed for the *Boston Globe* in 1967 he said, 'Almost all the people today who have any money in this country have been here only a generation or two and have little education, little taste, little sense of beauty.' He described Marblehead Harbor as 'just like floating swill' and lamented, 'At the present time there isn't one designer in the whole world that's any Goddamned good. No one knows how to draw. No one has any decency.'

Not, you'd have to say, a happy old man. Yet this was the man who in a 1927 letter to his father had written, 'History shows us that almost all improvements in mechanical devices have been condemned by people imbued with tradition ... I expect to bring out several new things in the next few years, and am not going to be discouraged by criticism.' He was neither the first nor the last revolutionary to get crusty in old age.

Which seems a shame because it's sad that a man whose work has given and continues to give so much pleasure to so many appears, at least in later life, to have enjoyed so little himself; that a man who spent much of his life kicking at cages should have turned against innovation, even if he didn't like some of its specific results; and that a man whose integrity shone through everything he ever drew, ever made and ever wrote should have bitterly questioned the integrity and value of those with whom he disagreed.

It occurs to me that had we met we would have had little in common. Yet just as I have learned to treasure individuals with whom I share little or nothing in terms of political ideas, social values or stylistic preferences but with whom I share other important things, I am confident that, sticking to boats, we would have got on very well, although he would have been rather old and I would have been rather young. While I find the credo carved in his wooden drafting table at Marblehead ('Let's call it the Republic again. Let's have law and order again. Let's have God-fearing judges again. Let's say the Lord's prayer again') vastly too conservative for my tastes (it might have been carved by George W Bush!) I have no hesitation in counting myself fortunate to have become the humble owner of a masterpiece designed by a genius.

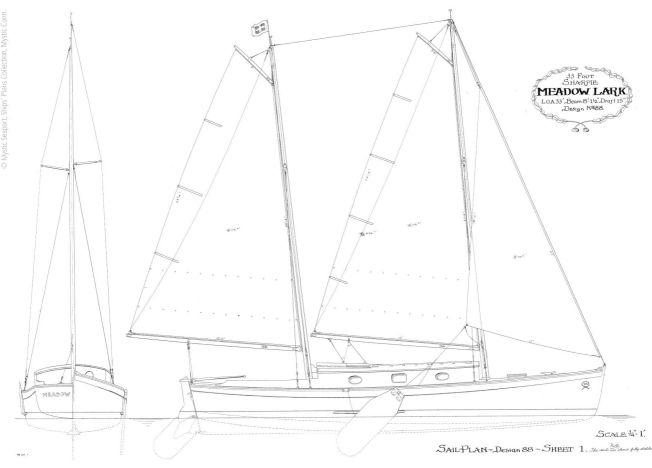

SAIL-PLAN ~ Design 88 ~ SHEET 1.

Herreshoff's design
for Meadow Lark.

Meadow Lark

Background

Had it not been for World War II, America's decision to enter it in 1941, the consequent decline in sales of *Rudder*, the decision of its new editor Boris Lauer-Leonardi to commission a series of 'how to build' articles from LFH, and the success of the series, there might have been no Meadow Lark.

The series began with eleven monthly articles on the H-28 ketch and the sale of hundreds of plans to prospective builders. The H-14 dinghy (two instalments in 1944) came next, followed by 21 monthly episodes on how to build the 55-foot three-masted schooner 'Marco Polo' and, in March 1947, fifteen articles on the 36-foot ketch 'Nereia'.

Bare bones

Design number 88, 'Meadow Lark', first published in *Rudder* in 1948, was a leeboard sharpie ketch, 33 feet on deck, 31 feet at the waterline with an 8' 1½" beam,

15-inch draft, an arced bottom, asymmetrical rocker and an external slab keel. LFH described her as a 'modified sharpie with a slightly rounded bottom and sides'.

Intent

LFH's statement of Meadow Lark's purpose was admirably forthright. His aim was, he said, to satisfy 'those who can visualize a different kind of yachting than ocean racing and would like to spend their vacations in pleasure with comfortable relaxation'. He might have said a very different kind because Meadow Lark is about as far removed from a racing yacht as you might imagine.

He explains that 'a great many people have asked for the design of a shallow draft yacht or cruising boat ... to cruise in some of the very shallow lagoons and bays in the Gulf of Mexico, Florida, Albemarle Sound, and the Chesapeake', and adds 'I can say from my experience that even in New England some of the most pleasant cruising grounds require shallow draft', telling us that Meadow Lark is intended for those who 'would like to anchor in sheltered places, or lie on the bottom of a sandy inlet, cook supper in comfort, and sleep without worry'.

What's in a name?

LFH says 'Meadow Lark' is a suitable name for a craft that could 'skim over the marshes and meadows as the joyful bird of that name does over many of our fields that border the Atlantic'. It certainly wasn't a bad name for a boat and I later borrowed it (abbreviated to *Meadowlark*) to christen the homeless, nameless, Columbia 21 I acquired in 2002. Indeed, birds and boats usually go well together. Take the 1899 Dutch-registered North Sea Klipper *Albatros* moored on Wells Quay fifty yards from where I am writing this, and the usual summer flock of *Kittiwake*,

Albatros: built in 1899, still sailing in Norfolk.

Heron, *Gull*, *Guillemot*, *Goosander*, *Mallard* and other flying boats that will soon join her for the short North Sea sailing season.

Nobody looking at the photograph of one of the first boats built to the Meadow Lark design 'driving to windward in a fresh breeze' with a lovely bone in her teeth could deny she was a good boat as well as a good name or query LFH's claim that she looked 'eminently practical' (Herreshoff 1973). I have seen better photographs of more elegant boats sailing in more challenging conditions but I can't recall a more wholesome image or a more urgent reminder it is time to get up and go sailing.

Antecedents

It seems likely, because he was undoubtedly familiar with them, that LFH approached the design of Meadow Lark with sharpie-hulled New Haven oyster boats in mind. He must also have been familiar with the racing sharpies that had been derived from the New Haven boats in the 1890s, and with the facts that they dispensed with the raised sterns that allowed working boats to carry loads of tonged oysters, featured less rocker and in some cases had more beam to carry more sail than the working versions (Parker 1993).

LFH may also have been familiar with Larry Huntingdon's 1890s experiments with round-bottomed sharpies. But whereas LFH's design carried significant camber to both ends, Huntingdon's 'quite small camber' was concentrated midships, decreasing towards the bow and stern (Chappelle 1939). LFH would also have known about Thomas Clapham's arc-bottomed, flat and flare-sided, externally ballasted and supposedly uncapsizeable sharpies that outsailed every other boat on the racecourse *and* survived gales and heavy seas with, according to Clapham's son, 'no other craft in sight'.

Clapham's sharpies confirmed the proposition that speed and seaworthiness were not incompatible and that, contrary to popular misconceptions, sharpies were as safe as, if not safer, than other boats. William J Starr praised 'the flaring sides and lifting ends' that gave Clapham's boats their 'reserve buoyancy and stability in spite of their relatively narrow breadth' and concluded that 'the secret of their speed with small driving power and their clean sailing was the perfectly fair segmental rockering of their bottoms from forward to aft, and perhaps fully as important, the perfect diagonal formed by the sweep of their sharp bilge when heeled under sail' (Starr 1915).

Starr's comments seem as applicable to Meadow Lark as to Clapham's designs of half a century earlier. She certainly had 'flaring sides and lifting ends ... segmental rockering from forward to aft ... and a sharp bilge'. LFH noted that 'as seen from on deck Meadow Lark is rather more triangular than most sharpies', and explained 'this is done to give a large cockpit', adding that 'with the rounded bottom she should not drag much water at a slight heel'.

Sail plan

Meadow Lark's ketch rig was carried on main and mizzen masts of almost the same height (31' 1¼" and 29' 4¼") spaced to 'give a long deckhouse and an unobstructed cockpit'. As LFH pointed out (Herreshoff 1973) this put 'both masts rather farther forward than is customary on a ketch' and gave her a schooner-like appearance. With stability in mind he opted for short and straight (rather than Dutch-style and curly) gaffs in preference to leg-o'-mutton sails to get 'sufficient sail area without excessively high masts'. And with sail power in mind he gave the main and mizzen sails the same areas, compensating for the mizzen's slightly shorter leach with a slightly longer foot. Both had 'quite deep reefs' that would, LFH thought, allow Meadow Lark to be sailed in a storm if both main and mizzen were double-reefed and the jib down. He opted for a loose-footed foresail (with virtually no overlap) but thought 'a self-tending jib would be an advantage where there are leeboards to handle'. He 'hoped' Meadow Lark could 'get along without backstays and relied on a springstay (triadic stay) from masthead to masthead to keep things upright (see picture on page 47).

Attributes

Although LFH does not have a lot to say about Meadow Lark's hull he is directly and indirectly forthcoming on its economy, safety and comfort.

LFH saw Meadow Lark as a practical option for a family without a lot of money but a strong urge to go sailing together in coastal waters. He stressed that 'the principal object of "Meadow Lark" is economy, for she should be cheap to build, easy to keep up, and could be hauled out by an amateur with a few planks and

Meadow Lark: deck plan and longitudinal section.

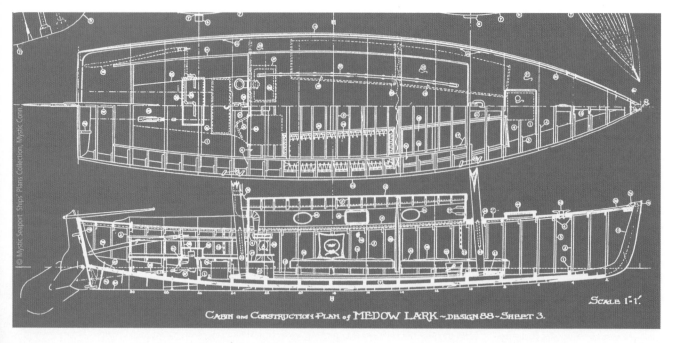

CABIN and CONSTRUCTION PLAN of MEDOW LARK ~ DESIGN 88 ~ SHEET 3.

SCALE 1"-1'

rollers'. He knew cheapness dictated simplicity and thought her 'slight curves [would be] nearly as easy to plank up as straight surfaces' while having 'greater strength'.

He also thought she was the 'the only type of yacht some fathers with two or three children could afford'; that she was 'perhaps the cheapest small moving home which combines safety with some speed'; that 'she would be cheap to service and keep up'; and that 'her strong hull might last fifty years and retain a good sales price to the end, which is the only thing that makes yachting cheap, for if you can use a boat for ten or twenty years and sell her for as much as she cost, you have done your yachting very cheaply.'

So soon after the war, with the American economy in transition and the global economy in chaos, he was almost certainly right in thinking Meadow Lark was a good buy – it would be interesting to know how many sets of plans were bought by expectant fathers. He was also right about relative costs because, as Reuel Parker pointed out many years later, 'Sharpies are remarkably easy to build – easier and in fact less expensive than any other boat type' (Parker 1993).

Concerning Meadow Lark's safety, it is curious that having noted that her 'freeboard aft is rather high compared to that forward' LFH says this is 'to discourage her tacking around when at anchor, a feature somewhat annoying in sharpies'. Why, one wonders, did he not add that the extra freeboard would also make the boat safer than it would otherwise have been – certainly safer than her working forebears? Was he more concerned with comfort than with survival?

Probably not, because elsewhere he seems acutely conscious of the safety issues commonly associated with sharpies. While silent on the trade-off between initial and ultimate stability he emphasises his efforts 'to get the weights as low as possible'. He says that 'when double reefed it is believed' (why does such a confident man retreat so often to the passive voice?) 'she can be sailed in a storm', adding, 'her spars and rigging will be as light as I dare make them simply to gain stability, which is a vital point on a boat of such shallow draft'. He notes that 'too high or long masts are a dangerous thing on such a shallow yacht', and concludes that sharpies 'must be handled carefully, for like many other sea boats it is possible to capsize them' (suggesting he might have been sceptical of Clapham's claims).

Perhaps assuming his readers would understand the risks, and/or believing he had performed a duty of care in mentioning them, LFH is also concerned about comfort. Mast height is as much a matter of convenience ('for inland cruising' high masts 'prevent one from passing under many bridges') as a safety issue (they could make her top-heavy). He points out that the chine forward 'is well below the waterline so she should not pound either when at anchor or when sailing in a small chop and it is believed the slight round to the bottom forward will cause less slap than most sharpies have in a seaway'. He does not predict how she might behave in heavier seas – perhaps assuming sensible cruisers would not sail in them or that the sharpie's speed would get them out of harm's way in a hurry. Best of all, he says, 'some of the ladies would enjoy a sail in "Meadow Lark" who would not go out more than once on some of the deep craft which lay on their ears and have to beat through rough weather because their excessive draft keeps them offshore.'

He was, however, as Phil Bolger says, 'working from hearsay and theory' when it came to perhaps the most distinctive feature of this distinctive design (Bolger 1983). LFH had drawn leeboards just once before – on the 11' 6" lugsail tender for the Marco Polo, where they seem to have worked well enough (although the tender was probably more often rowed than sailed). But on Meadow Lark they failed, being far too small (initially 5 feet 5³/4 inches) to dig deep enough on the weather side to provide an adequate pivot point when going about or to provide enough lateral resistance once turned.

The design for Meadow Lark's, leeboards and adjustable rudder.

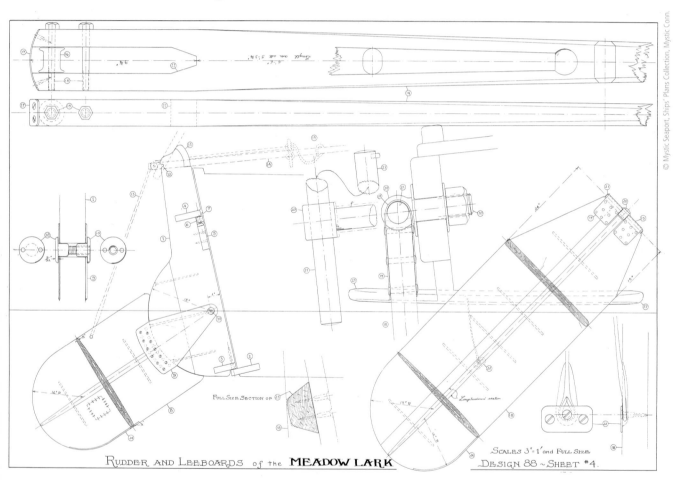

RUDDER AND LEEBOARDS of the **MEADOW LARK**

SCALES 3"=1' and FULL SIZE.

DESIGN 88 ~ SHEET #4.

The solution, which came not from LFH but from boatbuilders' experiments, was to lengthen the leeboards to 8' 10". LFH learned about the modification from builders brave enough to tell him he had been wrong (he did not take well to criticism). Bolger says he refused to alter the plans, 'simply noting the correction for use in future designs', but since the leeboards described in *Sensible Cruising Designs* (Herreshoff 1973) are 6' 6" long it seems he did, after all, stretch them

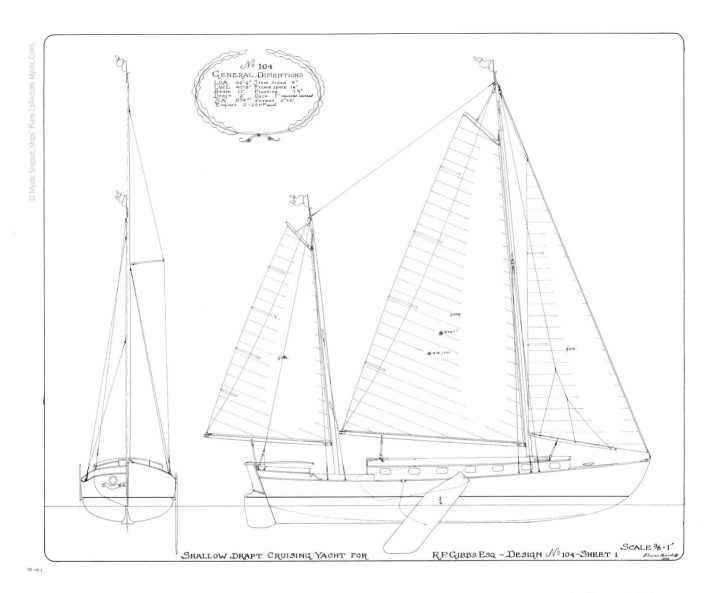

No 104
GENERAL DIMENTIONS
LOA 46'-6" Stem sided 4"
LWL 40'-9" Frame space 16"
Beam 11' Planking 1½"
Draft 2' Deck 1" canvas covered
SA 874 sf Frames 2"x2"
Engines 2 - 25 HP each

SHALLOW DRAFT CRUISING YACHT FOR   R.P. GIBBS ESQ ~ DESIGN No 104 ~ SHEET 1   SCALE ⅜ = 1'

– though not enough. LFH touched leeboards only once again – on *Golden Ball*, which he considered 'one of my best designs'.

Designed for an owner who already owned a *Meadow Lark* and wanted something similar but larger, *Golden Ball* was bigger all round (46' 0" feet LOA, 40' 9" LWL, 11' 0" beam, 2' 0" draft) and owed something to the fictional *Tranquillo* that (with the real *Rozinante*) played a starring role in LFH's *Compleat Cruiser* (Herreshoff 1956).

Golden Ball's leeboards were disproportionately longer than *Meadow Lark's* and, more important, were hung significantly forward of the midships position he gave them on *Meadow Lark*. Perhaps not surprisingly – it does not seem to have been his way – LFH said nothing about *Golden Ball's* leeboards relative to *Meadow Lark's*. Once more we can't ask and can't know but it seems highly likely his decisions about the size and placement of *Golden Ball's* leeboards were derived from *Meadow Lark* experience and that he consciously made them long enough

Herreshoff's 1958 design for Golden Ball.

for windward work, having placed them where they would get the boat on a windward course in the first place.

Golden Ball and Meadow Lark aside, few American yachts, before or since (with such exceptions as Bolger's Dovekie and Martha Jane and Kirby's Norwalk Islands Sharpie), have featured leeboards. Yet LFH refers several times to the fact they had been used for centuries past in Holland and on Thames barges in England, and in describing how to build Meadow Lark he wrote enthusiastically about their virtues:

> 1. They are cheaper and no great disadvantage in a boat that will do little quick tacking.
>
> 2. They take up no room in the cabin, whereas a large centreboard box sometimes quite spoils a cabin.
>
> 3. (And most important). Having no centreboard box allows the frames to pass from side to side so the bottom can be strong enough for almost any sort of stranding.

On Meadow Lark his seeming lack of interest in the design and placement of the leeboards – a critical feature that affected safety as well as performance – was odd. Perhaps he thought it enough that the problem had been resolved by others. Or perhaps, although he was a noted stickler for minutiae, he was more interested in the idea than the execution of the design.

Auxiliary power

At 33 feet on-deck Meadow Lark needed auxiliary power. On some slightly smaller designs – including the canoe-sterned 29-foot Rozinante – LFH decided long sweeps were adequate. His solution for Meadow Lark was practical yet compromised. As always, he made it clear you can't have everything:

> At first I drew out Meadow Lark drawing only twelve inches of water, but I found that this draft did not allow a large enough propeller to be efficient, so the draft was increased to fifteen inches, and this allows one and one-half inches of water over a twelve inch propeller ... Of course, such a high propeller will cavitate for a few seconds before the boat gets under way. The propeller also will not work very well in reverse but these are some of the disadvantages of shallow craft.

He was right. Meadow Lark does not go backwards very well, even with twin Kermath-powered screws. But how many other boats of comparable draft will do that? As he said time and again, life and boats are about choices, and the more honest we are about them, ourselves and each other, the better. And his candour almost makes you cry. How many designers – of anything – point out that something 'will not work very well' under certain conditions? It's a simple statement of fact. But it's also an effortless recourse to the truth. He could have left it out and the fact would have remained a fact. But our understanding of the man would have been poorer and our respect for him diminished.

Author and Meadow Lark addict Thomas McGuane (1981) was well pleased with a boat that was designed to 'skim over the marshes and meadows', and with LFH's tendency to describe trade-offs as 'annoying' and his belief that the best thing in a strange anchorage was 'not to be worried'. For McGuane, LFH was refreshingly down to earth, unpretentious, honest, straightforward and above all a designer you could trust because he really wanted you and yours to enjoy his boat. McGuane obviously did enjoy it. Likewise,

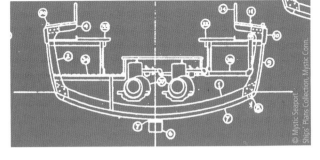

A section through Meadow Lark's cockpit, showing the position of the engines.

as far as I know, the other owners who had boats built to the original design. And so too, presumably, the dozen or so who opted for the 37-foot fibreglass version later produced by Allan Vaitses – although I somehow doubt LFH would have approved of a Meadow Lark hull made of 'frozen snot'.

Mudlark's Ghosts

You could however argue that by scaling up Meadow Lark, Vaitses produced a different boat. It was faster (one owner claims up to 9 knots) because a 37-foot hull is faster than a 33-foot hull, the more so in this case because he kept the beam at 8 feet, thereby accentuating the slipperiness of the original hull form. By increasing draft from 15 to 24 inches he retained shoal water capability while increasing grip. And by reducing the height of both main and mizzen masts while retaining their proportions he compensated for the greater tenderness that would otherwise have been caused by the reduced beam-to-length ratio. Look casually at a Vaitses-built 37 at anchor and you sense the differences but aren't sure what they are unless you can simultaneously see a 33. Go on board and it's game over: the bigger boat has standing headroom and a cavernous cabin. Yet another reminder that a modest increase in LOA yields a stupendous increase in interior volume.

Mudlark's 33-foot plank-on-frame hull conforms to the original design. Length, overhangs, sheer, beam and draft are as drawn by Herreshoff in 1948. But she is significantly different in three ways. Whereas in the original design the main and mizzen masts are almost equal height (the mainmast 31' 1$^{1}/_{4}$", the mizzenmast 29' 4$^{1}/_{4}$) *Mudlark*'s mainmast (33' 8") is a third higher than the mizzen (25' 7"). Whereas, correspondingly, Meadow Lark's main and mizzen sails are of equal size *Mudlark*'s mainsail (210 square feet) almost dwarfs her mizzen sail (122 square feet). And whereas the original coachroof had a single cockpit, *Mudlark* has a shorter coachroof and two cockpits, a seven-foot one that converts to a canvas-covered second cabin (think convertible) and a small steering cockpit abaft a full-width engine compartment.

The story of how 'Meadow Lark' became *Mudlark* is a ghost story. All the characters are dead but their dreams, ambitions, errors and achievements live on in an old boat that each of them, in different ways, at different times and in different places, helped create. There were four of them. But only one (the owner) knew all the others. Without him there would be no story and no *Mudlark*. Each

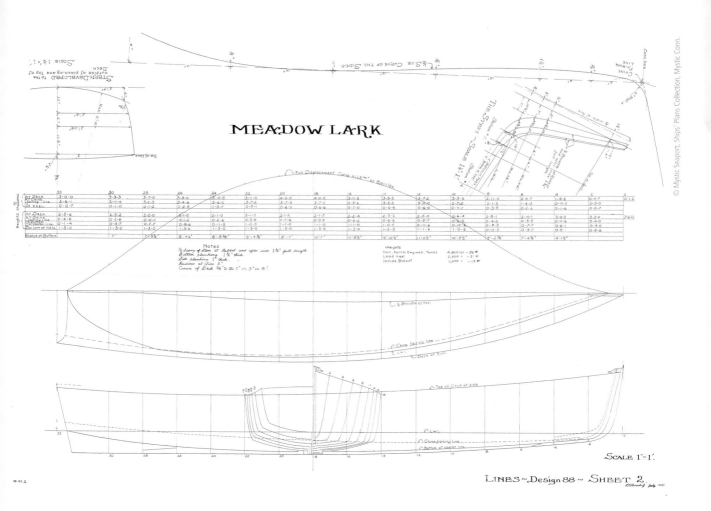

Meadow Lark's lines
and displacement curve.

of them – the designer we have already met, the owner, the draftsman and the builder – played indispensable parts.

It would be fascinating to bring them together, ideally on board *Mudlark*, to ask them to review and if necessary destroy my interpretation of what they thought, what they said and what they did. I can't talk to ghosts. But I can use what evidence I have to probe their thoughts, reconstruct their decisions and try to figure why they did what they did and why they did not do what hindsight suggests they should have done.

The time is 1951–54. The setting moves from Washington DC to Marblehead, Massachusetts, to Hollywood, Maryland, to the Chesapeake Bay. The *dramatis personae*, in rough order of appearance and excluding the unknown number who played bit parts, are Dr Peter Horvath, who plays The Owner; L Francis Herreshoff in the role of The Designer; Fenwick Cushing Williams as The Naval Architect and U W Smith as The Boatbuilder.

The story begins when a Washington DC physician, Dr Peter Horvath, reads the *Rudder* articles in which LFH explains how to build Meadow Lark and decides it's just the boat for him and his young family to sail on the Chesapeake Bay. Sometime in 1951 he contacts LFH and says he is interested in having one built.

But as they talk and as Horvath thinks more about it he decides he'd like a few modifications. He may see them as improvements or simply as differences.

Perhaps because he has no time to do it himself, perhaps because he doesn't want to do it (believing he got it right the first time, or not liking what Horvath wants to do with his design), perhaps because Williams needs the work, LFH asks Williams to draw plans for a modified version of Meadow Lark. Williams draws the plans. Horvath takes them to U W Smith. And U W Smith builds Horvath's boat.

It would have been nice to talk to them about the conflicts, resolutions and results and their relationships. To ask 'why did you want this?' or 'why did you do that?' or 'why didn't you think of the other?' But I can't because they're either in burial grounds or crematoria (at least one should have been buried at sea), which means that what follows is, of necessity, an historical reconstruction. But I know at least some of LFH's detailed thoughts on Meadow Lark because he recorded them in *Sensible Cruising Designs*. I know the *results* if not the processes of Williams's thinking about the modifications because I have a full set of his detailed plans. And I have a huge amount of physical evidence in the form of a 53-year-old boat with 53-year-old sails and a 53-year-old engine. Archaeologists have done wonders with far less.

Fenwick C Williams

Working in Marblehead, probably at LFH's offices because that was where Meadow Lark's details were kept, Fenwick Williams completed plans for the modified version in December 1952. Williams, born in 1901, was 'a mild mannered unassuming man with a life-long visual challenge' (Peterson and Bauer 1984). Self-taught like LFH, Williams had worked for John G Alden in Boston in the 1920s and through the precarious 1930s with Murray Peterson and Aage Nielsen in Marblehead, where his output included the 52-foot schooner *Gloucesterman*, another 49-foot schooner in 1934, the 24-foot yawl *Mary M* in 1933 (the basis for one of his best-loved designs, *Annie*), and some of his seventeen catboats, the craft for which he is perhaps best known.

Williams later said:

> It is extremely distressing for me to be known primarily as a catboat designer ... It is hard to imagine anything more disastrous professionally.

Yet his catboats proved as popular as they were distinctive, their distinctiveness a function of fine entries and 'lively' (his term) sheers and the fact they embodied his 'essential concept of a practical boat'. Peterson and Bauer describe them as 'addictive', adding, 'Once you've seen one, no other catboat will ever be the same. Once you've owned one, no other rendition of this hull can satisfy you.'

There is no record of Williams working on other sharpie designs, although he would have been familiar with the sharpie oysterboats of southern New England on which Meadow Lark was, in part, based. Nor is there any record of a formal relationship with LFH, which leads me to think the commission to modify Meadow Lark for Dr Horvath was part of a casual arrangement such as can readily occur in a small town like Marblehead, where, from time to time, professionals help each other out.

There is an ample record that LFH was generally unreceptive and sometimes hostile to proposed or actual changes to his designs. Builders and owners who sought his approval for modifications to design elements that were, in his view, unnecessary and/or undesirable on grounds or safety, performance, aesthetics or all of the above, would, like as not, go away pulling fleas from their ears. In the 1920s and '30s he dealt harshly with wealthy owners who wanted to change his metre yacht designs, fell out with the syndicate that owned his only America's Cup design, *Whirlwind*, and had violent quarrels with the owner of one of his best designs (*Tioga II*, later renamed *Ticonderoga*). There is, however, no record of his reaction to Dr Horvath's request for changes to Meadow Lark to make her (in Horvath's opinion) better suited to the Chesapeake Bay and the needs of his then young family.

So what did Horvath want? And what, with or without Herreshoff's blessing, did Williams do to satisfy him?

Dr Horvath's request

Horvath had clear ideas about his functional requirements and these requirements led to the most distinctive features of the modified Meadow Lark Williams designed for him.

The first was driven by the fact that he and his family would sail her on the shallow waters and creeks of the Chesapeake Bay. The Bay's sailing season is quite generous, not as long as California's or Florida's but much longer than New England's. The early and late months – April, May, September and October – are best, with moderate temperatures, generally reliable and usually moderate breezes, and fewer storms than occur in the middle months of June, July and August. But some people, Horvath included, like to sail for the whole period and to use the middle months which include the long summer school vacation, for more extended cruises than were possible on two-day weekends. Compared with New England the Bay gets hot in summer. Extended periods of 100°+ heat are not uncommon. And Horvath must have reasoned that Meadow Lark, as designed, was less than ideal for hot-weather sailing. So he asked for a modified accommodation plan.

Horvath's second requirement was more auxiliary power than could be provided by the twin Kermaths specified in LFH's original drawings. He needed to cope with the Bay's frequent calms, to get to shelter if attacked by one of the squalls that are common on the Bay and to ensure he could get back to his busy Washington DC medical practice as and when necessary. He therefore asked Williams for a bigger engine.

Mr Williams's response

Williams left the Meadow Lark's hull severely alone, preserving the sharp entry and low beam-to-length ratio that made her fast, the flare and buoyancy that made her safe, and the rounded bottom, moderate rocker and short overhangs that made her comfortable. He left it alone because Horvath wanted a Meadow Lark and the essence of the Meadow Lark was in her hull. I have no evidence to prove it but I doubt Williams would have agreed to change it anyway and I am sure – to the extent he was involved in the exercise – LFH would have refused to countenance changes. Four years after the design was first published in *Rudder*, not many Meadow Larks had yet been built but LFH was established in both the public mind and in his own mind as a man who trusted his judgment, and there was no reason – at that stage – to doubt the hull was right.

But if Williams's boat was essentially identical to the original from the deck down it was radically different from the deck up.

As drawn, Meadow Lark's cabin was long and low with room for four berths, a galley and (for those who could not make do with a cedar bucket) an enclosed head. There was adequate sitting headroom but you couldn't stand except in the companionway, and the heat generated by cooking could make the interior untenable. But the cockpit was seven feet long and LFH pointed out that 'by putting a tent over the mizzen boom two others could sleep aft, altogether giving sleeping accommodations for six people, which is quite remarkable in a boat of this size and cost'.

Horvath had asked for a smaller cabin and an unencumbered cockpit and Williams came up with the novel solution of a foreshortened cabin with berths for two plus a galley, an enclosed head and a hanging locker; a seven-foot passenger cockpit covered by a collapsible canvas roof and sides on a strong metal frame (more robust than a boom tent) with ample room for two berths on the lockers; an enclosed engine compartment housing a four-cylinder petrol engine; and abaft the engine compartment, a steering cockpit with room for the helmsman/woman and companion seats on either side. A boom gallows was mounted at the rear of the aft deck balancing a massive cast-iron, muscle-powered windlass at the bow.

The resulting profile was quite unlike the original. To some eyes at least it looked odd: whereas the original cabin had neatly occupied the middle third of the deck, creating a symmetrical balance between the three sections (foredeck, cabin, cockpit/aft deck), the shorter cabin seemed disproportionately small; the slight forward tilt to the coachroof gave the boat a mildly nose-down look rather like that of some modern cars; the long run of the cockpit coaming to the cabin roof seemed overextended; and the double cockpit seemed weird.

But it gave Horvath what he wanted. It gave him two cabins, both weatherproof (provided the covers for the open one were well made, well fitted and well supported); two huge (six-foot) cockpit lockers in the passenger cockpit/aft cabin; adequate internal storage in the main cabin; an engine compartment that could be accessed from four sides; and a private place for the helmsman.

So far so good, but what about the powerplant? Not the one in the accessible-from-all-sides engine compartment (which promised to be a big improvement on the semi-submerged twin Kermaths) but the ones that made a sailboat a sailboat. With the deck reconfigured, where would the masts be stepped? Could the original, nearly-equal-height main and mizzen be retained? How would the balance and draft of the boat be affected by the bigger engine? What would be the impact on the boat's centre of gravity? And what about those leeboards, which by the time Williams set to work were known to be too short to be useful? Above all, could he (even with longer leeboards) deliver the performance potential of the original hull, or had he sacrificed too much to Horvath's demands for functional accommodation?

Williams's sail plan distinguished Horvath's boat from any other Meadow Lark. There were still two masts, but whereas the original boat had an almost schooner-like rig and equi-area main and mizzen sails (the mizzen's shorter leach compensated by its longer foot) this one had a dominant main and a subordinate mizzen.

Fenwick Williams's revised design with a shorter cabin, longer open cockpit, and second steering cockpit. Fitting an engine required the mizzen mast to be stepped above the engine, not, as shown here, on the keelson (see detail opposite).

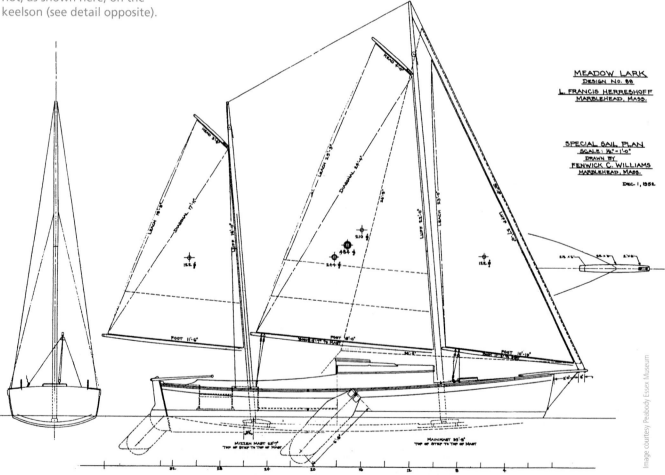

MEADOW LARK
DESIGN No. 88
L. FRANCIS HERRESHOFF
MARBLEHEAD, MASS.

SPECIAL SAIL PLAN
SCALE: ½" = 1'-0"
DRAWN BY
FENWICK C. WILLIAMS
MARBLEHEAD, MASS.
DEC. 1, 1952

As in the original Meadow Lark, the mainmast was keel-stepped on a heavy wooden block bolted to three frames eight feet from the bow. But Williams's 33' 8" mainmast was four feet taller than the original and carried more than 65% of the combined main/mizzen sail area, compared with only 50% in the LFH version.

The extra height of the mainmast and the correspondingly larger size of the mainsail were dictated by the need to compensate for the reduced area of the mizzen sail. This arose from the need to locate the mizzenmast three feet further aft than in the original, to step it over the engine compartment rather than (as in the original) on the keel, and to reduce the height above deck of the mizzenmast and thus the size of the mizzen sail.

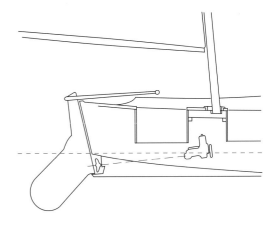

The relocation of the mizzenmast was determined by three requirements: to place it aft of the main cockpit and forward of the steering cockpit; to locate the aft bulkhead of the steering cockpit sufficiently forward of the transom to provide adequate depth in the cockpit (allowing for the rockered bottom); and (allowing for the placement of the stern tube and propeller shaft) to locate the engine where LFH had stepped the mast. Given its relocation, the height of the mizzenmast and thus the size of the mizzen sail was in turn dictated by the need to step it on a longitudinal wooden block attached to the fore and aft bulkheads of the engine compartment and to minimise the compression load on a structure inherently less supportive than the keel.

The modified step of the mizzen mast, accommodating the engine.

Performance implications

The Williams Meadow Lark illustrates what happens to a boat's performance when a sail plan is modified to fit an owner's priorities – in this case a different accommodation plan and a more powerful powerplant.

There is no surprise in the fact that Williams left the original hull form undisturbed. After all, Horvath wanted a Meadow Lark, and the essence of the Meadow Lark lay in her sharpie hull. In fact more than fifty years later you can almost hear Horvath insisting to Williams that he likes the hull exactly as it is and that all he wants are modified living arrangements and an engine he can rely on rather than those little Kermaths.

Nor is it surprising that Williams made minor changes to the original scantlings in light of the additional demands made on the hull by the modified sail plan and heavier powerplant. These changes included heavier and/or doubled frames and floors plus additional cross and longitudinal members in the engine compartment; heavier frames in the cockpit lockers to take the weight of the fuel and water tanks; heavier frames in the area of the mainmast step and a heavier-section mast block; heavy framing for the engine compartment bulkheads that supported the mizzenmast step; and heavier standing rigging to support the larger mainmast.

What is surprising is that a designer of Williams's experience and stature would have reviewed the scantlings for the hull, looked at the arrangements for ensuring the bottom and sides stayed together, and not asked LFH about the chine logs. Never mind that he was a catboat man, not a sharpie man. Never mind that Horvath had said he wanted the hull as designed. The fact that there was in effect no chine log should surely have leaped off the blueprint. But it obviously did not because he didn't change it and there is no record that LFH ever thought of changing it either. That said, it must be said in defence of both that I know the chine log was inadequate only because I have perfect rear vision – and that *Mudlark*'s chine log, for all its inadequacies, held the boat together for five decades.

What is far more surprising is that Williams seems not to have recognised that the modified Meadow Lark that came off his board in December 1952 would not only look different but would also behave differently than the original. Because, while the sail plan had changed, the dimensions of the rudder and the positions of the leeboards had not changed.

In light of reports from earlier builders and owners Williams slightly enlarged the leeboards to the new 'standard' size of 6' 6" (the eventual revised length of 8' 10" came later and appears neither in LFH's nor in Williams's drawings). But he suspended them in exactly the same (midships) positions shown in LFH's original drawings.

This meant that when partly raised, Williams's slightly longer leeboards would push the centre of lateral resistance or CLR (see box left) a little further aft than it had been on the shorter boards drawn by LFH. But when the boards were vertical (as they normally are on the wind except in shallow water) the CLR of the LFH and Williams boards would be identical.

The predictable performance differences arose from the fact that in the Williams sail plan the CLR remained unchanged while the centre of effort or CE (see box) was significantly further forward than in the original sail plan. This set up the conditions for lee helm.

It is inconceivable that Williams and Horvath, not to mention LFH, would have been relaxed about that. Sailors and designers universally and rightly regard lee helm as a curse, and because it is ultimately more dangerous, a worse curse by far than weather helm. Any boat that cannot sail out of harm's way is (unless and until the problem is corrected) an unsafe boat.

Stuck with Horvath's accommodation requirements and his demand for a larger, space-consuming engine, Williams had few degrees of freedom within which to create a safe, effective and efficient sail plan. He was stuck with a small mizzen sail because of where and how the mizzenmast was stepped. He was stuck

CLR AND CE

Centre of lateral resistance (CLR) – the geometrical centre of the boat while in the water.

Centre of effort (CE) – the geometric centre of a sail plan where wind pressure on the sails exerts its total heeling effect.

Co-locating the CE and the CLR results in **neutral helm**. Locating the CE aft of the CLR results in **weather helm**. Locating the CE forward of the CLR results in **lee helm**. In extreme cases efforts to counteract the effects of both weather and lee helm can lead to the rudder being used as a brake.

with the consequent need for a larger mainsail to drive the boat. He was somewhat stuck with the rake of the masts because while LFH had thought they would have

'two or three degrees more rake than shown on the sail plan' the extent to which they could be raked further was limited by the fact he left the chainplates where LFH had put them. But he was not necessarily stuck with the position of the leeboards.

There is no record he considered moving the leeboards forward to reduce or eliminate the larger gap between the CLR and the CE or to pre-empt the problems that subsequently arose from lee helm. Yet as a respected and experienced naval architect with a string of successes behind him and a reputation to protect for the future he must have seen them coming. It was neither in his nor his client's interests to produce a flawed design, but the evidence says that is what he did.

That was the worst of it, but not quite all, because the taller mainmast and higher centre of effort on the

> ## CG AND CB
>
> **Centre of gravity (CG)** – the single fixed point on or near the centreline of the hull where the full weight of the boat is concentrated, which moves only if people or objects on the boat move.
>
> **Centre of buoyancy (CB)** – the centroid of the underwater portion of the hull, which shifts laterally when the boat heels, the amount of shift being determined by hull shape.
>
> **Righting arm** – the horizontal distance between the CG and the CB.
>
> **Restoring moment or static stability** – the length of the righting arm times the weight of the boat.
>
> In calm conditions the CB and CG are opposed on the same line, cancel out and the boat remains level. When the boat heels the CB shifts away from the CG and the forces do not cancel but the shift creates a restoring moment on the hull, which exactly balances the wind. A 'stiff' boat develops a large restoring moment at small angles of heel. When level, the CG and CB are directly in line and the length of the righting arm is zero. If the boat heels the CB shifts, lengthening the righting arm, and, because the CB and CG are no longer in line, creates a righting moment.

mainsail meant that under *mainsail alone* the effective centre of gravity (see box above) was higher than in the original although the *combined* centre of gravity of the main and mizzen masts and the *combined* height of the centre of effort on the revised sail plan was the same as in the original.

The impact of Williams's sail plan on the Meadow Lark's centre of gravity was however trivial compared with its impact on the boat's balance. It was moreover offset by the fact that the Williams boat was heavier than the original. This was mainly because the Graymarine 18-hp Light 4 was considerably heavier than the twin single-cylinder Kermaths specified by LFH, partly because the five-foot-long monel fuel and water tanks that sat in the cockpit lockers weighed more than 100 pounds apiece, and partly because Williams incorporated a massive (80 lb) windlass on the bow. The weight of the windlass offset but did not cancel the extra weight aft of the centreline and Williams therefore added moveable lead ballast in the bows. LFH did not specify the design weight of Meadow Lark, but the Williams version (at 5 tons net) must have been significantly heavier. It certainly had more draft, the 15" of the original being increased by approximately nine inches to 24" (the same as in the 4' longer fibreglass versions).

Having decided not to move the leeboards forward, Williams must have suggested how Horvath might compensate for the gap between CE and CLR. He could have said the best way to go head to wind in light air (when lee helm would be strongest) was to use the engine. But since there were only 1,200 hours on the then 40-year-old Graymarine when I inherited it in 1993 it seems unlikely that was what Horvath did. He might have suggested getting the leeboards as vertical as possible when on the wind, which would have been sound advice for deep water but rather irrelevant to a shoal-draft yacht, and that would have helped. But the physical evidence suggests he concentrated most of his attention on using foresails to compensate for the imbalance of the new main and mizzen sail plan and also to cope with a range of conditions.

To provide for alternative headsail arrangements he drew a 30" spoon-shaped bowsprit so much wider and fatter than a conventional sprit it was best described as a 'bow platform'. It extended LOA to 35' 6" and added yet another distinctive element to the Williams design.

The upwind option was a club-footed jib bent to an 11' 3" jib boom. The head of the jib ran on an inner forestay to a block shackled two feet below the masthead.

The bow platform.

The tack was shackled to the topside of the outboard end of the boom and the clew to the topside of the inboard end of the boom. The outboard end of the boom swivelled on a plate near the forward end of the platform. The jib sheet ran through two blocks mounted on the underside of the inboard end of the boom to an athwartships traveller track three inches forward of the mainmast boot and from there, via a decklead, to a cleat on the coaming abaft the steering cockpit.

Club-footed jibs are mainly useful when short tacking and/or short-handed and are necessarily small because they cannot overlap. But in this application – where the aim was to bring the CE of the foresail as far aft as possible – small size was an advantage. The self-tending device also kept crew weight off the bow and allowed the crew to focus on helm, mainsheet, mizzen sheet and leeboards (although Williams knew leeboards could be left down when short tacking). That all made sense. What made less sense was the 4" diameter of the circular-section jib boom, which would not have been out of place on a much larger yacht. So much for keeping weight down and aft! Perhaps the idea was to discourage crew from getting on the wrong side of it.

Off the wind the club-footed jib was hauled down and the jib boom lashed on the side deck (or if likely to be needed again in a hurry left on the foredeck) and a 120% or 150% genoa was hanked to the outer forestay. Both genoas were later mounted on an early-edition Schaeffer furler shackled to the bow platform.

As in the original design both main and mizzen featured short (Dutch length but not Dutch shaped, i.e. curved) gaffs which made the centre of gravity lower than it would have otherwise been given the revised sail plan. All the original sails (which are interesting examples of sailmaking c.1953) have survived and, although understandably tired, are useable fifty years later.

Williams's taller mainmast and shorter mizzenmast might have called for heavier and lighter shrouds than LFH specified but Williams made them identical. The forestays (LFH only had one) and the triadic stay might likewise have been modified to cope with the different loads of the revised sail plan but were left unchanged. Williams's rigging plan was thus the same as LFH's, as were the terminals, turnbuckles and chainplates, which were also the same on both masts.

The roller furler.

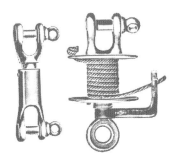

Williams implicitly shared LFH's optimism that Meadow Lark could 'get along without backstays for the masts are quite large in their fore and aft dimensions at the deck'. Williams's masts differed from the originals because they had respectively larger and smaller profiles with the same box sections as the originals. Williams's deck-stepped mizzenmast might have been considered potentially less secure than the keel-stepped original but, like LFH, he presumably concluded that sufficient rake would provide adequate assurance, and there is no evidence he was wrong because the original masts have survived in good order.

Living room

Commenting on the lack of standing headroom in Rozinante, LFH once said 'most sailormen I have known sat down when they ate, and much preferred to lie down when they slept' (Herreshoff 1973). He went on, in typical LFH fashion, to explain some fundamental truths about boat design, to emphasise you can't have it all and to emphasise the fact that if you want shoal draft you can't expect to stand up.

Many of his designs for boats under 40 feet, including Rozinante and H-28 as well as Meadow Lark, lacked standing headroom because LFH was unwilling to compromise safety and performance for the sake of standing up to do things you can do sitting down. I don't know what he thought of the trade-offs that went into the Williams version of Meadow Lark. While he may have feared they would compromise performance I doubt he would have objected to standing headroom in the convertible cockpit – although I wonder about his reactions to the impact of the canvas top on the boat's visual profile.

The cabin of the modified version, like that of the original, is a bent-over, mind-your-head, hands-and-knees environment. Once you get used to it, however, it is a comfortable place in which to move around and a very comfortable place to sit and sleep. Those who think otherwise could do worse than visit a restored eighteenth-century warship (such as USS *Constitution* in Baltimore or HMS *Victory* at Portsmouth), where space below decks excluded standing headroom and sailors were used to ducking their heads. Indeed, it was not until recreational sailing became more popular in the 1960s, '70s and '80s that standing headroom become almost routinely available on small (under 40 feet) production yachts, invariably at the cost of compromised performance and even (because they tended to have high freeboards) safety.

The cabin interior.

The galley was rudimentary by today's standards but included a sink, a stove and a hand-built copper-lined and stainless-steel icebox with lethally sharp corners, and a copper and stainless-steel food storage locker beneath it. The head compartment housed a sea toilet but no basin. A one-foot-wide hanging locker was built opposite the ice chest/food locker between the heads and the port berth. There was additional storage under the berths and in the forward area beneath the foredeck, where access was, at best, difficult. The small forepeak served as a chain locker and housed a circular drum for the anchor rode.

The port and starboard lockers in the convertible cockpit provided storage for a variety of things other than the monel tanks, including a purpose-built mahogany and oak cockpit table that, when not in use, was folded and stowed in a purpose-built frame in the port locker. There was also room for the miscellany of such frequently needed but hard-to-put-away items as buoyancy vests, buckets and seat cushions.

The engine bay.

The engine compartment was, to say the least, generous. The fore and aft bulkheads were built with two-inch oak frames and plywood facings designed to be removed for access to the engine, although rear access was less generous, partly because the hull was narrower than on the forward bulkhead, partly because the starboard bulkhead housed an engine control and electrical panel, and partly because there was a fixed seat on the port side. At either side of the laminated white oak block – eight inches deep, twelve inches wide and 30 inches long – on which the mizzenmast was stepped there were plywood covers that could be removed for access to the engine bay.

The steering cockpit, just two feet deep, had helmsman's seats either side (port side fixed, starboard side removable) and sliding doors for access to the lazarette under the aft deck. The straight tiller with rope and wire controls for the lifting rudder fell to hand in the centre of the cockpit. The electrical and engine control panel was adjacent to the bronze floor-mounted gearshift, which was coupled to the engine under a removable cockpit sole.

Engine

If, in 1953, you wanted an engine for a recreational sailboat you had a choice of a Graymarine, an Atomic 4, a marinised engine from an automobile manufacturer or one of the many products then made in very limited numbers by small firms with names now remembered only by people fascinated by old engines. Horvath's 18-hp Graymarine Light 4 turned a two-bladed propeller through a one-inch stainless shaft. Having been thoroughly restored it is still in the boat.

The engine before restoration.

The builder

More than thirty years after LFH published his 'how to build' series on Meadow Lark, Philip Bolger (1983), who worked with and knew LFH well, wrote:

> Meadow Lark was ... one of his disastrous attempts to 'simplify' construction for home builders. Every time he tried this, the design ended up more difficult and laborious than the plans he drew for skilled professionals. I've never heard of a home builder who succeeded in completing one of these hulls as designed and Meadow Lark only became practical when molded hulls were made available.

That insight was not of course available in 1953 when Horvath took his modified version to U W Smith in the then rural hamlet of Hollywood in St Mary's County, Maryland. Hollywood – its name prosaically derived from a large holly tree that, in 1878, stood in front of Thompson's General Store and Post Office in what was then Unionville – lies on a peninsula washed by the Potomac River to the southwest and the Patuxent River to the northeast. It is now a middle-class suburb of Washington DC.

Mr Smith ran the Hollywood Post Office for more than thirty years, building small boats in a barn beside his house in his spare time. On retirement around 1950 he turned to boatbuilding full time and when Horvath first approached him in 1952 had completed three cruising boats over 25 feet.

I have been to Hollywood. I have photographed his house. I have seen the barn next to the house where he built his boats. And I have to say I'm disappointed. There are, to be sure, worse places than Hollywood. Given a choice I'd take Hollywood MD over Hollywood CA but I wouldn't mind checking some other

Hollywoods (in AL, FL, MN, NY, SC and TX) before making up my mind which I like best. Politically speaking Hollywood MD is not even a proper place, because it is still directly managed by the Commissioners of St Mary's County.

What bothers me most about Hollywood is that it wasn't the right place for a boatyard, even a small, semi-professional one. Call it whimsy if you will, but I like my boatyards to be near water. Not necessarily neat and tidy. In fact I like to see some old boats too far gone ever to float again, a few heaps of material removed from boats being repaired, stacks of wood, a flapping tarp or two, some discarded engines and assorted marine junk. Neat and tidy yards (I know a few) put me off. They are after all *yards*, not showrooms, and should look like places where people work most of the time and tidy up occasionally. But whatever the yards look like, boats should be born (or repaired) near their element, so that when the day comes it's a short haul – on rollers, a truck, a crane or a travel-lift – to their launching (or re-launching) places. Mr Smith's barn (I've measured the distance on my car tripometer) was two and a half miles from the nearest launching place on Cuckold Creek off the Patuxent River.

Just why Horvath went to Smith is a mystery. Having sought out a master designer, and having persuaded a pretty good naval architect to do his bidding, it's surprising he chose to have his unique variant of Meadow Lark built by a man who was at best a semi-professional, at worst an amateur and a not very talented one at that. Perhaps he was in a hurry (I suspect he was a man who knew what he wanted and wanted it *now*). Perhaps other builders said they couldn't build it. Perhaps they looked at its balance and said they didn't want to build it. Perhaps alternative builders up and down the Bay had full order books. Perhaps he had come across an earlier Smith boat and liked it. Perhaps he was influenced by the proximity of the Patuxent Naval Yard up the road and the chance of getting hold of materials not readily available so soon after the war. Perhaps he planned to keep his boat across the Patuxent at Solomons Island (now overrun by developers but then an idyllic anchorage) about 80 miles from his home at Fairfax, Virginia, via what were then mostly minor roads. Whatever the reason, he went to Smith, who by my count was *Mudlark*'s fourth ghost.

Why Mr Smith did what Mr Smith did

The tempting answer to the question I asked myself almost every day I spent discovering (and uncovering) Mr Smith's handiwork, is that he didn't know any better. Yet this was not his first boat or even his first yacht, and the ultimate answer is I don't know and will never know. But I can conjecture and speculate. I can try to understand his circumstances and constraints and his options as well as his choices. I can only guess whether he made the decisions himself, consulted Horvath, or asked Williams or LFH for guidance.

There are two sets of questions: about materials and about techniques.

Materials

The first set of questions is about materials – the stuff that went into the boat – and the factors that led to what now seem weird (as well as sound) choices. LFH, perhaps more than most designers, tended to be highly prescriptive. When he said 'Tobin bronze' he meant Tobin bronze. When he said white oak, yellow pine or teak he meant to be taken literally. He often explained his reasons but sometimes left you up a creek without a paddle if you were unable to source the exact material he specified and had to use something else.

There is no record Williams saw reason to change any of the materials specified by LFH to build Meadow Lark, and it seems reasonable to assume the list of materials presented to Horvath by Williams and by Horvath to Smith along with completed plans for the modified design were identical to those specified by LFH in his 'how to build' article in *Rudder* four and a half years earlier. By no means all those materials found their way on to Horvath's boat. Some of the alternatives may have been sufficiently idiosyncratic to have shocked LFH (and perhaps Williams too) if they had known about them – which they probably did not. Many of the substitutions probably reflected the fact that, so soon after World War II, some materials were simply unavailable. Others may have reflected the fact that if you built your boat near a sympathetic Naval shipyard all sorts of things could be induced to fall off the back of Navy trucks.

By far the most striking deviation from LFH's norms was his use of black walnut for the frames and leeboards. 'What?' they say, 'Are you sure?' 'Yes, I am.' 'Extraordinary.' 'Yes it is.' 'How did it hold up?' 'All things considered, better than you'd think.' 'Extraordinary.' 'Yes it is.'

There is no denying black walnut (*Juglans nigra*) is a beautiful wood or that it makes fine furniture, gun racks, dulcimers, desk sets and other useful and decorative objects. But it is not a popular wood for boatbuilding. In fact it is virtually unknown in boatbuilding save for occasional use in interior trim where it looks and does well. *Mudlark* could in fact be one of the only boats in the world in which black walnut (or any kind of walnut) has played a starring structural role.

LFH said the 'lower section of the frames or what might be called the floor timbers are oak 2" in their fore and aft dimensions, and 3" up and down'; that 'the side pieces of the frames are sawn out of oak planks $1\frac{1}{2}$" thick and about 6" wide, shaped to include a partial knee'; and that the 'intermediate frames can be of oak about $1\frac{1}{4}$" square'. Every frame in *Mudlark* is made of black walnut, as are the leeboards.

He might have said Smith screwed up by using walnut, if for no other reasons than that oak was a tried and trusted framing material and that walnut was not a boatbuilding wood. Most carvel-hulled boats I know have oak frames. A purist might argue that besides violating LFH's rules, Smith violated the principle that traditional boatbuilders should stick to conventions refined by centuries of practice and that one of those conventions is to make frames of oak because oak has proved to be the best wood for the job. Why, they might ask, mess with what works?

Another perspective says that builders should be free to experiment; that there is no earthly (or heavenly) reason to exclude innovation; that the old way may not always be the best way; and that the real issue is whether the alternative solution works as well or better than the traditional one.

By that measure the test of *Mudlark*'s walnut frames (and leeboards, for which LFH specified white oak) is not whether they were made of oak but how well they stood the test of time. You could also ask whether they looked good, but that is a secondary matter because frames are functional (and by the time they came into my hands were painted white so you couldn't see them anyway).

Although in due course most of the frames rotted at the chine the rest of them stood up remarkably well and the leeboards, though not as good as new, remain fully functional after more than 50 years. So walnut worked. Smith's choice was surprising but sound. The question is, *why* did he make it? Did he have a walnut tree that blew down at a convenient moment? Did Horvath want walnut? Did he originally plan to varnish them to expose their looks? Or was white oak simply unavailable? More questions, no answers.

Frames apart, Smith seems to have stuck to LFH's prescriptions for the hull. I don't know what was on *Mudlark*'s original bottom but the replacement was certainly $1^3/_4$" white cedar. The side planks were, at $1^1/_4$", slightly heavier than specified but, as specified, were also white cedar. The sheerstrake was, as specified, $1^3/_4$" oak. The deck and house deck (cabin top) were, as specified (despite the shorter coachroof) $3/_4$" tongue-and-groove soft pine, covered with canvas (the deck but not the house was later covered with $1/_2$" marine ply). The 'deckhouse' (cabin) sides and cockpit coamings (the former shorter, the latter longer on the Williams than the LFH version) were, as specified, $1^1/_2$" cedar – an allowed LFH option. The cabin sole may originally have conformed to LFH's specified $3/_4$" softwood but by the time I got her was $3/_4$" marine ply, and judging from its age, construction and finish may have been original. Even the berth frames (two rather than four), for which LFH specified 'semi-hard wood', were wider ($1^1/_2$" rather than 1") than recommended but (as specified) 5" deep. The same construction was used in the cockpit lockers, which were much larger than in LFH's boat. Item for item, Smith obeyed LFH law in almost every respect, deviating only in the cabin and cockpit layouts, where the Williams boat and the LFH boat were fundamentally different anyway.

LFH initially drew the leeboards too short. Williams made them longer but still too short. Smith got them dimensionally right even if they were walnut and kept the hydrofoil profile. He also took care to ensure the hardware was heavy enough to cope with their additional length (8' 10" rather than 5' 5$^1/_2$" or 6' 6") and cannot be blamed (that was Williams's fault) for putting them where LFH had put them in what was, given the revised sail plan, the wrong place. All three got the rudder dimensionally right although Smith (with or without Williams's blessing) used an iron rather than the $1\,^1/_2$"-thick oak blade specified by LFH – but the oak rudder stock conformed to LFH's specification.

LFH specified $3\,^1/_2$" × $^5/_{16}$" carriage bolts to fasten the lower and side frames and shorter bolts for the deck beams. From what I could tell from their diminished condition when I took the lower ones apart (the upper ones were fine), Smith had followed the prescription and had also used 3" bronze wood screws for the side planking. Curiously, LFH did not tell builders how to fasten the $1\,^3/_4$" bottom planks to the bottom frames; Smith used more than adequate ($^1/_2$") galvanised bolts.

When it came to masts (box-section Sitka spruce), booms and gaffs (solid Sitka spruce), Smith followed Williams who, despite his taller masts and different sail plan, followed LFH except in making the main and mizzen masts and the main and mizzen booms and gaffs respectively larger and smaller than LFH had made them.

LFH offered a rigging and block list 'only ... as a guide', leaving 'each owner and builder ... to change things to suit best his conditions (such as what wires, ropes and hardware he can most easily acquire', adding, 'In the list I have not gone into as much detail as I usually do, and have not mentioned flag halliards, anchor warps, docking lines etc., or anchors.' Perhaps he thought people could work such things out for themselves.

Maybe not – because he then recommended 'two anchors of the Wilcox Crittenden Company's 2002 type – one 42 pounds and the other 30 pounds', and 'one anchor warp of $2\,^1/_4$" circumference, 25 fathoms long ... the two docking lines bent together for the other anchor'. So much for letting people make their own decisions.

Mudlark has a wealth of custom-made as well as standard bronze hardware. Although LFH specified many proprietary items (mainly Wilcox Crittenden and Merriman), each referenced by the manufacturer's number, he designed others himself – including the goosenecks, rudder pintles and gudgeons and leeboard attachments. The last included 'two straps of half hard phosphor bronze', about which

The port leeboard.

he said 'you may think $^1/_{16}$" is thin for these straps but their width gives them considerable strength while thicker ones would be difficult to bend properly'. He added: 'Some of the parts of these leeboard attachments may appear heavy, but besides the strains of a seaway they must stand the heavy strains which sometimes occur in lying beside a wharf.'

He explains, in his usual detailed style, how to make the non-standard items, and implicitly assumes the builder will have both the skills and equipment to do so. Whether Smith had either or both I don't know. The folklore that came with the boat (transmitted from owner to owner) says LFH made some of them. That is possible because he was a master metalworker. Whether it is also plausible depends on the likelihood he would have been willing to make them for a non-standard Meadow Lark about which he must have had reservations. But they are certainly there and somebody – LFH, Smith or Persons Unknown – made them well enough that they are still in use after more than fifty years. But even if LFH made some of those he designed he would not have made the mizzen boom gallows or other hardware that are peculiar to the Williams Meadow Lark.

Workmanship and techniques

There is no record that LFH or Williams ever saw the boat Smith built, which may be just as well because it's hard to imagine either would have been entirely pleased.

In 1953 Smith was almost certainly working partly with hand tools although several companies, among them Sears and Roebuck and de Walt, were producing stationary and portable tools for small shops, including band and table saws, thickness planers and jointers. Machining marks on frames and planks suggest Smith had at least a basic complement of big tools and it is reasonable to assume he had portable sanders, jig saws and grinders. But many of those tools – by comparison with those we have now – were crude and unrefined and Smith almost certainly did a lot of work with traditional hand tools like those my father – a carpenter and joiner – was using in England at the same time.

This means he would have worked relatively slowly and would have been deeply engaged in the workmanship of risk. Anecdotal evidence suggests he worked mainly alone – although he must have had help from time to time when working with and lifting large timbers.

By 1953 craftsmen had been managing the risks inherent in using hand-guided, man-powered tools in all branches and applications of woodworking, including wooden boatbuilding, for many centuries. And we know – from vessels at Mystic Seaport in Mystic, Connecticut, the Chesapeake Bay Maritime Museum in St Michael's, Maryland, and the National Maritime Museum in Falmouth, England – that they worked wonders with them, because those and other collections are replete with stunning, humbling examples of boatbuilding craftsmanship that leave me asking 'how did they do that?'

We know that at the time he built *Mudlark* Mr Smith had not spent a lifetime building boats. We know he was, at best, a skilled amateur turned post-retirement professional. We know other builders using much the same suite of tools Mr Smith may have used were building boats of remarkable beauty and durability even in the relatively austere circumstances of post-war America. And the physical evidence of the boat itself reveals a bizarre combination of competent workmanship, flawed techniques, errors of judgment and (arguably) an implicit willingness to shift construction risks from builder to owner.

The positive side is that with the apparent exception of the original bottom – about which nothing is now known except that it was replaced after two years – and leaving aside questions about materials I have already addressed, Smith seems to have used generally acceptable techniques and to have adhered closely to the dimensions specified by LFH. Properly dimensioned frames were properly sawn, and for the most part properly dimensioned planking was properly fastened. The deck was properly fitted. The keel was properly attached. The wood was as properly protected as it could be with a black tar-like substance that remained flexible fifty years later. The masts were properly stepped. And, from the partial evidence that remained when I came to restore the boat, the original plumbing and wiring systems were properly installed to then existing standards.

Had that not been the case it is inconceivable that in December 1999 *Mudlark* would have been in a fit state to go up the Tred Avon to Easton Point on her own bottom (rather than on a truck) under her own power (rather than that of a tow boat).

Whatever Smith might have done differently, whatever, with hindsight and applying today's standards with today's knowledge, he might have done wrong, he built a boat that lasted fifty years without a lot of loving care and attention. That was no mean feat, the more so if he was indeed an amateur with limited experience.

The most important negative side of his work was that having understandably failed – perhaps because they were simply unavailable – to use hull-long lengths of planking, he also failed to join the shorter lengths he decided to use (or had to use) with acceptable techniques.

Every green apprentice knows that when planks must be end-joined they must be fastened between frames with butt blocks. Smith's failure to use butt blocks, not in one but several places, was inexcusable. His decision to end-join planks on single frames was incomprehensible. He must have known this practice was inherently unsafe; that planks should never be toe-nailed in place; that the inevitable (and actual) result of doing this would be to split the frames; and that repeated efforts to refasten the plank ends would eventually weaken the frames as well as the hood ends of the planks.

Did this happen because he (or Horvath) disliked the appearance of butt blocks

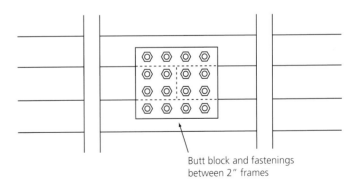

The right way to fasten planks end to end

Butt block and fastenings between 2″ frames

The wrong way

Fastenings in the frame

The use of butt blocks.

(they would have been internally visible)? Was he trying to save wood, money, time or fastenings? Whatever the explanation it was a bad idea. Horvath – assuming he had not agreed to it – should not have accepted it. Both were fortunate the hull was never (presumably) stressed so much that planks were sprung. But that could have happened, with potentially disastrous consequences.

The portlights.

The second apparent defect in Smith's workmanship was a gap between the inner stem on which the side planks landed and the outer stem or cutwater that was bolted to it. By the time I took it all apart the gap was bigger than it had been because the inner stem was by then badly abraded. But it was obvious the joint had never been tight and that, from the outset, filler had been used to close it. Although deterioration in the hood ends at the stem was partly the result of long-term abrasion it was also a function of badly made bevels and consequently weak joints which, in turn, had led to weak fastenings and split planks.

The third problem was that the opening portlights (six in all) in the cabin sides seemed to have been installed with a blunt axe. None fitted properly, all were stuffed with filler, all looked dreadful and must always have looked awful. The problem may have originated in the non-availability of suitable portlights. Those I got were undoubtedly original (Bob said they were identical to those once used by the US Navy), and because they fitted badly the wood around them had suffered.

By far the most serious structural defects – the weakness of *Mudlark*'s chines and the fact that the leeboards were attached in the wrong places – were not construction problems at all. They were design problems.

Section through *Mudlark* showing the weak chinelogs.

The first defect must be laid squarely at the door of LFH, because he drew them. The fact that, as I have pointed out earlier, Williams could have changed them but did not meant he was also complicitly to blame. The related fact that he accepted them along with every other detail of LFH's hull is not, in my view, an adequate excuse because he could have made an exception.

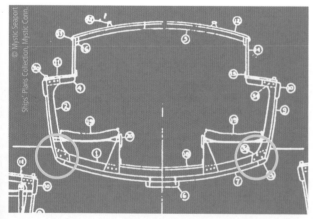

It could also be argued that Smith might have modified the design by building a stronger chine log. But that would be unfair. He was a builder, not a designer, and not even a well-established professional builder. If he had installed decent-sized chine logs they would have held the sides and bottom together, prevented the chines from leaking and enhanced the hull's integrity. But how could he possibly have brought himself to challenge the judgments of two eminent designers even if he had realised the chines were inadequate? He inevitably and quite reasonably assumed those guys knew better and he built the hull according to the plan. There is no way he should take even part of the rap.

Ownership

I have always thought the UK Driver and Vehicle Licensing Agency's term 'keeper' (for 'owner') applies better to boats than to cars. Particularly to boats that, by virtue of age and/or distinction, might be considered parts of a national or even global maritime heritage. I certainly think the term applies to *Mudlark* because, despite her faults, she is a Herreshoff and nobody I know would dispute the notion that every boat designed by Captain Nat or LFH is by definition a heritage boat to be preserved as long as possible, perhaps for ever, by those who become their keepers.

I feel much the same about old houses because they too are part of our history and should, in principle, be preserved. Cyclical teardowns and rebuilds in the context of what urban geographers call 'invasion and succession' result in the tyranny of a continuous present; everybody who has been to Brasilia or Canberra or for that matter Cumbernauld (Scotland) or Columbia (Maryland) understands that a place with no past is a place with no future. Accordingly, I think of my relationships with our Victorian house in Oxford, Maryland, and our converted granary in Wells, Norfolk, partly in terms of conservation and trusteeship.

And I think of my relationship with *Mudlark* and other elderly vessels in my care on both sides of the Atlantic in terms of custodianship as well as ownership. Maryland's Department of Natural Resources records me as *Mudlark*'s fourth

The converted granary in Wells-next-the-Sea, Norfolk. Our apartment is at the top and includes the tower and the gantry.

owner but I prefer to think of myself as her fourth keeper, to see her as a part of our shared heritage as well as part of my estate, and to see my responsibility as that of ensuring she will outlast me as well as preserving a financial asset with which, in due course, my heirs can do what they will (other than let her rot or consign her to flames).

I have no idea if any of that would have made sense to Peter Horvath who, after sailing what became an increasingly well-known yacht all over the Bay for 18 years, sold her in 1971 to John Bloggs, an officer in the US Coast Guard. Bloggs promptly changed her name from *Rozinante* to *Mudlark* (a good move) and took her up the Potomac to a pontoon berth at Washington Marina on Maine Avenue in Southeast Washington where he proceeded to turn her into a live-aboard home (a bad one).

Maine Avenue is now a trendy, upwardly mobile area populated by trendy, upwardly mobile young professionals. In 1971 it was less salubrious. A decade earlier, Washington, then a smaller city, had been ironically described by John F Kennedy as 'a combination of Northern charm and Southern efficiency'. And although Maine Avenue was less than a mile from the Tidal Basin where, every year, 3,700 cherry trees announce the triumphant arrival of spring, it was, metaphorically, on another planet.

Southeast Washington DC.

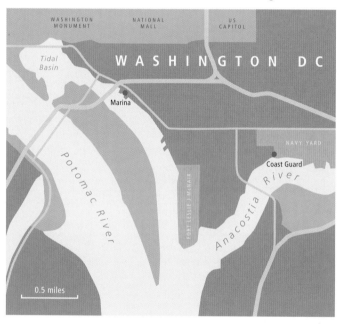

Southeast Washington, like every other sector of the city except the Northwest, was (and mostly still is) home to poor African-Americans. It had (and to a lesser extent still has) poor housing, poor schools, poor or non-existent public services, high unemployment, high crime and low life expectancy. It was and, despite partial trendification along the waterfront, remains a blot on the urban landscape, a social miasma and a national disgrace. Washington Marina was an enclave, a place apart from its immediate surroundings, a place where people who could afford boats kept them – and for some, like Captain Bloggs, it was home.

I don't know how LFH would have reacted to the notion that this modified version of Meadow Lark could be made into a satisfactory home, although in describing how to build the original, he had written:

> I believe 'Meadow Lark' is a type that will give much pleasure and perhaps is the cheapest small moving home which combines safety and some speed. I believe one can live aboard her the whole year around anywhere south of the Mason–Dixon line, and always find a sheltered creek or cove that would float her at the end of a day's run.

He certainly didn't look down his nose at the idea of living aboard a boat, having lived aboard a mastless cruiser on the Charles River in Boston in the winter of

1924–25. Nor did he think small cruising boats too small to be comfortable. In *The Compleat Cruiser* (1956) and elsewhere he wrote enthusiastically about adapting confined spaces to such quotidian activities as cooking, eating, sleeping and reading and how to live without elaborate bathrooms (he was understandably silent on other human needs). But even if he approved of what Williams did to Meadow Lark it is inconceivable he would have approved of what Bloggs did to *Mudlark*, still less how he did it.

It seems likely that Bloggs was in straitened financial circumstances when he purchased her from Horvath, that he had no intention of sailing her, and that his sole purpose was to use her as a home while serving at the Headquarters of the United States Coast Guard on 2nd Street SW, about twenty minutes' smart walk from Washington Marina.

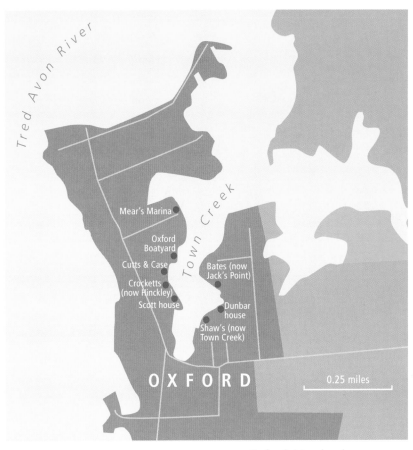

Oxford, Maryland.

Perhaps because he didn't really care about appearances, perhaps because he couldn't afford good materials, perhaps because he was a lousy craftsman, Bloggs erected what amounted to a plywood shelter in the passenger cockpit. I know he didn't buy Horvath's canvas and metal structure because Horvath's son gave them to Pete Dunbar after Pete bought the boat from Bloggs. The idea of living on the Potomac in a tent in Washington's cold winters would not have appealed to him (or anyone else). But it is hard to understand why he bought such a manifestly unsuitable boat if all he wanted was a houseboat.

Winter 1990.

In the event the relationship was soon over because in 1977 Bloggs sold her to Pete Dunbar, a marine biologist living on Town Creek in Oxford, Maryland. Pete had been looking for a Meadow Lark for some time because, in rather the same way Thomas McGuane decided a Meadow Lark was the perfect boat for the Florida Keys, he had decided she was the perfect boat for the shallow waters of the Bay.

By the time he found *Mudlark* Pete had been turned down by half-a-dozen other Meadow Lark owners

who did not want to sell. Collecting her from the Washington Marina, the return voyage of 150 miles took longer than expected mainly because the engine kept overheating as he took her, in stages, down the Potomac, up the Bay and turned left at the Choptank and right at the Tred Avon and eventually right again to the dock at the bottom of his garden on Town Creek in Oxford, Maryland.

Under power in Town Creek.

There he removed the superstructure, dealt with other urgent repairs, and sailed and maintained her without undertaking a major refit for the next 16 years. Because they lived on the water, the Dunbar family had less need of overnight accommodation than those who do not. In his ownership *Mudlark* was used for occasional overnighting but most often for day-sailing. She was hauled every year, given new bottom paint and put back in the water. Pete quickly removed what the surveyor described as the 'inferior construction' in the main cockpit and replaced it with the canvas structure first put there by Dr Horvath. With the canvas cover in place but the sides off, which was how Pete kept her most of the time, *Mudlark* looked very purposeful and in that form became a favourite of Jim Richardson, the renowned master boatbuilder of Cambridge, Maryland, whose yard lay an afternoon's sail up the Choptank from Oxford. 'Mr Jim' called her the 'banana boat', although there were no bananas under the awning where they would have been if the passenger cockpit had been a hold.

Pete Dunbar at the helm, 1990.

At the end of 1992 Pete, who had also by then also acquired a classic Hooper Island Draketail (and has more recently acquired a Rozinante canoe yawl, yet another LFH classic), decided to sell *Mudlark*. Which was how, on Easter Sunday 1993, having seen his advertisement in *WoodenBoat*, my family and I went to Oxford to see *Mudlark* for the first time.

Although *Mudlark* was not, as I suspected from the advertisement, a typical Meadow Lark, I was immediately boatstruck and had a gut-sucking certainty I would buy her.

Two weeks later, a test sail on the Tred Avon showed she pointed no better than I expected a leeboard ketch with no keel to point. But she picked up her skirts in a fresh breeze and everything, including the engine, worked. The sail confirmed a decision I had already made, although it was simplified by the fact it came after the surveyor's report. Infatuated though I already was I don't think I would have ignored a thumbs-down report from a surveyor with the reputation of Bill Thompte, who came recommended by Ed Cutts of the venerable Oxford yard of Cutts & Case.

But Bill had said what I'd hoped he'd say: she was basically sound. He also said my rough budget ($12,000) for putting her right was in the 'ballpark' – although I knew baseball analogies could be confusing if you didn't understand baseball.

'What you've gotta do,' someone had once told me, 'is give him your best fastball and then a slider on the corner of the plate.' 'Oh,' I had said, not having a clue what he was talking about but wondering how he'd react if I started talking about 'sticky wickets', 'boundaries' and 'googlies'. If Bill Thompte thought $12,000 was in the ballpark I'd take his word for it.

———◆———

McLean, VA, 30 April 1993

● Today I went to Oxford to see Pete Dunbar, this time with chequebook in hand. We didn't haggle. I paid the asking price of $6,000. *Mudlark* is mine.

Since my first visit I have been back three times. Mostly just to crawl all over her and talk to Pete about his years of ownership. I am in love with her essence, which is not to say her presence because I am conscious of her blemishes and shortcomings. But I think I have done the right thing. The next few weeks will tell.

Above the waterline *Mudlark* is white all over. And pretty much everywhere, though less on the hull than on the deck and cabin and in the cockpits, the paint shows the tell-tale signs of having been thickened, layer by layer, for many years, until it has crazed in random fractures that resemble an alligator's backside. It is not, as Mr Thompte pointed out, a pretty sight. Nor are the paint-flecked hand-cast bronze fittings or the crumbling hardboard in the cockpit. But none of those things are fatal flaws, provided of course, which he believes to be the case, the underlying wood is mainly sound.

Some rot must be expected in a 40-year-old wooden boat. I would have been very doubtful about a survey that said she was rot-free. Actually, there seems to be less rot

Mudlark, white all over.

than I had feared. The deck and house appear sound. The engine compartment bulkheads in the main cockpit look awful but can, I think, be put to rights with new wood. Best of all, Bill thinks the bottom is intact. Also, the masts and spars. The bad news is that he says there are some partially rotten boards in the topsides and that the chineboards (which are on the outside of the hull) must be refastened.

The chineboards give me pause. There are none in Herreshoff's drawings and

I have never seen a hard chine hull with chineboards before. They look like an afterthought and (the answer is blindingly obvious but being boatstruck I don't want to admit it) I wonder why they were added. Presumably they're meant to strengthen the chine by reinforcing the joint between the sides and the outboard bottom planks (of course they are, stupid). But is this the right way to do that? And why do they look so heavy? Perhaps they're also meant to add weight – which they do – but it's an odd place for ballast isn't it?

———◆———

In due course I spent more time thinking about chineboards than anybody has ever spent thinking about chineboards in the history of the world. But for now, leaving aside the considerable amount of cosmetic work that would be needed to make the cabin serviceable, I was convinced *Mudlark* was a manageable renovation project. By that, I meant – or I think I meant – making her seaworthy (that should really be *waterworthy*, because I had no intention of taking her to sea). Also making her presentable to 'well-kept workboat' rather than 'proper yacht' standards. I knew that all too many old-wooden-boat projects started out as straightforward fix-ups but turned out to be far more ambitious, but I was determined to stick to the essentials and thus recover the 'essence' I knew was there. I was also determined to sail her that fall.

———◆———

It can't happen very often that you buy a boat from an owner who lives next to a boatyard and then get the boatyard to do what a former colleague of mine at the World Bank delightfully used to call the 'needful' (i.e. what needed to be done). But a week after I bought *Mudlark* I moved her exactly 90 feet from her old home to her (at least temporary) new one at Shaw's Boatyard.

In June 1993 there were six boatyards on Town Creek (see the map on page 77). As you entered the creek, which runs roughly nor'nor'east–sou'sou'west from the Tred Avon, you came first, on the west bank, to Mear's Marina where we were once towed by a US Coast Guard cutter after we lost our steering on a timeshare boat in the middle of the Choptank and found (yes of course I should have checked) there was no emergency tiller. That was before Ronald Reagan decided the US Coast Guard would no longer act as a seaborne AAA and that towing services for recreational boaters would henceforth be commercial. It was the only Reagan policy I ever agreed with.

A bit further up the creek you came to the Oxford Boatyard (locally known as OBY) which had been in business since 1870 although boatbuilding on the site probably went back to soon after Oxford's founding in 1673. In 1694 it became one of only two ports of entry in Maryland and flourished with the surrounding tobacco plantations. After the Revolution, tobacco was replaced by wheat, businesses failed, cattle grazed in the streets, the population dwindled and its colonial jewels were fortuitously preserved. They also survived Oxford's nineteenth-century renaissance when the oyster fishery flourished and some new Victorian jewels were added to the crown.

The next bight on the right was home to the Cutts & Case Shipyard. Owned and operated by Ralph Wiley for more than 35 years, the yard was acquired by Ed Cutts Senior (Case was a lawyer and sleeping partner), who moved his family to Oxford from Long Island, New York, in 1965. Cutts established an international reputation for innovation, notably by using Kevlar cords in a patented technique to build and repair exceptionally stiff hulls. Later the yard became locally famous for its giant window display of classic craft large and small, including *FOTO*, Stanley Rosenfeld's former photographic chase boat that had been restored by Ed Cutts.

Mudlark hauled out at Shaw's, summer 1993, showing external chineboards.

The south side of the bight was then occupied (it is now the Hinckley Corporation's Chesapeake Bay facility) by the Crockett Brothers Boatyard. Near the head of the creek (the site of the former Applegarth yard) was a 'trawler basin'. Shaw's Boatyard was almost directly opposite it on the eastern side of the creek and Bates Marine Basin, the last but not least of the six yards, was about 100 yards closer to the Tred Avon on the same side.

Some people see big differences between boatyards and marinas. Decent boatyards have pontoons and piers in good repair, electricity, water, toilets, showers and laundry facilities. They should have workshops and ship's stores or chandleries that sell bottom paint, cordage and hardware. They might (useful) have petrol and diesel. They should (my preference) look like places where work gets done, and usually lack swimming pools, children's play areas and acres of deckchair-covered grass.

Marinas tend to have those things and are more likely to sell ice creams and Chardonnay than bilge paint and wiring. Mears is the only marina on Town Creek and for those who find what they want there (a place to keep a boat but not to get work done) it's just fine, although I have the sense some people look down their noses at it – which is too bad.

Among the boatyards there was in 1993 a distinct and not so subtle hierarchy.

OBY was top dog but Cutts & Case was the place if you had a wooden boat. Crockett's came next, being bigger and cleaner with better marine supplies than Bates (actually a branch of OBY) or Shaw's, which was at the bottom of the heap – which suited me just fine.

Yes, Shaw's finger piers were tired and some of the pilings wobbled. Yes, the water and power connections were unprotected (but worked). The showers and toilets were – let's settle for crude. And there was a ton of mess lying around which I liked. There was no travel-lift, the crane was old (after *Mudlark* survived her lift-out I learned it had toppled over the year before when they misjudged the weight of the boat they were trying to lift). And it had a fairly new-looking shop where I assumed (wrongly) *Mudlark* would undergo surgery. For now she was sitting in a slip and all that remained was to transform a somewhat tatty middle-aged boat into a reliable long-term proposition.

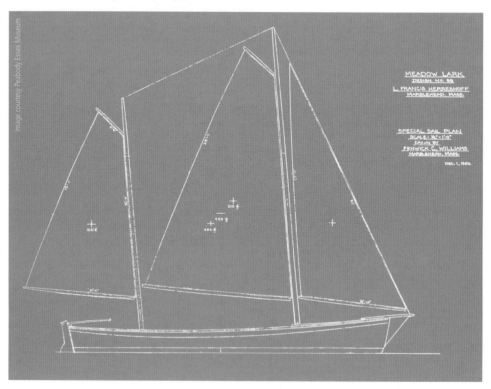

Fenwick Williams's sail plan for the modified Meadow Lark (cabin not shown here).

3
The first seven years

Numerologists, astrologists, Borders rugby players and some biologists seem to be hung up on sevens. I actually have no idea if human organs reconstitute themselves every seven years or why seven-year intervals were used to compute Jubilee cycles in ancient Israel. On the other hand the early stages of my own life seemed to have evolved on a roughly seven-year cycle and my relationship with *Mudlark* seems to have a seven-year rhythm. Seven years elapsed between the start of my ownership and the crisis that led to my decision to restore her. Another seven will have passed by the time we head down the Bay to the Intracoastal Waterway, the Carolinas, Georgia, Florida and possibly further west on the Gulf Coast Intercoastal to Texas in 2007 (with the return trip, however far we eventually get, by road).

In retrospect, the first seven years are a history of denial, prevarication, inexperience and incompetence, which was, I suppose, hardly surprising because up to that point I had done very little work on any of the boats I had owned. I was Granny Smith apple green, but was about to start learning. Partly by doing the right things the wrong way, partly by not doing the right things at all, and partly by doing the wrong things (sometimes right, sometimes wrong). I can't claim I wasn't warned – by people who (I think) wished me and/or *Mudlark* well, but as I am fond of telling other people, you only learn from mistakes. Over the next seven years I would make a lot of mistakes, and I sometimes made the same mistake more than once.

—◆—

Oxford, MD, 12 May 1993

● Bob Bauernfeind has known *Mudlark* since Pete Dunbar brought her to Town Creek in 1978. At that time Bob owned what is now Shaw's Boatyard and before that worked for many years at the Applegarth Boatyard across Town Creek building skipjacks.

During the years of Pete Dunbar's ownership Bob had hauled *Mudlark*, painted her bottom when Pete didn't do it himself, and from time to time done repairs. By the time I moved *Mudlark* to her new home at Shaw's, Bob was an employee of Karl von Kirchoff Senior – known as 'Von' (to distinguish him from Karl von

Kirchoff Junior, known as Karl) – who had acquired the lease from Ken Shaw, who had bought the yard from Bob a few years before. I met Bob there one afternoon, introduced myself and said I understood he would be repairing *Mudlark*. 'I'll be one of them,' he said, meaning others would be involved too. Modesty, I would soon learn, was but one of Bob Bauernfeind's many attributes.

We chatted briefly about the boat. He said he knew her well and that he thought she'd been a good buy. She was, he said, echoing Bill Thompte's conclusion, basically sound and added, 'She's a Bay-built boat.' I asked why that mattered. 'Because wooden boats don't travel well,' he said.

This sounded contradictory; boats are built to travel. But Bob explained that boats that have lived in the warm waters of, say, the Gulf of Mexico, or the cold waters of Maine, do not usually take well to be being moved to the Chesapeake. I hadn't thought about that before. I knew boats that have lived in fresh water don't like salt water and vice versa. But the only factor I had borne in mind when looking at boats-for-sale advertisements was how far away they were and the logistics of going to see them and the costs of moving them if I bought them.

I am waiting for Von to haul her so we can get started on the strange and wonderful process that lies ahead. What shall we find? I have every confidence in Bill's survey, but until we can attack the paint we shan't have a definite idea about what may need to be fixed. I'm mainly worried about the hull. I know (because it's in his report) there are at least a couple of bad boards on the topsides. But until we get the paint off we shan't know whether other places have rotted out.

Von says he expects to finish spring commissioning this week and will then get *Mudlark* out of the water. I suppose every new owner of an old wooden boat feels as I do at this stage. Apprehensive about finding things I don't want to find. And excited because the work of getting her back in shape is finally about to begin.

It's really warming up now, so the heavy work will be done at the hottest time of the year. I'm glad I shan't have to do the work on the hull myself, although I didn't even consider it. Grinding paint off bottoms and topsides is heavy and unpleasant even in cool weather. And work on a hull as big and old as this is a job for a boatbuilder, not a well-intentioned amateur. I've never even touched a caulking mallet, let alone used one. I'm happy to work on the cabin, deck and cockpits myself – I shall leave the masts as they are – once the hull is ready.

Me, I'm going to Norfolk for six weeks with my family.

———◆———

In mid-June, I took off for England. From there, I kept in touch with Von at weekly intervals to check on progress, always with a gnawing, stomach-churning sense of anticipation. But Von would tell me about the weather, about what had been done and what remained to be done, and would sometimes add bits of real-time reportage: 'They're just getting their respirators off now,' he said one afternoon, making me think, in the relative cool of the Norfolk countryside, about what it would be like to wear full protective gear in 95 degrees of humid heat.

Karl took photographs at every stage of the hull repair project and there was a complete record of what had been accomplished in my absence and what (although I couldn't see a lot of it) I was getting for my money. It wasn't just the new planking. It was also the caulking, the new fastenings, the sistered frames, and of course the new paint.

The first task had been to take the hull back to the wood because the only way to tell if Bill Thompte's assessment was right was to examine the planking above and below the waterline. Although LFH had specified white cedar for the bottom and mahogany

Back to the wood.

for the sides of Meadow Lark, I knew through Pete Dunbar (who knew through Pete Horvath's son) that the bottom planks had been replaced within two years of her initial launching. I didn't know what wood Smith had used initially or if Smith or someone else had replaced the bottom. My instinct would have been to go elsewhere but perhaps, implicitly at least, it was a warranty issue and Horvath had insisted he re-do it. All I knew for sure was that white cedar had been used the second time around.

Several days of grinding by the three-man team of the two Bobs (Bauernfeind and Crowder, a ship's carpenter who had worked at OBY and Cutts & Case) and Karl Von Kirschoff made it clear the bottom was sound. There were no bad boards and no surgery was needed. That was a relief, but the sides were another matter.

Rot in the transom.

Thompte's survey had pointed to a rotten board on the starboard quarter near the transom. But as the paint came off, it became obvious that, as I had feared, there were other problems too. Not enough to make me regret my decision. But enough to point to more money on repairs than I had bargained for.

The top board on the five-plank white oak transom was bad at both ends. It had to go. Likewise two on the port side and two more on the starboard side, in addition to the one I had known about. In all, by the time we were through, she would get a total of 150 board feet (about 8% of the total) of new white oak and cedar planking.

I hadn't reckoned on replacing or repairing frames. But after Bob Bauernfeind had looked at some of them from the outside-in (where planks had been removed) he decided to sister six broken ones. I saw none of what he saw because by the time I returned the hull was sealed up again. But I had Karl's photos and could see what they had found hadn't been pretty.

Perhaps it was a willing suspension of disbelief, perhaps dumb ignorance, but it didn't occur to me at the time to wonder what Bob would have seen had he removed the chineboards and looked at the underlying planks. It was probably as well I didn't because I have no idea what I would have done about it. Sometimes ignorance, if not bliss, is at least a way of moving on.

———— ◆ ————

Oxford, MD, 7 August 1993

● I could hardly wait to get down to Oxford today, the first Saturday since our return from England, to see for myself what a difference six weeks had made. But my reaction on seeing her again was, to say the least, mixed.

The transom has been stripped and varnished, and likewise the sheerstrake, which was previously painted a shade between magenta and burgundy. Now, although I can see a lot of knots in the pine and a lot of filler where the strake has been damaged by 40 years of impacts with docks, pilings and for all I know other boats, it has six coats of varnish. The bronze rubrail mounted on the sheerstrake has also been cleaned and polished and (at least until it discolours again) looks great.

The hull has been painted, as specified, in Interlux Brightside Sea Green. The bottom has been antifouled in Pettit Trinidad Red (75% cuprous oxide) to match the colour of the canvas top of the cockpit awning and the sail covers that came with the boat. The waterline stripe is Interlux Boot Top White, which bothers me because I was planning to use Interlux Brightside Hatteras Off-White on the cabin sides and I think they should match, but it's a detail I can live with.

But there is an almost obscene difference between what has been done and what remains to be done. The toerail is the most spectacularly rotten feature, but the decks are cracked, discoloured and flaking; the coaming and the cabin sides are still slathered in crazed white paint, as is everything inside the cockpits. In some ways she looks worse than before.

———— ◆ ————

The following Tuesday I slipped down to Oxford to see *Mudlark*, wearing her new paint and varnish so that, below the rubrail, she looked almost like a new boat – but not quite, because the hull was close to but not perfectly fair – gently picked up by Bob Bauernfeind's crane in new slings bought for the occasion, and returned to her element. Not, for several days at least, without support because if she had been set down without restraining slings, she would have sunk rather quickly, having been out of the water nearly two months in hot sun. But she quickly took up enough moisture to stop most of the leaks, and by the end of the week was floating unsupported at the work slip.

All I had to do was fix the rest of the boat. How long? Three weeks? Three months? Three years? Piece of cake, I said to myself. Nothing there that can't be put right pretty quickly with hard work and enthusiasm. But she absolutely must be ready by early October when the Cracknells visit from England. I had eight weeks.

The bronze rubrail.

On Saturday, entering stage-left armed with the first of the tools and materials I would gradually load on board, I got stuck in to the bit of the project called 'Everything Above the Rubrail.'

Have you ever found yourself facing an impossible task knowing it's an impossible task yet unwilling to admit it to anyone, including yourself? Then you know how I felt. With even a modicum of experience I would have known before I started there wasn't a snowball's chance in hell I could have the boat in anything remotely approaching a fit condition for our friends to sail and – hell's bells – live

In slings, before returning to the water.

on for two weeks. In Norfolk a few weeks earlier it had been easy to say things like 'Of course she'll be ready by then' and 'I've got two months before you come and that'll be ample time to sort things out inside'. The sad thing was I believed it. The worst thing was they believed me.

First draft: what not to do

The first job was to repair the deck. The yard removed the old toerails, which had to come off because they were full of rot and looked awful. I agreed with Von I would prepare the deck and that the yard would repair it by letting in new pieces of plywood where (as Thompte had told me) rot had taken over. The yard would then cover the whole deck with fibreglass cloth and 'microballoons' (I hadn't a clue what they were but understood they were mixed with epoxy), lapping the cloth over the deck edges to make a good hull–deck seal and provide a base for the new toerails.

Using a heat gun and Pro-Prep scrapers – I found the bigger hardware store ones weren't sharp enough – I scraped paint, degraded glass cloth and a layer of black

The toerails, as they were.

rubber compound from the plywood, which, except where it had rotted, was in very good condition. It was tedious and boring but the scale wasn't enormous. The largest areas were the aft and fore decks – the side decks were mercifully narrow. Yet I felt slightly ridiculous using such tiny tools; it was a bit like shovelling a snowdrift with a teaspoon.

The deck prep took three weekends but by late August it was ready for the plywood repairs and fibreglassing and by the time I got there the following weekend it was, except for paint, finished. Meanwhile the clock was ticking and the day of the Cracknells' arrival in early October was rushing at me. I always find it's good to have deadlines (I can't do without them) but this one was looking absurd.

Oxford, MD, 1 September 2003

● There's nothing for it. I have taken three days' leave (fortunately the Bank provides plenty, being generous in that as in other ways) to try to accelerate progress. Bob Crowder is doing a wonderful job on the mahogany toerails: the scarfs are almost undetectable and the wood has a lovely grain. He's also repairing a broken section of coaming on the port side which seems to have cracked when the boat was lifted. Plus a few more 'while you're at it why don't you' jobs (the equivalent of 'while you're below could you' requests yelled down the companionway on a blustery day). Things like reinstalling the traveller track for the club jib and installing new deck ports for water, fuel and waste.

I'm working on the cockpit, scraping, sanding and doing my best to create paintable surfaces, knowing I shall have to take off whatever paint I put on them because I don't have time (or know how) to do it properly quickly. The name of this game is to get things cosmetically acceptable before the Cracknells arrive; that means quick and dirty, once over lightly and let's call this a rough first draft.

As I work on the coamings I realise they will need a lot of work, as will the cabin sides and coachroof. It's a shame I don't have time to get all the alligatored paint off. Instead, I'm putting filler in the cracks although I'm not sure if I'm using the right stuff. But it will have to do for now. The forward bulkhead of the engine compartment is a real mess. It's a weird design with removable lift-off sections secured in place by sliding bolts. It's great for getting at the engine but the central section is very heavy and there's nowhere to put it once it's off. Then I

The engine cover.

suppose that doesn't matter if you only want to get at the engine. I've replaced the broken bits of perforated hardboard on the bulkhead but have left the rest to be replaced later.

McLean, VA, 19 September 1993

● It's Sunday evening and I'm knackered again, having worked unbelievably hard (by my standards) over the weekend. The steering cockpit got a lick of paint yesterday and that was that. The control panel, now I've looked at it closely, is awful, what I originally saw as its antique charm being more than offset by the

The controls.

crudeness of its workmanship, the difficulty of cleaning it and (although Bob Buaernfeind says it's OK and I trust him) the possibility the whole thing may be unsafe. I'm fairly sure it doesn't conform to whatever code exists for these things. Perhaps the Smithsonian would like it.

I've decided the spars will have to stay as they are. I just can't touch them now although their white paint is badly faded. But I have asked Bob Bauernfeind to check the wiring and to replace the decklights on the

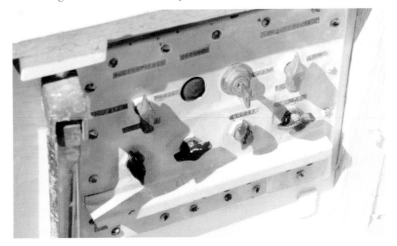

undersides of the spreaders on the mainmast. I should add a VHF radio aerial too but there's not much point because I'm not going to buy a radio at this stage. I know there should be one but the Cracknells will only be day-sailing and won't be exploring too far. Anyway I'll give them my mobile phone so they should be OK.

I've also decided the bronze fittings on the masts, the jib, main and mizzen winches and the stanchion for the boom gallows will have to stay paint-flecked. Pete Dunbar tells me he thinks some of the fittings were cast by LFH. They will, however – even if they were hand-cast by the Great Man – have to wait until I have time to clean them.

The cabin needs a huge amount of work, so much I hardly know where to start. But Bob Crowder is making a folding door to replace the curtain that previously hung across the toilet area. Somehow I don't like going to the loo in public. He's also boxing in the pipes at the back of the new toilet Karl is installing. The old one didn't work and looked very tired. Karl is fitting a holding tank in the portside cockpit locker because it's now mandatory to have one, although the 'Y' valve gives me the theoretical option of dumping waste at sea. The valve is only legal if the overboard option is closed and these days the Coast Guards are getting more picky about compliance.

That is just as well, because although the Chesapeake is not a closed system, it's not an ocean. Indeed the whole of the Bay is legislatively within the three-mile limit where waste disposal is illegal. When (in the early 1980s) the US Government finally made holding tanks mandatory, they forgot to ensure there were enough pump-out facilities (a bit like banning parking on public roads without providing off-street parking). In fact, there were, initially, only a handful of pump-outs, which meant even if you wanted to comply with the law there was no place to empty your holding tank once it was full. It also meant that when, for whatever reason, the Coast Guard boarded your vessel they would say something like 'You do have a holding tank don't you?' and 'It isn't discharging overboard, is it?' That was then and this is now.

Anyway the head will look a lot better (I'm also installing a teak cabinet and painting the shelves and sole). The galley already has a new Origo alcohol stove and a Fynespray water pump, both high-line items that look good and work well, but the countertop, sink, drawers and icebox are as found. The copper lining in the icebox and the metal cupboard beneath are hard to clean but at least I've removed the dirt and polished the stainless.

Oxford, MD, 3 October 1993

● Well that's it. I've done my best and things look better. But that was the last weekend before Richard and Alison arrive and I'm not really finished. In the last couple of days I've painted the cabin overhead, cabin sides, bulkheads and berth lockers and hung small cargo nets either side of the mainmast. I've asked Karl to install new electric lights on the bulkheads and a couple of

Weems & Plath brass oil lamps I got at Fawcetts in Annapolis to add a bit of character (and a bit of light).

I think Bob Bauernfeind doesn't quite approve of all this attention to cosmetics and that he feels I'm hung up on how things look without worrying about important matters like sails and rigging and engine. It bothers me because I'm developing serious respect for his experience, knowledge and judgment and don't want him to think badly of me. I want to tell him I really do understand priorities and that I'm only doing all this now because the Cracknells are coming. But even so I'm still not ready which means (damn it) I shall have to finish the remaining jobs with Richard's help next Sunday.

McLean, VA, 11 October 1993

● I've known Richard Cracknell a long time and I am delighted he's going to sail *Mudlark*. He's a far better sailor than I shall ever be, Dean of International 12 Square Metre Sharpie class helmsmen, former British and European champion, Norfolk Wherry skipper and an outstandingly good teacher who never shouts or panics and has the rare skill of imbuing the greenest of helms with a confidence they thought they'd never achieve.

He and Alison arrived yesterday on their first trip to America and early this morning he and I drove down to Oxford to take care of a few last jobs.

A few last what?

Richard was very polite but almost visibly stunned when he saw *Mudlark* for the first time. As we stood on the dock I waited for him to say 'what a lovely boat' or something like that but he just kept looking. Sensing I had oversold the boat and undersold her defects, I broke the silence: 'She's a bit rough cosmetically'.

The brass oil lamps.

'That's not what I'm looking at,' he said. 'I don't think this boat is ready to go to sea.'

If you've ever auditioned for a part in a play and been told you not going to get it, gazed expectantly at a team list and haven't found your name, torn open an envelope to learn the college has rejected you, or turned hopefully to the driving examiner having just run over a cat, you'll understand how I felt. But I wasn't really surprised. I'd known all along that two months of part-time effort would never suffice to do the job properly even if I'd known what I was doing. So my disappointment was akin to that of the actor who never expected to get the part, the cricketer who knows he should be dropped, the applicant who never expected to get in, and the examinee who expected to fail. Richard was only telling me what I already knew.

The question was, could we, working together for a day, somehow make things – if not right, then at least minimally right enough to allow Richard and Alison to spend some time on her? We could only try. And try we did for the next twelve hours. I was astonished by the list of things I hadn't done and the longer list of things I hadn't thought of. Things like checking the anchor rode and anchors (a big CQR and a good-sized Danforth); ensuring that the sails could be bent on the spars, that the shackles had pins, that the leeboards were on the right way up, that the winch handles were accessible to the winches – the list went on. We stopped for a quick lunch and worked through dusk. It was a tired and subdued drive back to McLean.

The next morning we returned to Oxford, this time with Alison and a supply of food and drink, and said to let us know if they needed help and wanted to come back to Virginia before next weekend. I drove back to my office at the World Bank feeling slightly sick. The bottom line was that I had foolishly induced two friends to come to America to play with a boat that wasn't ready and would at best give them a miserable experience. It wasn't fair and I was entirely to blame.

Things didn't go well. *Mudlark* didn't sink and most of her gear worked most of the time. But they were wretchedly uncomfortable, cold to boot (that wasn't my fault, because mid-October is usually fine for sailing on the Bay), and the engine refused to cooperate because the fuel was dirty (the tank hadn't been cleaned before being refilled). As a result they set out three times and returned to the yard before the problem was diagnosed and a plastic tank rigged up to provide clean fuel, after which they were able to spend a night away from the dock. And when they did get out they were hit from behind by one of those freak Chesapeake squalls that came out of nowhere and Richard was just able to get the sails down in time while Alison, alone in the steering cockpit, hung on grimly thinking, she told me later, not about getting drowned but about wrecking my boat.

———◆———

Second draft: the return of the bumbler

I learned a lot from the Cracknells' visit. About them, myself, boats in general and *Mudlark* in particular.

I learned that Alison and Richard were (and are) even nicer friends than I'd thought (they were, in the circumstances, remarkably forgiving).

I learned that there were limits to my time-tested belief that by promising the ridiculous I could achieve the impossible. When the job at hand was on familiar territory; when I knew my way around the subject, when I was pushing envelopes I had pushed before, it usually worked, although I was sometimes a bit late. But when, as in this case, I was on unfamiliar ground, largely ignorant of both substance and method and playing with envelopes that were quite likely (metaphorically speaking) to explode in my face, it was a different matter. I had failed because I didn't know what I was doing, and instead of moving the goalposts I had kept my head down and raced towards them, knowing I would never cross the touchline.

I learned that boats are far more complicated than I had thought; that their complexity is partly a function of size; that length overall is a misleading guide to volume; and that while two masts have many advantages, and may be essential to safety as well as offering convenience and flexibility, they mean more work. Although *Mudlark* was not my first wooden boat she was my first cruising boat and my first relatively big boat. She was also the first boat on which I had ever tried to do a significant amount of work myself – as opposed to getting someone else to do it. Besides lacking experience and relevant skills, I was quite unprepared for the amount of work I had to do and did not know how to make the best use of my time.

And I learned that because *Mudlark* was an old and tired boat there was no way to get around the fact she would not, could not, respond to someone who charged headlong into a project to get her ready in what amounted to a few days. A newer boat, in better condition, with basically reliable systems, could perhaps have been dusted off and turned around quite quickly. Not this lady. She needed far more time, skill, effort and money than I had imagined might be needed. I was by no means the first or last boat-sick fool to rush in where older and wiser heads would not have thought of treading. But at the end of what I began to call (being used to writing successive versions of books and papers) my 'first draft', I realised it was time for the second.

For the next two years I kept the boat at Shaw's, worked on her a lot, sailed her a little and found my place in the cast of characters who populated that boatyard – and, I daresay, most boatyards in the Known Universe.

WHO'S WHO AT THE BOATYARD

Sailors are people who believe recreational sailing craft are either devices for thrashing around plastic buoys to win races whose winners are determined by obscure mathematical formulae or devices for sailing with friends and family mainly in sight of land proving nothing to anybody.

Boatmen are so seriously fascinated by boats of almost all kinds (but mainly by boats of intrinsic value to those who own and sail them) that they believe well-maintained boats are far too precious to be actually used and, as a result, rarely if ever go sailing.

Nautical hermaphrodites are sexually normal people who enjoy sailing and boating who may be good at both and may spend a lot of time (and money) on maintenance and improvement but also like to use their boats as much as possible.

Teeth-suckers are know-it-alls who do not own or work on boats who spend significant parts of useless lives giving unsolicited advice to people who own, sail and work on their own or other peoples' boats and who, having sharply inhaled between clenched teeth, start most sentences with 'I wouldn't do that if I was you ...' (the syntax is worse than the suck).

As a group they confirmed my long-held belief that most people who hang around boats are exceptionally agreeable. But I also realised, more than before, that they were quite diverse and that I had more in common with some than with others.

A few weeks after the Cracknells had gone back to England I set about building a winter cover for *Mudlark*. The Lowes store in Easton, ten miles up the road, became the source for 2" × 4" pine studs, lengths of copper pipe, an assortment of copper coupling devices and bright blue tarpaulins. It took several weekends. I started without a plan, made it up as I went along and ended up with a flimsy structure that seemed likely to collapse in the first blast of heavy air.

It actually lasted until February, although I did running repairs throughout the winter, refastening ties that had come undone and replacing the plastic (ex water, milk and chlorox) bottles I filled with creek water to weigh down the tarps. In mid-

February I declared victory by saying the winter was over and spring was about to start and began removing the by-then very wobbly and decidedly Heath-Robinson apparatus I had put together in the fall. It snowed as soon as I removed it.

Once the ice and snow had disappeared for good I took stock of what I had done. I got a little help from Bob Bauernfeind, who strolled down the dock one Saturday afternoon and said it was a pity I had spent so much on the boat only to have it wrecked by the timber and metal framework. He was quite right, so much so I apologised to him and Bob Crowder for having messed up their work. The toerails had taken the biggest hits, where they had been gouged by shifting 2×4s, and it would be a while before I figured how to repair them. The lesson was that I couldn't build a boat cover for *Mudlark* without a plan that took account of the low deck house and the two masts, and without the right materials and construction methods. Next year I'd have to do something else.

That spring, I was later starting work again on *Mudlark* than I had intended because I sidetracked myself by refinishing an 8-foot lapstrake plywood skiff that had been well built by Pete Dunbar to the Cabin Boy design. I had bought her from him at the end of the previous year to use as a tender to *Mudlark* (nameless, she became *Lesser Mudlark*) and took her to my McLean workshop to clean, re-varnish and repaint over the winter. As everyone who has tried to clean around copper roves and get at tiny spaces between thin ribs knows, it's a tiresome and frustrating job. I was determined to do it as well as I could but the job cut into time I had meant to spend at the yard. Her most distinctive feature was a saucy sheer, accentuated by the fact that Pete had left the stem very proud, giving the little boat a jaunty appearance. Once finished, I took her to a canvas shop on Kent Island – where the owner had to fend off offers to buy her – to get a new cover.

As the weather warmed I spent more weekends on the boat. In April, other owners started to come down to greet each other by saying 'Happy Spring', just as, in December, people say 'Happy Christmas'. Having often said there were few places more seductive, absorbing or joyful than an American college campus (by which I mean a liberal arts college like Washington and Lee, Swarthmore or Middlebury) in spring, I learned American boatyards have comparable charms.

Looking back, it seems remarkable that after the mess I had made of things in the late summer I started the second draft of 'Everything Above the Rubrail' without a proper plan. As a result I found myself doing a bit here, a bit there, rather than working systematically on one task before moving to another. I did however distinguish between the things I would tackle myself and the things I would get the yard to do, the main item in that category being the engine and the fuel system.

Removing the massive monel fuel tank – five feet long, a foot and a half in diameter, and weighing over 100 pounds – from its wood frame meant taking the top off the port cockpit locker, releasing the turnbuckles that held it in place, lifting the tank off the boat onto the dock and trundling it to the yard in a wheelbarrow.

Lesser Mudlark, a Cabin Boy skiff designed by John Atkin.

Von then sent it to a specialist firm in Delaware for cleaning. The reports that came back weren't encouraging. It was not, as I already knew, a purpose-built tank. It was an industrial heat-exchanger with internal baffles that proved very hard to clean. It was also, it turned out, illegal because the law said the fuel had to flow from the top rather than the bottom. That meant it had to be retrofitted. Bob Bauernfeind pointed out that even when that had all been done I'd still have a dodgy tank. 'Why not get a new plastic one?' he asked. 'Because I want to preserve the boat as is,' I said. Lesson: listen to the voice of experience.

As to the engine, there was no question. I would keep it. Partly for the same reason I wanted to keep the tank, partly because I didn't want the expense of a new one. So I asked Bob to overhaul it and he did and said that although one cylinder was bad, it would serve me well enough, bearing in mind its simplicity, strong build and low hours from new. In due course the tank came back, and was reconnected to the engine. At the dock, it ran well and sounded good.

The electrical system also needed a complete overhaul. Bob installed a power inverter and shore power connector to allow me to run power tools in the boat. He also urged me (revealing his real opinion) to get rid of the control panel because it was a piece of junk and, more important, unsafe. But I wouldn't have it, insisting, 'I want to preserve the boat as is.' Bob, doubtless against his better judgment, did as I asked.

Although, for the work I did myself, I lacked a plan, I had goals: to repair and refinish the passenger cockpit; to do the same in the steering cockpit; to paint the cabin properly – which, as in the cockpits, meant re-doing most of what I had done before in a hurry; and to review, refinish and as necessary replace the sail-handling and anchoring systems.

My decisions about what I would do next were largely guided by what I felt like doing on the weekend in question and partly by what I felt comfortable (i.e. confident) doing. Not, therefore, by what was most urgent, because I had decided I was not going to sail the boat again until all the important jobs were finished and that the order in which I did them did not therefore matter. In retrospect it would have a good idea to develop a sequence based on a critical path analysis that would have told me 'this before that'. Or to have thought more about the logic of painting things that might have to be removed, getting scuffed or damaged in the process.

Instead, I bumbled on, sometimes spending a day at the yard and driving back, usually very tired, in late afternoon, sometimes staying overnight. But it wasn't easy to get there at all because there was an inevitable conflict of loyalties – to *Mudlark* on one hand and, far more important, to Glynis and my children on the other. By the spring of 1994 Carey was at Cambridge and Caitlin was in the sixth form at Rugby. But Cameron was barely twelve and Catriona fifteen and obsessed with her horse. Sometimes, when Glynis went to a weekend riding event with Catriona, Cameron and I would spend the weekend on the boat, but there wasn't a lot he could do and I knew he was not – at least not yet – into boats and that much of the time he was bored. These, however, were early days, and in due course Cameron would become an important actor in the process of remaking *Mudlark*.

There was also a house to consider, and a garden, neither small. The house, in McLean, Virginia, near the CIA, had 5,000 feet of living space and from time to time required maintenance and improvement, most of which I chose to do myself. The half-acre garden also seemed to need constant attention and to repay neglect with vicious ingratitude: the woods at the back would drop trees, shed branches and throw leaves across the lawn which, facing north, was hard to keep green. My periodic efforts to grow shrubs and flowers on the south-facing front were only partially successful, not least on account of the plagues of Japanese beetles that devastated roses and other plants.

Last but often first there was my job at the World Bank, which consumed vast amounts of time and energy every week and often weekends too. By the time *Mudlark* entered my life I was a decade past my last operational job as Chief of the Bank's Urban Development Division for Latin America and the Caribbean and had become Director of Organisation, working directly with the President and his senior management team on a variety of issues affecting the Bank's organisational performance.

I loved the job, relished the responsibility and thrived on the often short deadlines and high expectations. But by Friday night I was often exhausted and it was a rare weekend when at least part of Saturday and Sunday was not consumed by reading and or writing documents designed to help the institution make sound decisions about how it should organise itself to address constantly changing and invariably difficult challenges.

I did a lot of painting that spring. A lot of scraping and sanding too. Having discovered the virtues of the Pro-Prep scrapers with interchangeable heads I also found the Swedish-made orange-handled Sandviks (easily found when dropped, and now marketed as Bahco) were very good if less versatile, although I found both hard to sharpen. I continued to find cheaper conventional scrapers – including the big black plastic-handled ones from Hyde and the wood-handled Skarsten ones I bought in England – less satisfactory because I couldn't get an edge on them. I know they work well in other hands because I've seen the results, but I found the extreme sharpness of the small ones indispensable.

I also began to collect sanders. Having started with the rather ordinary pad and orbital tools from Black and Decker and a Sears belt-sander I had used for jobs in the house, I soon realised there were better options. Pete Dunbar recommended Porter-Cable and I bought their standard orbital. I also found a file sander in a McLean hardware store and bought that but steered clear of expensive tools, believing cheaper ones were just as good and that the best tools were only meant for professionals. However I ventured as far up the line as another Porter-Cable sander with interchangeable rubber profiles for getting at the odd shapes you find on wooden boats, but I was less than pleased with it because the sandpaper kept falling off the profiles.

Then, in an old copy of *WoodenBoat*, I saw a review of the Fein oscillating sander with a triangular head that ran at 22,000 rpm and promised truly superior results. It too had interchangeable heads including a really small triangle that would, I thought, be just the thing for those correspondingly tight places I was trying to clean. Bob Crowder told me he had one and offered to let me try it but I said no, never having held, much less used, a $200 tool before. Then I bought one, and wished I had done so sooner because it's a superb tool; a few years later I bought another with all the attachments. I guess it just takes time to learn that the best tools work better, last longer and, in some cases, do things other tools can't.

I spent as much time preparing surfaces as I thought I could spare if I ever wanted to go sailing again but did not, at that stage, learn it was by no means enough. Because the surfaces I was preparing to paint and varnish had been neglected for a long time, they needed far more work than I imagined they needed or was willing and able to do. It was ultimately a case of doing the best I could in the time available – 'time available' being arbitrarily determined in light of competing demands. 'Time available' for *Mudlark* was the residual of the hours of the day minus time spent working, minus time spent with my family, plus or minus time spent or not spent on house and garden.

I discovered that sandpaper came in more gradations than fine, medium and coarse, that grades were defined by numbers and that I should work through them, spending a lot of time on the highest ones to get a good painting surface. In practice I used a lot more coarse than medium and a lot more medium than fine and hardly anything above 180. When I heard someone on National Public Radio's *Marketplace* saying, as they did every evening, 'Let's do the numbers' I wondered if he knew sandpaper had numbers or that those numbers were at that stage far more important to me than those that described the US stock market.

It also took me time to learn that cheap paintbrushes produce poor results. It's not that I hadn't read (in several books) or heard from several people (including Bobs Bauernfeind and Crowder) that it always pays to buy the best; I just couldn't bring myself to pay $15 or $20 for a paintbrush. The cheaper ones looked much the same. More than once I decided the plastic bags containing an assortment of cheap brushes were excellent value, only to find you get what you pay for. So I tried better ones, but in that first season did not get beyond understanding that better brushes usually had wooden handles and that, depending on their intended use, some had chiselled heads. This put me in the $8 to $10 range but not above. Buying slightly better brushes induced me to clean them in brush cleaner but not to store them in kerosene or other suitable liquids. I just wiped them off and wondered why they were stiff next weekend.

By the time we went to England again in June 1994 *Mudlark* was looking a lot better and, with the powerplant working more or less reliably, we had taken her out for a few family weekends, never going far – partly because I was nervous about leaving the yard too far behind and partly because the Tred Avon and its creeks offered some of the best cruising on the Bay and there was plenty to explore within ten miles of Town Creek.

Returning in August (by that stage of my Bank career it was normal for me to break my vacation to return for important meetings, and that year I had done so twice), the regime continued. Sometimes I could slip away for an extra day at the yard but the never-ending process of remaking *Mudlark* slowed to what I could accomplish in, on average, about five or six days a month – and that was not much. Almost before I knew it October was coming round again and it was time to think about building a better winter cover.

The second was better than the first. I abandoned the copper tubes, sticking to wooden posts and rails, this time ensuring I got a high ridge between the masts to clear the cabin roof which had by then been refinished and repainted and rimmed with teak battens. The cover stayed on, the boat was not damaged, and

Mudlark, circa 1995.

I came to terms with a less intensive relationship than I had envisaged but one that gave me a better balance between boat, home, and work.

1995 came and went in much the same fashion as 1994, and by this time *Mudlark* was looking almost presentable. The deck and cockpits had been prepared and painted, as had the deck and cabin. I had done nothing to the spars, rigging or sails. I had however begun to realise that the sails, while interesting, had outlived their natural span, although I got the genoa repaired after it tore from its roller furler in a storm and was rescued by Bob Crowder and Pete Dunbar (who heard it flogging before major damage was done).

I asked Bob Bauernfeind where I might get it fixed and he told me to see Downes Curtis at his loft on Tilghman Street in Oxford. Downes and, until his death a year earlier, his brother Albert, had been making and repairing sails for working sail craft (mainly skipjacks and bugeyes) for more than fifty years. His other customers included a catalogue of the Great and the Good of East Coast sailing who for decades had come, as I did, to his rickety building near the Oxford Boatyard, drawn by its reputation and perhaps by the fact this was no ordinary sailmaker, nor for that matter an ordinary man. The loft's success – at a time when, except on stage and field, few African-Americans achieved it – was a function of excellence. Yet it was remarkable because, well into the 1960s, a decade after the

US Supreme Court ordered schools to integrate 'with all deliberate speed', Talbot County had clung to segregation and successful black-owned businesses were extremely rare.

I found Downes on hands and knees on the floor of his loft and showed him the sail. 'Ain't seen one like this in a long time ... that's good work,' he said, pointing to a hand-sewn cringle and the soft leather edge-protector around the clew. 'You in a hurry?'

'Well, no, not really,' I said.

'Couple of weeks OK?'

'Sure.'

'You come back in two weeks and I'll have it ready.'

I got it back a year later. But hey, my sail had been repaired by a legend!

At the end of 1996 I retired from the World Bank after 25 years to devote myself to a wider range of activities than I could enjoy while working for a superb, demanding, but (like all organisations in my experience) flawed institution. I wanted to spend more time writing (having written two books while working for the Bank), to work in the private and voluntary sectors (having spent my whole life in the public sector), to return to academia (having been a university lecturer in my twenties when it seemed like a premature retirement), and to spend the rest of my time (as I told friends) playing with my boats.

Third draft: the chequebook years

My new lifestyle – which is what it was rather than a new career – involved more travel, much of it transatlantic, than my later years at the Bank. This meant more time in England, where three of our four children were by then living (Cameron having progressed to a Pennsylvania boarding school). It also meant I began to think about doing more boating in England as well as more boating in America.

1997–98

By the spring of 1997, having jumped into my new life with both feet, I was busier than ever with a raft of projects: advising the Secretary General of the International Red Cross in Geneva; advising the president of a multinational oil company; studying the feasibility of bringing the last sail-driven freighter in Europe, the Dutch-registered *Albatros*, to a permanent berth in Wells-next-the-Sea, Norfolk (see photograph on page 48); being a research fellow at the London Business School, where I was writing a monograph on knowledge management with my colleague Professor Michael Earl; writing a weekly (later biweekly) column on American life for the *Eastern Daily Press*; and doing monthly broadcasts for the BBC.

All of that gave me less time than before to work on *Mudlark*. I was however financially able to pay for more work to be done on her. Over the next three years I commissioned Bob Bauernfeind to do a series of what I saw as major jobs and did a few myself. But we had also by then acquired a house with a dock on the far side of Town Creek, which meant we could spend nearly all our weekends there, and even if I was not doing the work I could stay close to it – which made me feel better.

In the preceding two years I had often looked across the creek from Shaw's at a house with a lawn that sloped gently to the creek and thought how nice it would be to be able to walk down the garden to one's boat and work on it using a workshop at the house. On leaving the Bank I was in a position to buy such a house and Glynis, who was by then as fond of Oxford as I was, liked the idea. Then one day in April 1996 I drove by that very house, found it was for sale and, more or less just like that, bought it. We moved in the end of the year but I decided to leave *Mudlark* at Shaw's over the winter – and covered her for the duration.

In April 1997, I moved *Mudlark* across the creek to her new home and soon afterwards I took her up the Tred Avon to the head of navigation at Easton Point, where, in the marina boatshop, Bob Bauernfeind and his business partner Tim McManus had started a new business, trading as Classic Crafts.

During the winter I had noticed that *Mudlark* was leaking more or less all the time, so much so that I kept her on permanent shore-power life support, having limited our outings the previous year to single nights because, although bilge pumps work on batteries, the batteries don't work indefinitely unless they can be recharged by the engine.

At the Oxford house jetty.

I asked Bob to do two things: to check the keel bolts that both he and I thought might be the source of the leaks and to overhaul the engine, which had been unreliable, having once left us anchored at the entrance to Town Creek with no wind and no power until we were thoughtfully towed to our dock by a passing motor cruiser. The incident had been instructive because I learned that afternoon that nobody who sailed past seemed to notice I was flying the American Yacht Ensign upside down to signal distress. This led me to conclude they didn't know their signals, and I told Glynis I was buggered if I was going to yell 'help!'

I also asked Bob to repaint the hull, top and bottom. As in 1993 I said I would deal with everything above the rubrail, and also decided it was time – while they were out of the boat – to have a go at the masts, and that I would fit an inner forestay, because I was by then convinced that *Mudlark*'s reluctance to go to windward in anything less than a stiff breeze (above force 3) was a function of the fact that large foresails with clews shackled to the outboard end of the bow platform pushed the CE too far forward.

I was in effect starting over, doing again what had been done at Shaw's in 1993.

Bob removed the keel bolts and rather to my disappointment found they were fine. This meant the leaks had another source. But he diagnosed why the engine had been unreliable and got new valves, a new fuel pump and various other bits and pieces from Dave Van Ness at Van Ness Engineering *Metalark.* in Ridgewood, New Jersey, who specialises in rebuilding and remanufacturing Graymarine engines. It would have been a good time, now the engine was out, to refinish the engine beds and the adjacent area of the hull, but I chose not to.

It was a foolish decision but perhaps understandable in light of two facts: that I was not yet ready to admit the awful possibility there was something seriously wrong with the boat; and that I was not yet ready to deal with the consequences of such possibilities. The result was that three years later I was faced with (for the boat) a life-and-death crisis I could not ignore. It amounted to a willing, even wilful, suspension of belief.

The work on the engine took longer than expected. So did the work on the hull, and *Mudlark* ended up spending the rest of that year and part of the next at Easton Point, although when Bob and Tim lost the lease on the boatshop she was moved, on the marina's travelift, to their new premises next door. *Mudlark* got a better cover that winter because it was much easier to build a frame without having to worry about the masts getting in the way and to tie things down when she was ashore.

Mudlark's extended stay at Easton Point led to the acquisition of another boat. One afternoon, arriving at the yard, I found an aluminium speedboat of about fourteen feet with the most seductive backside I had ever seen – on a boat. I wandered over. There were quite a few dents in the hull but the exaggerated tumblehome at the stern was wonderfully pleasing, the 15-hp Yamaha outboard looked to be in good condition, the cushions were clean, the dashboard was varnished, and I fell in love again. I learned she had been built by a long-extinct company called Feathercraft in Atlanta, Georgia, in about 1947. I asked Tim who owned her and he told me it was an airline pilot who lived next to the yard and wanted to sell. I asked how much? Tim said $2,500. 'Can we go for a drive?' 'Sure.' We did. I talked to Glynis. She said 'Why not?' And we had ourselves a new old boat.

Tim, who knew quite a lot about aluminium boats, said I would not be able to keep her at my dock because aluminium and salt water, even the semi-saline salt water of the mid-Bay area, don't do well together. So I arranged for Tommy Campbell to store her at Oxford under a tarp for the winter and the following spring got Bob and Tim to put together a floating dock from a kit that would keep *Metalark* (as she became, having previously been nameless) out of harm's way.

That spring we used the new boat a lot, enjoyed her speed, liked looking backwards at the spume thrown up by her flat-bottomed stern, learned to take it easy on turns (because I wasn't sure about her ultimate stability) and only broke down once when we ran out of fuel, which was not a huge problem because we could paddle ashore in this very light hull.

I started on the masts in the spring of 1997, took detailed photographs of every fitting and where it went, and stripped several layers of tired white paint. Progress was slow because I was travelling every couple of weeks and spending as much time in Europe as in America. It was also tedious work because I had to re-wrap the masts every time I left them for more than a day and by the time I was ready to refinish them it was getting cold again and yet another year had unbelievably vanished.

In April and May 1998 I carved a chunk of time from my schedule to finish the job and decided to coat them with epoxy and varnish. I had, by then, been using the Wood Epoxy Saturation Technique (WEST) system for four years on repairs to the superstructure. But I had never tried clear-coating and somehow failed to understand amine blush.

There was no excuse. The Gougeon Brothers, inventors and manufacturers of WEST, make it clear that blush – a waxy film thrown by the epoxy curing process – must be removed before another coat of epoxy is applied – unless the previous coat has not cured, in which case you can apply another while there is still time for a chemical bond between the layers (Gougeon Brothers 2000). Once cured, blush must be removed by washing it carefully with clean water and wet-sanding the surface to ensure a mechanical bond between successive layers of epoxy. It was all there in the excellent instructions but I missed it. The result was that the second coat delaminated from the first and I had to take it all off, get back to clean wood and start again.

With four coats of epoxy on each mast it was eventually time for varnish but, unbelievably, I failed again, this time to ensure the varnish stuck to the last coat of epoxy. It didn't stick because although I had learned about amine blush I failed to remove it from the top layer of epoxy before applying varnish. Another removal job, this time to get back to the epoxy surface, which was fortunately hard enough to allow me to heat and remove the varnish without softening the epoxy. But how stupid could I get?

Then came the challenging task of reinstalling the hardware, having first cleaned and polished it. The photographs I had taken before starting were useful but didn't show which machine screws to use in which threaded inserts, or for that matter which screws to use in which holes, all of which had been filled with epoxy but lined up with the fittings. The option of using new fittings didn't occur to me because they were almost all original and sound and I saw no reason to discard them, partly because there was no need, partly because I had no idea where I might find new ones and partly because I remained intent on preserving and restoring the boat in its original condition. How stupid could I get?

June 1998 came and we went to England, leaving the boat at Easton Point.

Returning in August, I prepared to re-launch her and take her back to Oxford. The launch went without incident but as we were lifting the masts onto a trailer to take her to the bulkhead where they would be re-stepped using Jack Frost's crane a waterman known to Tim wandered along and said he would help. Seeing and smelling he had been drinking all day (it was mid-afternoon), I said we did not need help. He ignored me and eventually went

THE WOOD EPOXY SATURATION TECHNIQUE (WEST) SYSTEM

The WEST system was initially developed by the Gougeon Brothers in Bay City, Michigan, in the 1960s for building iceboats. Since then it has been used in a wide range of marine and, increasingly, non-marine applications.

WEST System epoxy cures to a high-strength plastic solid at room temperatures, by mixing specific proportions of liquid epoxy resin and hardener. Using a simple 'cookbook' approach, the handling characteristics and the physical properties of the cured epoxy can be varied to suit working conditions and different coating or bonding applications.

The basic ingredient is the resin (105 Epoxy Resin). Cure time is adjusted to the working temperature or working time required with specially formulated hardeners, three of which were used in *Mudlark*'s restoration:

- slow (205) – for use in lower temperatures or for longer set-up time
- fast (206) – for higher temperatures/faster set-up
- clear (207) – for clear coating under varnish

The strength, weight, texture, sandability and colour of the cured epoxy depend on fillers, and the following were all used on *Mudlark*:

- microfibres (403) – used to create a multi-purpose adhesive
- high-density filler (404) – for maximum physical properties in hardware bonding, filleting and gap filling
- filleting blend (405) – for glue joints and fillets on naturally finished wood
- colloidal silica (406) – a thickening additive used to control the viscosity of the epoxy and prevent epoxy runoff in vertical and overhead joints
- low-density filler (407) – a blended microballoon-based filler used to make fairing putties that are easy to sand or carve
- microlight (410) – a filler for creating a light, easily-worked fairing compound especially suited for fairing large areas

The viscosity of the resin/hardener mixture is varied by adjusting the amount of filler added.

off. Bob, who rarely criticised anyone said, 'Glad he's gone. Y'know, it's guys like him that give watermen a bad reputation and spoil it for the others.'

Bob came with me to Oxford in case anything went wrong with the rebuilt engine, but nothing did and we got to my dock in about an hour and a half. The Tred Avon is an exceptionally pretty river, mostly wide and well marked, and the waterside estates that line both banks were at their abundant summertime, white-painted, red-roofed, best with tall flagpoles flying Stars and Stripes. Whatever people think about America it's hard to imagine they wouldn't be moved by a slow passage down that river in August. Who couldn't like a river with creeks that had names like 'Peachblossom' and 'Plaindealing'?

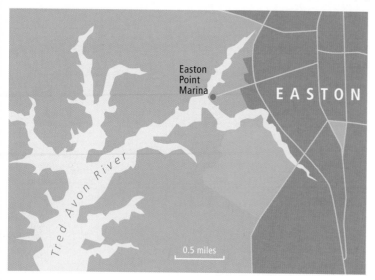

The Tred Avon River and Easton, Maryland.

That fall we sailed *Mudlark* more, not going far but enjoying the improvements we had made. Everything seemed to work, although in light airs she continued to miss stays, which sometimes meant we had to wear around. Not elegant, actually embarrassing when people were looking – which they usually were, because she tended to attract attention. I experimented with the leeboards and confirmed she sailed better to windward when they near vertical. But the main improvement came when I hanked an ex-sharpie jib on the new inner forestay, pushing the CE back towards the CLR, and found a big improvement. Perhaps I was finally getting the hang of it?

1999

In the spring of 1999 I acted on an idea that had been taking shape in my mind for some time. Cameron would be leaving Westtown School in Pennsylvania in June, and during spring break in March we went to Britain to look at universities. He had already applied to several American colleges but, partly because his sisters had enjoyed their decisions to go to Britain for degrees, he wanted to consider his options. While he was spending a day being interviewed at St Andrew's I drove across Scotland to look at a Maurice-Griffiths-designed Lone Gull II at Lochgilphead, a small town on Loch Fyne.

Having agreed with Glynis it was not a bad idea (I can't claim she ever said it was an *excellent* idea) to buy a cruising boat to keep in Norfolk, since we were now going to spend more time there, and also (she says she never agreed to it) that it would be a great idea to sail from Norfolk to Russia, I had spent the winter looking at possible boats.

During visits to Britain in January and February I had poked around frozen yards across the south and southwest, which was where most of the possibilities seemed to live. I spoke again with Alan Platt and asked him about the 27-footer he had built but he knew of none on the market and agreed the 24-footer might be a bit small for my future needs. I got lots of friendly advice from Wooden Ships in Devon and Classic Yacht Brokerage in Worcester. I looked at a Pilot Cutter in Bristol, a Pintail at Christchurch, a Hillyard at Bosham and finally a Lone Gull II at Emsworth.

Leaving Emsworth, I was deeply convinced I wanted a Maurice Griffiths boat, and ideally a Lone Gull II. MG had after all sailed most of his life on the east coast and had kept his yachts on drying moorings much like the one I would have in Wells. And there was an appealing wholesomeness to his boats. They were strong, designed to survive bad conditions, and brilliantly thought through; I was particularly taken by the signature raised deck incorporated in many of his designs including Lone Gull II, and by the emblematic 'loco cab' on some of them, Lone Gull II included. So I told the brokers that was what I wanted and remarkably, within days, Classic Yacht Brokerage and Wooden Ships had jointly come up with a Lone Gull II at Lochgilphead.

Lochgilphead, in the west of Scotland.

Graham King had almost given up on me by the time I reached him. It had taken longer to cross Scotland than I expected. He explained he was only selling *Moonfleet* because he had degenerative arthritis and could no longer handle her safely,

adding that her restoration was incomplete for the same reason. But my inspection showed – and this time I had some idea what to look for – that unlike *Mudlark* she was in sound condition. Her pitch pine on oak hull was cosmetically rough but showed no signs of rot and sounded fine, her spars looked excellent, the blood-red sails were crisp and the two-cylinder Sabb engine looked good. True, she needed paint, but my impression was that she was a good buy as well as a good boat. I told Graham that, subject to survey, I'd buy her. We shook on it.

Moonfleet.

Research showed an interesting history and some notable previous owners including a well-known marine photographer – which probably explained why she had appeared in and on the cover of several nautical magazines. I asked William Cracknell, Richard and Alison's son, who was by then an established boatbuilder and repairer in Wells, to go up to Scotland to have a look at her, and in the event Richard went too. They came back impressed and reported that apart from damage to the rudder and the trailing edge of the starboard bilgekeel it would not be a huge task to get her afloat. That, however, did not mean the task was trivial, because all the paint would have to come off. I set aside part of the summer for the job and paid the broker. A few weeks later, while I was in America, *Moonfleet* was trucked to Wells by a local boat mover and by the time I arrived in June was blocked up and covered beside William's boatshed on the Wells Industrial Site.

Besides buying *Moonfleet* I was busy that spring with a raft of commitments outside the USA and realised I would be unable to do the next job on *Mudlark* – to paint the superstructure – myself. I could, however, do the preparation work as I wanted it done (I understood by then the secret to a good finish is preparation, preparation, preparation), and get Bob and Tim's outfit to paint and varnish her while I was in England. In May and June we sailed her occasionally and I worked on her quite a lot until I took her up to Easton Point again with very detailed instructions about which paint and varnish to use in which colours and how many coats of each I wanted on the deck, cabin top, cabin sides, coamings and cockpits. I opted to use Interlux Brightside again on all the painted surfaces except the deck and Pettit Captain's Varnish on the brightwork. I looked forward to seeing her rejuvenated on my return.

We got back just before Labor Day and on the first Friday evening, full of expectations, went down to Oxford (where we had agreed the boat would be by the time I returned). I half-ran to the dock in the fading mid-evening light, reached the boat and froze.

The shock lasted about two minutes. The detailed inspection took about five. The sprint back to the house and the phone took about five seconds. Breathless, I asked for Bob and through near-clenched teeth asked him to get there as soon as possible. By the time he arrived on Saturday morning I was calm but still angry and above all deeply disappointed that the yard I had trusted had let me down utterly and completely.

The surface of the deck resembled a cross between a cow with a blotchy hide and scruffy camouflage on a military vehicle designed to operate in a desert. There was paint on woodwork that should have been varnished and varnish where there was meant to be paint. The metalwork I had spent days and weeks cleaning was new-paint-smeared. With two exceptions – the cabin bulkheads to either side of the companionway – the painted surfaces were streaked and the paint seemed to have applied with a rough brush. Some of the varnish resembled transparent jam. It was the worst finish job I had ever seen.

I am not, in my own view – others may disagree – exceptionally hard to please, and I like to think I make reasonable allowances when people do manifestly imperfect jobs and expect me to pay for them. But when Bob walked down the garden and started (good move) by saying 'the buck stops here, it's my fault', I could only tell him it did and it was. I said I was not going to pay a cent; that I thought I might have a legal case (causing grievous bodily harm to my boat); but that I would settle for having them re-do everything in the next three weeks before the Cracknells paid a return visit.

To his credit Bob made no defence and said he and Tim would start on Monday. They did and the second time around delivered an acceptable job on schedule, although they didn't have time to erase all the errors. In due course Bob explained he had given the job to a yard employee who had done a lot of good paint and varnish work in the past (I had seen it for myself and the man in question had even taught me to lay on varnish 'like an aeroplane coming in to land'). Bob had not – because the employee had not previously needed it – supervised him closely and had only seen the results at the end of the previous week when he took the boat down to Oxford, by which time it was too late to do anything about it. He said he had been waiting for my call and was actually surprised I had not been more upset.

———◆———

I think Richard and Alison probably enjoyed their second visit to Oxford more than the first. They stayed in the house, walked down the garden to *Mudlark* and went sailing, and this time the engine worked and the boat behaved itself. But, said Richard, the leaks were serious. He spent some time examining the bilge, crawled forward to look carefully at the forepeak and became convinced the problem was in the chines. It was hard to be certain but there seemed to be a continuous trickle of water along the chine; it was worst near the bow.

He also said he thought the boat had been badly built; 'Look at the chine log' he said, 'it's much too small to hold the sides and bottom together'. We measured the chine logs against the drawings in *Sensible Cruising Designs*. They conformed to LFH's specifications. So it was not so much a question of badly built, more one of badly designed.

'But come on,' I said, 'Herreshoff couldn't have made a mistake with something like that. He was the best there ever was. And this wasn't his first hard-chine design. His model was a workboat and workboats were built strong enough to be fit for purpose. Why would he have undersized the chine logs, which are after all just about the most critical bits of a sharpie hull?'

But Richard insisted and I realised my reaction to his suggestion had less to do with the measurable reality of the boat than with my reluctance to consider the possibility that LFH might have been wrong.

I asked Bob what he thought and he said, having thought a lot about *Mudlark*'s leaks, that Richard was right and that we should have looked at that explanation a long time ago. We knew it wasn't the keel bolts. We knew it wasn't loose fastenings or bad caulking. By elimination it had to be the chines.

Glynis and I went sailing in *Mudlark* with Richard and Alison on the last Saturday of their visit. There was a fresh breeze as we romped down the Tred Avon and in to the Choptank, where there was a three-foot swell. The two electric bilge pumps ran constantly yet we seemed to be taking on slightly more water than they could cope with and I realised that although there was no immediate danger of sinking, the boat was not seaworthy. It was all very well keeping her on life support at the dock, but what sort of life was that – for her or me? It was a moment of truth, and like many such moments an unwelcome one. The truth was that *Mudlark* needed urgent attention without which she would eventually sink. It was also an end to denial and to years of kidding myself she was a good old boat full of character, a bit uncomfortable but basically sound and what if she did ship a bit of water, all old boats do that don't they?

It took a few days for all that to sink in, and for me to come to terms with the new and awful reality that if I didn't take action soon, all the time, effort and money I had poured into her since 1993 would be for nothing and that I would have to see myself as a foolish dreamer with an infinite capacity for self-delusion, self-deception and self-destruction.

I had more conversations with Bob. How urgent did he think it was? Very. Could it wait until next year? If she was his he'd get her out fast. If I decided to have the chines repaired how far could I take her? Not far. Best get one of the Oxford yards to do it.

I called the three yards I thought could do the work. Cutts & Case (too busy before next spring), Oxford Boatyard (not really interested), Campbell's Town Creek Boatyard, as Shaw's had now become (possibly, but very busy until March or April).

Back to Bob. Could I wait? No. So what about other yards further away? He would advise against taking the boat out of the Tred Avon at the end of the year (it was now early October).

'So where can I go?'

'You could do it yourself.'

'Who, me?'

'Suppose I act as your consultant?' (Bob had retired a few weeks earlier.)

'Let me think about it.'

I consider my options: (1) Let the boat sink at the dock. (2) Haul her, remove anything of value that could be sold and get someone to break her up. (3) Try to persuade Tom Campbell at Town Creek Boatyard to reconsider his schedule and at least haul her for the winter before doing the work in the spring. (4) Do it myself.

Not (1), not (2). I tried (3).

Tom warmed a bit but said he had no space to haul her. The yard was fully booked and so was the shop. Did he have any other ideas? Had I thought of trucking her overland? Well no I hadn't, but to where? Tom mentioned yards further up the Delmarva I had never heard of. So I was left with option (4).

———•———

I look at my record. The last seven years have been a history of muddled thinking, confused priorities, crass ignorance, denial of the obvious and prevarication. It was one thing to mess about with paint and epoxy, and repair and rebuild coachroofs, coamings, lockers, and other bits of boats that only get wet when it rains – I had even become reasonably good at it. But I had always said I would never touch a hull because if you haven't got a hull you haven't got a boat. So why should I – or anyone else – believe that despite this background I am likely to make a success of doing what is unarguably a boatwright's job, using materials I have never seen and tools I have never touched in a location that doesn't even exist? Unless of course I could find somewhere on the river and organise my life to make time for what was at least a three-month task?

Bob suggested I call Tim and ask about space in the big shed he had rented from Jack Frost for a new business at Easton Point. Tim was sorry but his space was full for the winter. Had I called John Saulsbery about the possibility of renting part of his heated boatshop for three months? I said I hadn't thought of that but it sounded like a great idea.

John and Georgiana Saulsbery owned and operated Easton Point Marina. The boatshop where Bob and Tim had operated a few years earlier had subsequently been leased to a couple of young guys who had tried and failed to establish a boat repair business. It was now up for lease. Tim offered to approach the Saulsbery's on my behalf. I said 'yes please'. Tim called back the next day to say John had told him two other guys were interested in taking long leases and that he'd know about them by the end of October.

It would be an ideal solution. Partly because the space was dry and – a great rarity in boatshops – heated. Partly because I already knew John and Georgie (from the several months I had spent there working on *Mudlark* when Bob and Tim had leased the shop). Partly because the rent ($500 a month) seemed fair value. And finally because I liked Easton and the idea of getting to know it better.

Easton (see map on page 104) – Talbot County's seat of government – had thus far mainly been a place where we bought supplies on the way to Oxford weekends. But I was intrigued by its historic area and by the fact that, every November, Easton hosted the world's largest waterfowl festival, complete with decoy auctions and the world championship goose-calling competition. Once off the highway you found a leafy town with gracious Federal houses, good small hotels and some nice shops and restaurants.

Easton Point lay about a mile from the town centre, to which (appropriately) it was connected by Port Street. This street crossed the bypass highway (named 'Ocean Gateway') on its way to the river about half a mile from Easton Point. At the junction with the highway there was, on one side, a cluster of nondescript buildings surrounded by heavy yellow vehicles for moving earth, ploughing snow and digging trenches that belonged to Talbot County's road-maintenance department. On the other side there was a new development of 'shelter' homes for the elderly which some marketing genius had named 'Londonderry'. Beyond them, towards the river, there were some much older houses, all decrepit, some uninhabited, that were home to poor African-Americans. Closer still to the river there was an oil storage depot, a road-maintenance gravel plant that grunted material brought up on barges, two boat storage yards, Jack Frost's modern, well-maintained shed where Tim had a business, a crab dealer and two gas stations.

It seemed inevitable that sooner or later the old homes, the industrial plants and the storage facilities would be pushed aside to make way for waterside or at least 'waterview' (the distinction is crucial) houses or apartments because people around here, ourselves included (we had been lucky to arrive before the pressure really started to build), wanted to live on or near water and were willing to pay for the privilege. The marina and boat shop were at the bottom of Port Street on the right. A public launching ramp and parking area were on the left.

I flew to Holland for a week of meetings, wondering if it would work out and if it did what I might have let myself in for. The day I returned Tim called to say I could have it. Well, excellent, I thought. Having spent years messing about with boats all I had to do now was to learn how to mess about with a hull. No lease, just a verbal agreement to pay $500 a month for the next three months for half the shop. I arranged that Bob would take the boat up the river once the present occupants of the shop had moved out, and I went to England for Christmas.

4
Remaking *Mudlark*

2000: the deconstruction story

In July 1957 I had an urgent desire to go for a long walk in Scotland. Not just any long walk but a specific, celebrated walk from the Lin of Dee, near Braemar on the eastern side of the Cairngorms, to Aviemore in the Spey valley on the west side. Aviemore was then a small and rather nondescript roadside village with a youth hostel, a bar and a few houses. Its future as a sometime ski resort lay far ahead.

The walk, 28 miles from end to end, follows a rough track known as the Lairig Gru. I wanted to do it because I had heard it was challenging and for some reason I wanted a challenge. It turned out to be one of my better ideas but I could not do it without proper footwear and needed suitable boots. Lacking the means to buy them, I decided to get a job for the first couple of weeks of the six-week-long school holidays.

A car breaker a mile or so from my home in northwest London wanted workers. I was hired there one day, turned up the next morning and retired that evening. The link between that experience and the first stage of deconstructing *Mudlark* to prepare her for restorative surgery proved tenuous but it was on my mind as I considered the task ahead.

When I arrived at the breaker's a very large man gave me a very large hammer and said, 'See 'at car over there? Break it up!' 'How?' ''It it, stoopid!'

It was fun for half an hour. I started by knocking the 1950s headlights off the tops of the mudguards. Then I smashed the windows and door hinges. Then it got harder because there was no obvious way to break anything else. The answer, said a monosyllabic Irishman who knew more variations on 'fuck' than I imagined existed, was to fetch the oxyacetylene torch.

Not being used to industrial deconstruction, it took me a few minutes to realise there was no safety equipment. No gloves. No goggles. 'Shouldn't we have some protection?' 'Thas fer fookn woosis. Owld at.'

My job was to hold the bits being cut off while the Irishman wielded the torch (without, I thought, much expertise) and as he did so talked, as best he could with a limited vocabulary, about accidents, mainly amputated arms and legs (caused by things dropped from the ancient crane that stood gibbet-like in a clearing amidst the wrecks) and burns (caused by people holding on too long when the torch got close). Was he having me on?

I decided not, and I may actually have quit before knocking-off time – and I certainly didn't go back. Not even to ask for my day's pay. I had, after all, survived. I forget who paid for the boots – probably my grandmother – but the Lairig Gru was as good as I'd hoped. I've been meaning to do it again for nearly fifty years.

Comparatively speaking, the first stage of deconstructing *Mudlark* was a stately minuet to the boot-stomping crudeness of smashing old cars. But as boatyard jobs go it was pretty crude.

———◆———

Oxford, MD, January 2000

● I've returned to the USA with Glynis and Cameron, who has offered to help for a couple of weeks before returning to St Andrew's. I'm very happy to have him with me. For one thing he's a good deal bigger and stronger. For another it's an opportunity to spend time alone with him, and I know from experience that as children age there are fewer and fewer such chances.

I may not have the right tools for the job. No stationary tools except the Sears radial arm saw in my McLean workshop, which will have to stay there (it's too big to move). A selection of sanders including a big Sears belt sander, two pad sanders, a couple of orbital ones, the detail sander with interchangeable heads, my (pride and joy) Fein triangular sander, a couple of electric drills, a couple of sabre saws, a heat gun and an indifferent collection of hammers, screwdrivers, chisels, handsaws, awls, squares and other odds and sods. Most of the power tools are standard Black and Decker items collected over the previous twelve years

Adjustable jackstand.

while working on the McLean house and mini-projects to spruce up *Mudlark*. But Bob has firmly said that to do the job properly I'll need a table saw for ripping the new chineboards, a band saw for cutting them to shape and a power planer for bevelling their edges.

This morning we drove up to Easton to take stock of the shop and get our bearings. Larry Russ, a very friendly man who runs the maintenance side of the yard, was already there. He showed us where to turn on the lights (fairly obvious) and the heating (not obvious) and where I could plug in to power outlets (mostly well hidden). Although I had been in the shop many times when Bob and Tim had leased it I had never of course looked around enough to know the layout.

We found *Mudlark* supported by three stacks of wooden blocks under the broad lead keel and four pairs of adjustable jackstands on either side and another at the bow. You never see jackstands in Britain where, in my experience, boats are chocked with makeshift wooden blocks and wedges. The results are stable enough but a big advantage of jackstands is that by moving one at a time you can move them around to scrape, repair or paint the bits hidden by the stands without fear of dropping the boat on the floor.

⸺◆⸺

The chineboards looked even worse than they had in the water now the liberal coatings of aquatic slime and mud had dried in the warm air of the shop. The task ahead was to (1) remove the boards without damaging the hull, (2) make good underneath and (3) laminate two overlapping layers of marine ply on the sides and bottom of the chines to create a new leakproof solution to my weeping bilge. Three months looked like being plenty of time.

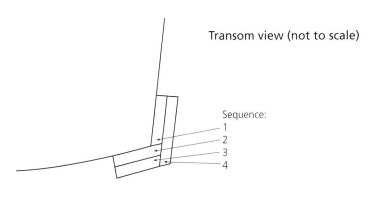

Transom view (not to scale)

Sequence:
1
2
3
4

I assumed the chineboards were fastened through the planking to the walnut frames, which were on 24-inch centres in the bow and stern sections and 12-inch centres midships where the engine and water and fuel tanks imposed higher loads. But before we could get at the screws we had to find them, and because the chineboards were below the waterline that meant removing the antifouling that covered them.

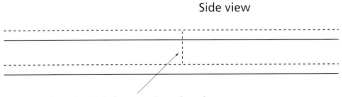

Side view

Outer board overlaps join between inner boards

Section through the chineboards.

The year I bought *Moonfleet* (1999) I removed (or more accurately paid someone else to remove) thirteen layers of multicoloured antifouling from her bottom, which, as far as I could tell, had never been cleaned back to the wood in twenty-five years. The task of cleaning the topsides had gone quite quickly but removing the antifouling was a much bigger job for two reasons. One was that Lone Gull II has an ample underwater profile (much bigger than Meadow Lark's). The other was that paint had been applied but never removed. I estimated that if Catriona (who was helping me almost full-time) and Cameron (who was helping part-time) and I kept at it, it would take at least three weeks to finish the job. With summer slipping away that was far too long and I decided to risk sandblasting.

Soft pine bottoms like *Moonfleet's* can be wrecked in minutes by a blaster who lacks finesse – and finesse is not an attribute commonly associated with sandblasters. But we got lucky because William Cracknell came up with a local father-and-son team with a reputation for careful work who had worked on wooden boat bottoms before. They paused frequently to check for gouging, left the last layer of paint more or less intact so as not to go right down to the wood and took just an hour and a half to do the job. Before hiring them it crossed my mind to try to locate the English farmer whose ultra-safe method for bottom cleaning had been written up in a boating magazine. But I couldn't find the reference and needed to press on. I later learned that his name is Farrow, that his method is called the Farrow system, that it's very effective, and that it costs a lot more than I paid. I was pleased with my decision.

There was no question of blasting the antifouling off *Mudlark*'s chineboards in the confines of the shop. The options were sanding or scraping. We couldn't burn it safely (or so I thought) and it was too hard to scrape without softening so it was back to Lowe's for goggles, respirators and 50-grit paper for our sanders.

———————

Even limiting sanding to where we thought the fasteners lay beneath the paint, the air was soon full of red dust, and despite the respirators we had to stop frequently for gulps of cold outside air. I now wished I had chosen (on the spurious grounds that it had more copper than anything else legally available and therefore had to be the best bottom paint) something other than Pettit Trinidad. But what is bad for marine wildlife and vegetation is also bad for people, and what is good for boats that leave their slips frequently and/or are scoured by strong tidal flows is less good for those that sit around. I now knew that because *Mudlark* had done a lot of sitting a slow-release, soft or sloughing (ablative) paint would have been better. But that was hindsight and the job at hand was to get rid of the hard stuff with as little prejudice to our (particularly Cameron's) health as possible.

Once we had located the frames from the outside things went faster and we learned where to look for bungs. But it still took three days to locate them all. It was now time to get the bungs out and then the screws. 'So let's get some more tools,' I said and off we went to Lowe's and came back with more bits for the power drivers, a couple of big screwdrivers, a heavy hammer and some small chisels.

From hard ...

I started by assuming the bungs were wood. Some were. Others were epoxy. The wood bungs popped out. The epoxy fillers had to be dug out. I found it impossible to make clean holes. The epoxy had also filled the slots in the bronze screws, making it hard to get a grip on them.

If at that point I had taken time to search the *WoodenBoat* index for wisdom I would have found McClave's excellent article on how (and how not) to remove bungs (1983). But for neither the first time nor the last I failed to make good use of the extraordinary reservoirs of knowledge in back numbers of *WoodenBoat*, *Classic Boat* and *Water Craft* sitting on the shelves of my Oxford library. Instead, I implicitly chose to learn by doing, raising the question of why, if I couldn't be bothered to use the back numbers (and indexes), I bothered to keep them.

Cameron: 'Dad, I'm having trouble getting these screws out.'

Me: 'So am I.'

About a third of the screws came out with varying amounts of effort. The rest refused to budge. I wasn't sure what to do next.

'Bob?'

'What's up?'

I explained the problem.

'I'll come and have a look.'

About an hour later Bob's truck came to a scrunchy stop on the gravel outside the shop. He said we had two choices. I could drill holes around the screws to expose the heads, remove the surrounding wood and then either unscrew them or twist them out with locking wrenches. Or I could cut through the screws (leaving most of them in the wood) by sliding a Sawzall (a.k.a. reciprocating saw) under the chineboards, taking care not to damage the planking.

'Just like that?' I said.

'You'll get the hang of it'.

I had used hole saws before (on house door locks) but had never touched a Sawzall or a locking wrench.

I decided to try holes first. They would obviously ruin the wood but I was happier sacrificing chineboards than planks. A quick trip – the first of what seemed like thousands – to Easton Hardware, which would, I thought, have a better range of hole saws than Lowe's. Because hole saws have central bits I had to drill to one side of each recalcitrant screw and then remove the waste wood from the bit. Each hole took about ten minutes. Reckoning there were about 90 screws on each chineboard and we had removed only about 30 in the first pass there were 150 to go. At our current rate it would take another 40 hours to get them off; longer if I ran into problems.

I decided to bash on. But some of the screws broke when we attacked them with locking wrenches and others just wouldn't move. Three days later we were getting fed up. So we switched to Plan B. Back to Easton Hardware for a de Walt reciprocating saw (I learned that 'Sawzall' was a proprietary name for a Milwaukee tool and Easton Hardware didn't stock it).

The saw was quicker, and I found that by using a flexible bimetal blade and ensuring it came out at the bottom of the six-inch wide chineboard before I started sawing laterally it made quick work of the bronze screws. But I didn't know if I was damaging the planks until I got to the first of two scarf joints joining the three sections of chineboard on each side and to my relief found nothing that couldn't be put right with epoxy. Anyway the bottom planks would in due course be covered by the new laminated chineboards and nobody would see what was under them.

We spent the next two days sawing through the remaining screws until all six sections of both chineboards were off, revealing perhaps the most extraordinary mixture of colours and textures I have ever see on a boat – or any other wooden object.

I have however seen bruises that resembled the random, ugly, awful mixture of blacks, purples, yellows, reds and greens, part smooth, part wrinkled, part crevassed, part putrefied, the product of God knows how many years of neglect. The colours were the colours of who knew what kinds of goop, filler, putty and patent nostrums guaranteed to keep water out that had manifestly failed to do their job. The wrinkled and crevassed bits had dried out years, perhaps decades, earlier and had set so hard they had to be heated before they could be scraped. The softer bits came off fairly easily, but it took another four days to get close enough to the wood to see what I had to deal with and to reach the first of many moments when I asked myself what I really thought I was doing.

To harder ...

Starting at the transom and working forward, I had inadvertently saved the worst till last, because as the gunge came off it became obvious that the chineboards had done little to prevent water flowing through huge gaps – some more than $1/8"$ wide – in the seams between the side and bottom planks. But the scale and nature of the horror was not fully evident until I reached the foremost plank on the starboard side ... and asked why this boat was not on the bottom of the Bay.

The plank that had been covered by the chineboard was cracked, soft and sodden. The fastenings were loose. The wood around them was discoloured. It explained (at least in part, because I had not yet seen the rest of the bow) why there was always water in the forepeak.

The port side was much the same and as I scraped the crud away I thought this boat had deserved to sink because it had been badly built and poorly maintained. Yet somehow she had told me, just in time, to get her out of the water, before it was too late, rather as a dog at an animal pound pleads to be rescued. But it was poor consolation for the fact that my game plan lay in ruins.

I had rented the shop for three months to replace the chineboards. I had removed them only to find they had concealed an as yet unknown amount of deterioration. To repair the damage would take a lot more than three months' rent, a lot more than three months' work and a lot more skills than I could acquire in three months, three years or perhaps three lifetimes. What I had thought was a relatively easy (though for me difficult) job to fix a relatively small (though to me serious) problem was turning into a mountainous challenge that seemed to grow before my eyes.

I could not then know that what I could see was just part of what I would have to contend with. If anyone had told me there was much worse to come and that it would be more than three years before I was ready to replace the chineboards, I might, overwhelmed by the magnitude of the task, have considered quitting. But I didn't know. And even had I known, I'm not sure I could have turned my back on a boat that, just in time, had cried out to be rescued.

And harder ...

By the time Cameron and I finished cleaning the bottom-most planks, the edges of the outboard planks and the seam between them, it was clear that the extent of the deterioration was uneven. The stern sections were not nearly as bad as the forward sections although there were areas of softness. But the bow area was much worse than it had seemed at first blush.

Another consultation with Bob and a decision to remove the bottom bow plank on the starboard side to see what was going on behind it. The starboard plank came off, and what I saw through the eight-inch by eight-foot hole shook me like a hard grounding on a North Sea sandbank.

The previously invisible outside edges of the side frames were broken and rotten at the chine. The bolts that had once fastened them to the bottom frames were so badly corroded that when I tapped some of them they crumbled in piles of rust. The stem was wizened, cracked, shrivelled and eroded to the point it was a wonder anything had stayed fastened to it. The bottom planks were badly eroded.

Bob Bauernfeind examining the state of the woodwork at the bow.

Another consultation. 'Looking good!' said Bob when he saw what I was looking at.

'Right,' I said weakly. 'What now?'

'Take the bottom-most plank off on the other side And you'll have to get these out too (the second planks up on both sides). Then you'd better look at the bottom and the stem'.

'So I take everything apart?'

The bow from the starboard side with the bottom and side planks removed.

'Don't see as how you've got much choice.'

I obviously needed a plan of action, and decided to attack the planks first, then the bottom. The planks came off, revealing more of the same, although once they were removed it was easier to work on the bottom because I could reach between the frames like a surgeon reaching into a thoracic cavity. The only good news was that the upper parts of the side frames were sound, suggesting that if the chines had not leaked the walnut frames might have stayed good throughout.

Now it was time to look at the bottom, and I decided to work bottom-up. LFH gave Meadow Lark an external keel in the form of a slab of lead that began six feet short of the bow, where it was about six inches wide and three inches deep, broadened to about twelve inches wide and six inches deep midships, and then narrowed and shallowed aft, where it was faired to the deadwood.

My immediate interest was the wooden forekeel between the stem and the forward end of the keel. It was in two pieces but had surely not been made that

The sheet of copper between the forekeel and the planks.

way, the two-piece arrangement presumably being the result of a botched repair when perhaps someone before me had tried to stop the leaks. A short piece (nine inches) was held in place by boat nails. A longer piece (three feet) was joined to the stem and fastened with three-inch bronze screws.

The short section succumbed to a pry-bar and a heavy hammer. Once the longer piece was off too I found a sheet of quarter-inch plywood and above it a badly corroded sheet of copper, liberally coated with something resembling tar, sandwiched between the plywood and the bottom planks above it. More evidence that someone else had tried to stop the leaks. Needless to say the bottom planks were terrible.

'Bob? Could you come over again?'

'Good thing you hauled her ... y'know what ... this boat should've sunk.'

'Really? So what should I do?'

He told me.

A Quixotic moment. Was Bob seriously saying I should get on my horse, grab my lance and charge at a project so obviously beyond my dreams and means? He was. Was he really saying I had to rebuild the bow forward of the end of the slab keel by replacing at least part of the stem and at least part of the bottom planking, add new side and bottom frames by sistering the old ones, and replank the sides? He was. Did he also mean I should replace the cutwater (outer stem)? He did. Was he crazy? Was I crazy? Both of us? Did it matter?

The game plan

I took time off to consider how I would rebuild the stem and bottom, sister the side and bottom frames, replank the sides, and shape and fit a new cutwater. I also considered, more seriously this time, whether I should continue. Having in the past applied Macbeth's conclusion 'I am in blood stepped in so far that should I wade no more, returning were as tedious as go o'er' to circumstances ranging from the completion of long walks to persistence with economic policies to gutting out organisational changes, I decided there was really no choice, and with Bob's help I developed a reconstruction plan with three elements:

- A 6" × 10" cross-keelson, shaped and bevelled at either end to fit the curves of the hull, epoxied and bolted to the forward ends of the bottom planks, which (except for the central plank, which would be left a foot longer) I would saw off level with the forward end of the keel.

- A sawn and shaped stem-cum-keelson (much longer than the original stem, to provide a stronger tie to the rest of the boat) extending from a scarf joint at the remnant of the original stem (the lower, abraded, part of which would be cut away) to the central bottom plank, where it would be half-lap-joined to the cross-keelson and notched on the underside to the depth of the central plank and epoxied and fastened (with half-inch stainless bolts) to the central plank and cross-keelson.

- A new bottom made of 1³/₄" × 1³/₄" strips of wood edge-glued and screwed to the centre bottom plank and the lower section of the stem/keelson reinforced with two layers of quarter-inch marine plywood epoxied and screwed to the underside of the strips.

It doesn't sound like much, and to a seasoned shipwright would have been little enough. But it was far, far more than I had bargained for. It implied major challenges to my meagre skills. It meant I would have to acquire and learn to use tools I hadn't thought of buying or using. And it was brutally clear it would take a long time, at least several months, because I had other things to do too. I told John and Georgie Saulsbury I would like to stay longer, perhaps much longer than I'd said, and was relieved when they said 'no problem'.

Before I could start rebuilding there was more deconstruction. Once the bottom planks, rotten frames and the bad part of the stem had been removed the boat resembled an open-mouthed shark and the remaining frames looked like bad teeth in an upper jaw. But one glorious day in mid-April when the shop door was open and the sun was shining and the water was sparkling and I would have liked to be on the water, there was nothing left to deconstruct. At least in the bow.

All I had to do now was build a new front end.

———◆———

I rarely make important purchases without doing research first, these days on the Internet, and with a band saw and table saw in mind plus a power planer and a right-angle drill for getting in tight spaces between the frames, I spent a lot of time checking websites and user reviews. I opted for a folding table saw from Home

Depot's Ridgid range, a Taiwan-made JET 12-inch band saw from Woodcraft, a Bosch power planer and a Milwaukee right-angle drill which fitted my hand.

Tools on board, the next thing was wood. One choice was easy: I would not use walnut to sister the frames – or for anything else. Partly because it was not a boatbuilding wood. Mainly because it was hard to get in the dimensions I would need. So after consulting Bob I decided to use white oak wherever walnut had been used originally. I chose mahogany for the new keelson that would be scarfed to the cut-off stem at one end and half-lapped to the cross-keelson at the other, which would also be mahogany.

I went looking for wood at Warren's Woodwork in Easton, where over the next three years I became a sufficiently regular customer they eventually knew what I was doing. Both there and at Chesapeake Woodworkers ('a candy store for woodworkers') at Hurlock I found I was welcome to browse through the stacks. Not once in many visits did any of the yard guys get impatient as they worked

The laminated mahogany stem.

their way to the board at the very bottom of a stack only to find I ended up taking the one at the top I had seen first. That kind of service is rare these days, as is the freedom to pick and choose.

Warren's provided the wood for a massive baulk of mahogany (36" × 8" × 24") for the new stem/keelson and another for the cross-keelson, the bigger one made by laminating two pieces together. It took several days to reach the point at which I was ready to cut it on the band saw. Before risking a substantial and perhaps not easily replicated purchase on a tool that was still new to me I cut a few other shapes on smaller timbers. But Cam was about to return to St Andrew's, having helped me yet again during his spring vacation, and having put it off I decided to cut out the rough shape on his last afternoon. He took the weight of the timber as I pushed it through and managed to avoid removing more than I wanted to remove. The result was something I could work with handheld tools.

I chose the new Bosch power planer for much of this task because I found it made quick work of surplus wood and I could easily control the depth of cut. I also appreciated the fact it ejected waste from either side. I later found (when I bought and used other power planers) that this was a huge advantage because it meant I was not blinded by flying chips and shavings.

The planer also taught me to keep my hands out of the way of rotating blades when, one Sunday morning, I lifted it off the stock with my right hand and had a mid-air collision with the fourth finger of my left hand. Just the slightest of glancing blows but enough for the first of several visits (don't believe anyone who says boatbuilding is not a blood sport) to the Emergency Room at Easton Memorial Hospital. Feeling queasy (I hate the sight of blood, particularly my own), I returned to Oxford and less sympathy from Glynis and Catriona than I thought I deserved (although Glynis stopped short of her grandmother's line that it served me right for working on the Sabbath).

The first step towards a restored hull was to install the new keelson/stem. Hours of measuring, checking, fitting, re-measuring and adjusting. If I got anything less than a tight joint between the old and new stems I would weaken the boat in a critical place. I had not then read Ruhlman's *Wooden Boats* and Nat Benjamin's reported insistence on 'onion skin' fits between wooden surfaces, but if I had, I'd have said that was what I wanted. I didn't get it quite right but there was certainly no daylight.

The new cross-keelson.

After what seemed weeks but was actually several days of planing and sanding, I had a reasonably tight dry-fitted joint between the stem/keelson and the cross-keelson. I then epoxied and bolted them in place.

The new bottom plank in place near the bow.

The power planer was also my tool for bevelling the sides of the $1^3/_4$" $\times 1^3/_4$" strips of white oak for the new bottom. Once they had the right bevel to maintain the bottom curved through the bow, each strip was edge-glued (with WEST epoxy) and fastened with countersunk 316 square-headed stainless screws, although I took care to omit screws in areas that would be cut and bevelled to match the original curves (lengthwise and vertical) of the hull and provide a base for the new chineboards. Bob came to look and said it was OK, which was all I wanted to hear – and all I needed to know.

———————

There was at last some visible progress, and I enjoyed spending a few minutes after I got to the shop each morning looking at what I had done and thinking it wasn't half bad. Although I knew very well it wasn't something with which a professional would have been satisfied, I thought my work was fit for purpose. The boat wouldn't fall apart when it crashed off a wave and wouldn't come unstuck because glue joints were weak or screws the wrong size. For the first time I believed I had done something with my hands that would stand the test of time and that what I had done, though quite unremarkable, was 'workmanlike'.

Alan Platt had used that word to describe the fit-out of his Finesse designs. It was a word I had always taken to mean sound, solid, durable and honest rather than fancy or elegant (although I thought the Finesse was those things too); a word that, above all, described a working value.

When I set out on this project I thought that whereas in the first seven years of ownership I had done the best I could in the time I had, my aim now would be to do *the best I could in whatever time it took to do it*. But I had not defined 'best'. It obviously did not mean 'best possible', because I was incapable of mastery. The standard by which I would judge my work was therefore a personal standard which might not coincide and did not have to coincide with anybody else's standard, and which certainly wasn't derived from abstract definitions of either satisfaction or excellence. And as I looked, with some satisfaction, at the rebuilt bow I realised my standard for this project was that the result should be 'workmanlike'. A few years later, when, for the first time, I began to cook with recipes, I decided my aim was to produce food that was 'edible'. Workmanlike and edible were, in my book, much the same thing.

With age and experience I had learned the best can sometimes be the enemy of the good and that the good was often good enough. Indeed, I had sometimes encouraged staff at the World Bank to trade off timeliness and elegance in favour of timeliness, and to use the 80 : 20 rule to manage marginal returns. That approach was consistent with the approach I had decided was right for *Mudlark*. If it didn't sink it was OK. If it was edible it was satisfactory.

My morning musings often went on all day because I never listened to music or anything else when doing physical work (neither, when he was in the shop, did Larry). And they led, in due course, to two other conclusions. One was that it was now obvious this was no longer a three-month chineboard replacement job but an open-ended adventure. The other was that, in jumping to the conclusion that *Mudlark*'s leaks could be stopped by replacing the chineboards I had violated an important personal principle.

The principle had been born of frustration with the fact that when confronted with issues, many people – including some whose education and training should have enabled them to know better – had a perverse tendency to leap to conclusions, sometimes prompting me (when they fortuitously got the right answers) to paraphrase T S Eliot by saying:

> The last temptation is the greatest treason:
> To get the right answer for the wrong reason.

If your country was suddenly attacked you didn't commission a six-month feasibility study of alternative defences. If your house was on fire you didn't waste time asking how it started. If your boat was sinking you didn't get out the construction plans to look for potential weaknesses before you started bailing. But most problems weren't like that. The presenting problems – the ones people complained about – were often symptoms rather than causes, and unless causes were understood intuitive solutions often failed, and the usual result of reaching for answers to half-understood problems was frustration.

Yet in November 1999, when presented with evidence that *Mudlark* was getting ready to sink, what had I done? I had decided, on the basis of what I could see, that the leaks were attributable to weak chines, and that the solution was to replace the chineboards. The diagnosis had been correct: the boat leaked because the chines were weak. But I had never considered the possibility that one thing would lead to another.

Only so much goodness can be expected from self-flagellation and I was left with the practical question of how, now, to define the job, knowing I would probably run into further problems. Given the unknowns a firm schedule was impossible. The best I could do was to paraphrase Yogi Berra and say it wouldn't be over till it was over. But despite the uncertainties, my objectives were to get the boat back in the water in a sound and seaworthy condition as soon as possible and as inexpensively as possible, the second and third objectives being clearly subordinate to the first. I wasn't going to cut corners to save time or money if that would prejudice safety or durability.

Long conversations with Bob and longer conversations with myself helped shape a rough plan of what I would do to reach those goals. Starting out, I had known I would have to repaint the hull, because replacing the chineboards would inevitably make a mess of the existing paint on both bottom and topsides. Now, looking at the gaping bow and knowing I had to replace planks, the question arose of how I would go about doing that. My initial impulse was to say I'd put things back together the way they had been put together in the first place, using cotton caulking and screws to install the new planks before repainting the topsides. But Bob persuaded me this old hull needed all the strength it could get and that a non-traditional approach would be better.

One non-traditional approach would be fibreglass sheathing. Bob was not keen on that unless we removed the keel to lay glass cloth across the hull to create an impermeable layer between hull and keel. Wrapping it around the keel was not, he said, a good idea because it would be impossible to get a tight fit.

I rejected that option on three grounds. First, I didn't want to take the keel off, because it was yet another task I hadn't bargained for. Second, I wasn't happy about working with glass cloth. I had no experience of it, didn't like what I had heard about working with it and readily imagined getting wrapped in it as I tried to stick it on the bottom. Third, I didn't like what I'd read about the risks of encapsulating hulls with fibreglass cloth, particularly the risk that moisture could be trapped between glass and wood, prompting the glass to fall off.

The alternative was to get all the paint off the topsides and bottom, fill all the seams with epoxy and clear-coat the planks with multiple layers to create an impermeable seal. If I did that the planks couldn't breathe but some of the things I had read said wood didn't need to breathe. I liked this option. It would mean a lot of work, because I knew that epoxy would not stick to paint and that the quality of the result would largely depend on how well I prepared the surfaces. But it seemed a relatively straightforward process, one I could both understand and execute.

So I had a game plan. Or so I thought. I did not of course have a contingency (if this, then that) plan. Still less a set of multiple scenarios for managing a range of plausible outcomes, partly because it would have seemed ridiculous even to think about them but mainly because I lacked the knowledge and experience I would have needed to think about them intelligently. A game plan was enough.

The hardest job I've ever done

There are worse jobs. Mining coal in Siberia. Making clothes in Chinese sweatshops. Cutting cane in Cuba. I have done none of them but what I did next was by far the hardest, most arduous, unpleasant, ache-inducing, nausea-provoking job I have ever done. Exhaustion brought on by hours, days and weeks of drafting and redrafting reports, negotiating and renegotiating loans, lobbying for organisational change and dealing with its human consequences was nothing compared with the seemingly endless task of removing every scrap of paint and other foreign substances from the bottom of my boat.

Mudlark's wetted area was tiny for her 33-foot length because the bottom was so shallow. Had it been comparable to say, *Moonfleet*'s wetted area the job would have been far worse. On *Moonfleet* I had got most of the job done by sandblasting. But blasting the bottom had not been an option for getting antifouling off the chineboards in the confines of the shop and was certainly not an option for the bottom. Nor could I have taken her out on a low-loader, blasted her bottom and put her back because Maryland's rigorous environmental laws would have made that illegal. Yet had I known at the outset the job would take almost two months and would be so miserable I suspect I would have looked for options even if there were none.

It could have been worse. There could have been even more layers of antifouling to get off. There could (but for her gently rounded bottom) have been even less space under the hull. The floor on which she stood could have been too rough to allow me to scoot or crawl around on a trolley. The jackstands could have been wonky enough to make me worry about having her collapse on top of me.

It could have been worse but it was bad enough. And it was certainly worse than it would have been had I used less toxic antifouling. I already knew, because Cameron and I had removed Pettit Trinidad from the chineboards, that it was noxious stuff. But whereas our only goal there had been to expose the bungs over the screws (and we had not completed the job because I had eventually decided to cut through them instead) cleaning the bottom was a vastly bigger task.

Soft scraping had its own risks because burning off antifouling released foul and, I assumed, poisonous fumes. Hard scraping was only useful in the initial stages where I was removing loose material. So I relied a lot on sanders but found it very hard to lie on my back, wearing a half face respirator to use some of the power tools I tried to use. Notably the eight-inch Fein orbital sander Tim had generously lent me and my de Walt belt sander. That was partly because they were heavy to hold over my head and partly because they released choking, blinding clouds of paint-dust. Even the smaller sanders were hard to use in that position and all of them generated far more dust than I could tolerate for more than a few minutes at a time. It got worse as the weather warmed up and my protective clothing did not change with the season.

It took time to learn the importance of protection. I quickly found disposable masks were useless against the dust and fumes of copper-laden paint and that plastic goggles, apart from a tendency to mist up, got covered in paint dust and needed frequent cleaning as well as demisting. So I bought myself a full face visor that misted less quickly and could be wiped without removal.

It took me a while to learn to cover my head.

One afternoon in May, soon after I had started on the bottom, I wandered over to the marina store for yet another bottle of cold water and met Georgie who said 'You look like a red racoon.'

'Huh?' I said.

'Go look at yourself.'

'You know, you're the second person to say that.'

'Say what?'

'That I look like a red racoon' (the first had been a colleague at the Bank after I had spent a sunny weekend sailing on the Bay wearing glasses).

She was right. I was red all over. My clothes from head to foot, face, hands and hair. I wiped some of it off and worked on for another couple of hours and then went back to Oxford and showered for a long time. The next day, and for several days after, I did the same thing. Then one morning I noticed my hair, normally grey, had turned yellowish green. Could it be the shampoo? Was it jaundice? It didn't occur to me there was a connection between my day-long exposure to red dust and the startling (people stared at me in the supermarket) change in my appearance.

Then someone said, 'I think your bottom paint is making your hair green.'

'But the paint's red, not green.'

'And what happens to copper when it oxidises?'

My hair was still green when, to the huge amusement of my friends in Oxford and Norfolk, I went to England for the summer, leaving the project behind me for a few weeks. But by then, having understood cause and effect, I had learned to protect my head no matter what, and had even asked my Washington doctor whether I had done myself permanent harm. 'No,' he said. 'But make sure you cover up when you're near that stuff.'

Before I left for England the bottom was clean. Using what became a vast array of tools, including metal picks, files and every scraping device I could find in tool and automobile stores, I had succeeded in removing every bit of antifouling. But it was a truly rotten job I would never do again. And I would strongly advise anyone faced with a comparable situation to find an alternative to what I did.

Time out

The plan for the fall of 2000, after I returned to the USA, was to carry on where I had left off. But carving out most of the spring to work on *Mudlark* meant I had put other things on hold and I wanted to get back to them.

Having been elected a Senior Associate Member of St Antony's College, Oxford, in May I stayed on in England in September and became a co-convenor of a university seminar programme on globalisation and global governance. I also went back to advising the president of a multinational oil company and to giving speeches on knowledge management and other topics to public- and private-sector audiences in Europe, the USA and Canada. As a result, I had neither time nor energy to do much work on the boat. And perhaps, after the rigours of the spring, less inclination.

During a short trip back to Norfolk, however, I found the energy to buy a tender for *Moonfleet*. It seemed a shame to have a boat with beautiful wooden davits with nothing to swing in them. Then one morning when I looked across the street at John Crook's chandlery I saw a stunning clinker pram dinghy of about eight feet, complete with a heavy rope gunwale fender. I had found what I wanted. She was called *Outje Boutje*, which I thought meant she was Dutch, but it turned out she had been built at Wootton Bridge on the Isle of Wight and that the name meant

'Little Boat' – although Dutch sailors from Friesland who came in to Wells later told us it was grammatically incorrect.

I was relieved to know I would not have to spend another several weeks rolling about a concrete floor dodging jackstands and getting covered in bottom-paint debris. But I squeezed out some time at Easton and, given the game plan I had adopted in the spring, began the next job of checking the topsides planking, refastening it where it was good and removing and replacing it where it was bad.

I already knew that besides the bad bow planks there were other suspect planks on both sides. I knew too (because even with paint still on the topsides I could see where planks began and ended) that for reasons Mr Smith had taken to his grave he had butt-jointed several planks on two-inch frames. This meant each plank had half a frame apiece (i.e. one inch) and, inevitably, the frames had split as new fastenings had been added in efforts to keep planks and frames together.

One of the butt blocks.

Bob suggested I deal with the consequences of Mr Smith's handiwork by building additional frames alongside existing ones to provide proper landings for planks on frames, and by removing and replacing inadequate butt blocks where they landed between frames. I agreed. But before I could do that I would have to get the paint off the topsides because I needed to inspect each fastening and the wood around it and to find out how much bad wood was under the paint.

Removing Interlux Brightside from the topsides was, if not a doddle, a straightforward and pleasant contrast to getting antifouling off the bottom. I actually enjoyed wielding a heat gun (my old Black and Decker packed up and I bought a Steiner from Annapolis Paint which cost about three times as much but

The topsides with the paint removed, with the masts lying above.

would, I was told, last a decade or more) with one hand and a Pro-Prep or Sandvik scraper with the other. In my disjointed and rather infrequent sessions at the yard between September and Christmas, when we returned to England, I finished cleaning paint from the hull, leaving bare wood.

After the shocks of the bow it was fairly good news. The frame-fastened joints were not as bad as I expected. Most of the fastenings had somehow stayed put, although a few were loose and there was rust around them. As far as I could tell without removing paint from the inside of the hull, which might expose more rotten or split planks, I would have to remove only three planks in addition to the four I had already removed either side of the bow. One was on the port side at the stern, another portside midships, the last on the starboard quarter. All were cracked and had split ends that would not take fastenings, so I decided to make new joints between frames landed on proper-sized butt blocks. I cut out the bad ends, leaving at least six-foot spaces for new planks. Not without difficulty, because despite other shortcomings Mr Smith's planks had been properly spiled, bevelled and fitted, which probably explained why they had not come adrift. The butt fastenings alone would not have held them in place.

As the end of the first year approached, the mild euphoria I had experienced in the spring when I looked across the shop at the partially rebuilt bow had worn off, and the cup that had been at least damp now seemed dry again. Apart from the new stem/keelson, cross-keelson and bow bottom all I could see were huge gaps where I had removed planks. But – I wearily told myself – deconstruction was a precursor to progress.

I would start work on the frames in the New Year.

2001: Deconstruction (continued)

In January 2001 I was thumbing through one of Cameron's classic car magazines when I saw a full-page advertisement in glorious technicolor for the 'Inca Trail', a 26,000-kilometre circuit of South America, starting and finishing in Rio de Janeiro. I showed it to Glynis, who said 'We're going'. And that (almost) was that.

Not quite, of course. The rally (for fifty classic cars and fifty 4×4s) was scheduled for November–December 2001. Before then we had to buy a suitable vehicle (a 4×4 because I had no idea how to choose or maintain a classic), and find the not insignificant sum required to pay the organisers. Glynis also had to negotiate time off from the Washington International School and we both had to arrange our lives to accommodate a three-month absence from our usual activities.

Glynis had been quick to say yes to the rally because when we had lived in Colombia for four years in the 1970s we had promised ourselves that when the moment came we would get a suitable vehicle and drive around the continent. In the course of my work at the Bank I had been to every country in the Americas except Suriname and Guyana but that had mainly meant cities – and we knew from experience the most interesting travel is in the spaces between them. The Inca Trail promised just that.

As the second year of the project began I knew it would be incomplete, that the second half, including summertime in England and the rally in the fall, would involve yet more time out, and that whatever I was going to do to the boat in 2001 would have to be sandwiched between other commitments in the first semester.

I was still travelling a lot – spending time at St Antony's, consulting, advising, speaking – and there was no way I could devote as much time to *Mudlark* as in the previous year, when I had thought it would all be over in three months. But she was still in the shop, still costing as much as some families spend on rent for houses, still waiting to be fixed, and I had to make as much progress as possible in the time I could spare. So, on an 'as and when' basis, I spent whatever time I could from January to June 2001 on the next major task of replacing and sistering the frames.

I am ashamed to say that after the boat had been brought up river and blocked in the shop at the end of 1999 the first thing I should have done in January 2000 was to strip the rigging from the spars, remove everything movable from the interior and either chuck it out or store it somewhere else. I failed to do that. The masts, complete with standing and running rigging, had been laid on top of the cabin, nothing whatever had been removed from the cockpit or cabin and although I had covered them, there was a liberal coating of sawdust, paint dust and generic boatyard residues.

Now, to get at the frames, I had to access the interior, and to do that I had to get the masts off the boat. This would have been the obvious moment to remove and store the running and standing rigging, move the masts elsewhere and leave the boat itself and the area around it free of clutter. So what did I do? With Larry's help (with the forklift) I took the masts off the boat and laid them on trestles alongside the boat, complete with rigging, and covered them with tarpaulins.

Most of what I had done to *Mudlark*'s cockpits and cabin in the first seven years was cosmetic. And now, standing in the main cockpit, I looked at my work and saw it was not very good. Perhaps the experience of wooding the hull as though my life depended on it had changed the way I looked at things. Perhaps I had finally understood the truth that a successful surface is 80% preparation, 15% materials and 5% effort. And even as I looked at it again for the first time I realised that if I was to do this hugely bigger project right, there was no way I could simply spruce up the paintwork and leave it at that. Nor could I leave the engine in its present condition. Doing things right meant doing the right things, which meant doing everything the right way.

I suspect many restoration projects evolve to the rhythm I adopted the first year I owned *Mudlark*, when I had said to Bob Crowder 'while you're at it why don't you ...' Because once you've done one thing you see an opportunity to do another and the project grows like a snowball – as do the costs and the time spent on it. This project had evolved too. Having started as a three-month process to fix the chineboards, it had grown to include a new bow, new planks and other things I hadn't yet thought of.

I'm not sure I believe in epiphanies but in light of experience I believe in moments of truth. I'd had one, in October 1999, when I realised the boat would sink if I didn't act. I'd had another in 2000 when I decided my approach to this kind of work and specifically to this project would be 'workmanlike'. Now, in 2001, I had a third.

Standing in the cockpit, I realised that everything I could see and some things I couldn't see would have to be rebuilt or replaced. Partly because it would be stupid to go to all the trouble, time and expense I had committed to the hull to end up with mediocre living and working spaces. And partly because I could not repair the frames with the existing internal structures in place. The question was whether to remove them with a view to putting them back once I had repaired the hull, or to dump them at the Talbot County landfill.

The plywood boards on either side of the engine compartment would have to go because they were worn out. So would the control panel, which had never been any good. The massive oak framework for the engine compartment needed repair but was basically sound and I would keep it. True, there was nothing like it in the original LFH design, but the framework stiffened the hull (as did the cabin bulkhead) and provided a base for the mizzenmast as well as a compartment for the engine.

The spruce frameworks for the cockpit lockers were sound and could stay; again there was no alternative to keeping them unless I wanted to rebuild the cabin (which I didn't). But the monel tanks would have to go, along with all traces of the electrical and plumbing systems.

I moved forward to the low step of the companionway and looked into the cabin. The sink and the countertop in the galley would have to go ... but what about those hand-fitted stainless-steel panels on the bulkhead ... and the stainless-steel icebox? Let's have a closer look ... you know, it's a shame ... but the metal's corroded and it's very unlikely the plywood beneath is sound ... so it will have to go. So will the sea toilet. And the hanging locker with those useless shelves between the starboard bunk bulkhead and the heads. And what about the berths and the drawers under them? Just have a look, will you? The drawers don't fit and never will. They must go.

So what's left? Well, if you put it like that, not much. But how could there be? All that stuff in the cabin and the cockpit has to come out if we're going to repair the frames so we can refasten the planks. It's all in poor condition and is basically worthless. End of story.

It's well known that solo sailors spend a lot of time talking to themselves. It may be less well known that solo restorers do so too.

By June I had pulled out the fixed contents of the cabin and the cockpits and stripped the bulkheads of the engine compartment. It all took far longer than I expected. The consolation was that I had followed my head. The plywood under the icebox came off in dried, rotted chunks. The stainless-steel and copper linings of the icebox and food locker had been worn through in places with lots of pinholes. The main cabin bulkhead that had been hidden by the galley was also in very poor shape, as was the bulkhead on the other side of the companionway that had been hidden by the box Bob Crowder had built behind the toilet.

There was a similar story in the cockpit lockers. I needed Larry's help (with the forklift) to get the fuel and water tanks out of the boat and thought (briefly) about the guy who was building a boat in his backyard, got tired of lifting heavy objects, decided he needed a forklift and gave his wife a used one for her birthday.

Once I had stripped the facades of the engine compartment I could get at the massive oak lamination that sat between the bulkheads and supported the mizzenmast. Its plywood cover yielded to a pry-bar and revealed another reason to be grateful I had hauled her when I did.

Having once wondered if Williams had shrunk the mizzenmast to reduce the load on the superstructure, and having concluded that other factors had been more important, I was now glad it had been no taller, because the laminated mast step which had been hidden by the cover was rotten. It would not have broken in the immediate future but it was only a matter of time before it would have fallen

The rotten mizzenmast step.

apart with potentially dreadful consequences. I unbolted the block but kept it as a pattern for a new one just as I had kept other things (like the outer edges of the cabin bulkheads) for the same purpose.

I then removed the remains of the filthy, stiff and useless wiring that had been added but never removed over fifty years, having already cut out some of it as I removed the internal structures. Now, I pulled loose ends through exposed bulkheads until I had a grungy mass of ancient wire, some as old as the boat. Why, I wondered, didn't people take out old stuff when they installed new stuff?

The plumbing met the same fate. When I bought *Mudlark* she had a manual Whale pump and two electric pumps, only one of which worked. Bob had installed two new electric pumps, one with a float switch, the other a fully submersible Rule automatic. Connected to shore power through the inverter, they had kept her from sinking at the dock. I now removed all of them, together with the hoses

Matilda.

and the bronze through-hulls on the topsides. Somehow, in my years of messing about with the boat, I had neglected to ask why there were so many through-hulls – or if they served a purpose.

At the end of June I left for Norfolk with mixed feelings. I had made progress inasmuch as the deconstruction job seemed largely finished. I had got rid of the old and tired internal fixtures, removed a lot of grunge and cut out a lot of rot. I had not of course touched the engine. But it too would also have to come out because I couldn't repair nearby frames while it was there and because it would have to be restored anyway. But all of that and the non-trivial task of sistering the frames would have to wait until we returned from South America.

While in England we ran headlong into one of those can't-pass-it-up-may-never- happen-again opportunities when (this is a problem when you live across the street from a chandlery) I saw what looked like a miniature Dutch sail boat. Hurrying across for a closer look after breakfast I found it was exactly that, a black-hulled, heavily built blunt-ended Tjotter from Friesland with blood-red sails and beautiful hand-carved spars and scrollwork including a scoll that said 'Matilda' – which just happened to be the name of our first grandchild. I made a deal with Glynis that when Matilda came to visit at the weekend we would put her in the boat, see if she smiled or cried and then decide. She didn't cry, and we had another boat.

2002: The frame's the thing

We had a wonderful trip but after a long absence found piles of urgent things to be done in England and the USA when we returned, and it was not until early February, with snow on the ground at the marina, that I pushed open the heavy metal door of the shop, switched on the lights and saw *Mudlark* exactly as I remembered her.

'So where have you been?' she said.

'Sorry, I had other things to do.'

'Like gallivanting around South America while I've been sitting here freezing?'

I had arranged my schedule for the next few months to give me at least several weeks working on the boat, and despite the long absence I knew what I had to do because, before leaving for the rally, I had written myself a detailed note on a paint-free area of topside.

The previous year I had spent so much time getting stuff off the boat I had not looked closely at the frames other than those at the bow and in a few other places where I had removed planks. Which was probably just as well because as I examined them, scrapers, wrenches and hammers to hand, I realised, to my growing horror, that nearly every frame in the boat would have to be repaired. All the frames were walnut, all of them had been sawn, and each had two parts joined by bolts at the chine.

The angles between the side and bottom frames varied from about 110° to about 130° and in almost every case – the exceptions were in the back half of the boat – constant moisture from the weeping chines had induced rot and corroded bolts to the point there was almost nothing left of them. Despite all the previous surprises, I was amazed to find so many rusted nuts snapped off as soon as I tried to turn them, and that the remnants of many bolts either refused to budge or emerged as wizened images of the useful fastenings of fifty years before. I asked myself, yet again, why this boat had not sunk, because many of the frames as well as the chine cover boards had ceased to hold bottom and topsides together. I realised it had not happened because enough frames had survived. But I wondered what would have happened in a hard grounding.

There was another moment of truth as I considered the fact

The old frames.

that there were 64 frames and that every repair would mean determining where the rot began and ended; removing the remnants of bolts that had held the two parts of the frame together; removing the screws (in the side sections) and bolts (in the bottom sections) taking care not to damage surrounding wood; cutting away the bad wood on one or both sections – at that point I had no idea how far it would extend across the bottom frames and up the side frames – ensuring the cut allowed a flat scarf joint with the sister piece; measuring and shaping new pieces of white oak, getting the bevels right; clamping and drilling the bottom and side sections for new fastenings and finally bolting, screwing and epoxying them in place.

At the same time I would have to add additional side frames to provide new landings where planks had been butt-jointed on single frames. A lot of wood, a lot of shaping, a lot of epoxy, a lot of nuts and bolts and probably a lot of drill bits, including some long ones where I would need to go through several thicknesses of old and new frames. And, oh yes, a lot of work in prime backache-inducing positions.

And I'd thought I was only going to replace the chineboards.

———

It took just a few days of banging, cutting and prying to confirm that reframing the boat would be a huge task. Again, an easy job for a seasoned boatwright, a serious challenge for me. I decided to start with what I thought might be the easiest bits by working at the bow, where I could get at the frames from all sides while standing outside the boat. The task there was also made easier by the fact I had installed a new bottom and could thus fit new bottom frames without having to remove old ones. It was complicated by the fact I had no side planks against which to match the bevels of the new side frames (each one of course different), although I could approximate the curves with battens fastened to the stem and side planks. I took

New frames clamped in place.

the new side frames up to just below deck level and installed triple frames where there had been (and would again be) butt joints. Each new frame was triple-coated in clear WEST epoxy and hung out to dry.

It was then time to get at the hard stuff. I decided I might as well work backwards from where I left off working on the forepeak and do several bays at a time – starting with the half-dozen bays between the forepeak bulkhead and the back end of the foredeck. This area had about two feet of headroom and was by far the most cramped part of the boat except the lazarette – and I wouldn't have to worry about that for some time.

Having suffered occasionally from lower-back problems for more than forty years, I was cautious about levering myself in and out of this space, lifting my legs in place one at a time. I also made a point of ensuring I had the tools and materials I expected to need before I settled down to a session but, being me, invariably forgot something.

The first step at each frame was to assess the damage by probing to determine where bad wood ended and good wood began. The second was to cut out the bad wood to provide a flat surface for bonding, using one of several saws including jigsaw, Rotozip, 3⅜" Makita circular saw and 'E' blade saw attachments for the Fein Multimaster.

That done, I removed *all* the paint from the remnants of the old frames and the surrounding areas to expose clean bonding surfaces, using heat gun and scrapers.

I later realised I should have removed all the inside paint from each bay at that stage but had not then decided to epoxy the inside as well as the outside of the hull.

By trial and error I found the best way to fasten the sistered sections was to:

- clamp the new and old bottom pieces in place;

- drill through the bottom planks into the new and old bottom pieces;

- epoxy and bolt the bottom pieces in place;

- clamp and drill for bolts to join the bottom and side pieces together;

- drill through the topside planks to fasten the side pieces; and

- epoxy and bolt the side pieces to the bottom pieces and to the topside planks.

Initially, in late winter and early spring, I used WEST 105 and 205 (fast) hardener, but as the temperature warmed I used 206 (slow) hardener to allow more time for set-up. I added 403 (microfibres) adhesive filler and 406 (colloidal silica), having learned that without 406 the mix tended to flow out of the joints. Set-up became more important as the temperature rose because I also had to ensure I had time to extract myself from the hull, get outside to shove in epoxy-coated galvanised bolts and get in again to add washers and nuts and fasten them before the epoxy kicked. An unanticipated benefit was that because this meant a lot of climbing up and down ladders I got fitter and felt better. An unexpected problem was that if I was slow cleaning residues it set up like rock and was very hard to remove later. I was however careful about getting all the screws and bolts in place before the epoxy kicked off, to ensure adhesive and fasteners worked together.

On both the bottom and side frames I left most of the old fastenings in place, seeing no reason to disturb them if they were still working. Considering so much else had been wrong with the boat I was amazed so many of the original fasteners were still good. I nonetheless checked every screw in every frame, removing and replacing loose ones – although a lot of the old screws wouldn't have come out even if I'd wanted to remove them.

In theory I should have cut wooden bungs to fill the countersunk screw and bolt holes in the sides and bottom. In practice I did only a few before deciding that since the outside of the hull would be epoxy-coated and it was extremely unlikely anyone would ever refasten this boat again I should fill them with thickened epoxy.

Once out from under the foredeck my working conditions improved but the bays were nearly five feet high and each one thus took more time and materials. Whenever I started moaning to myself on that score the thought of what I would have had to pay someone else to do what I was doing brought me up sharp. Indeed that question had occurred to me in many forms since I had innocently begun a simple project to replace the chineboards. What would Cutts & Case or OBY have charged to rebuild the bow and reframe and partially replank the hull? What would they have charged for the work I did not yet know would have to be done?

I knew my hours were not boatbuilders' hours. Something that took me a day might take a professional an hour, something that took me a week might take a professional a day. But even then the hours would surely have added up and I would have faced a much larger bill than I could afford. There was no other way I or anyone else could or should have contemplated doing what I was doing, although whether it was a labour of love, as casual observers assumed, I was not sure. On the other hand it was not a labour of despair.

True I had sunk a lot of money, time and effort in the boat since I bought her. True I had sunk far more of each in the last two years than in the previous seven. I could still have walked away telling myself it was a rational decision, that I had taken on much more than I thought, that I had tried my hardest and had learned a lot but had reached the point where I had to cut my losses. But that never crossed my mind. I would finish the job no matter what.

Norfolk, June 2002

● Here we are again with *Moonfleet*, *Matilda*, *Pocahontas*, *Outje Boutje*, *Tinqua* and in honour of our grandson a new addition named *Felix*, a sea kayak made up from a kit from Chesapeake Light Craft in Annapolis that I imported from America. Enough boats to keep us all happy although, having not sailed her for several years, I have finally decided to sell *Tinqua*. The problem is we are over-boated. *Matilda* goes out twice in eight weeks and in late August returns to Teddy Maufe's barn at Branthill Farm until next year. *Moonfleet* gets less use than she should. I tell myself it's because I have yet to refinish her interior but somehow I can't find the time or energy for it. I think the problem is that having spent so much of the last six months on *Mudlark*'s frames I lack the will to take a busman's holiday.

I should probably be embarrassed by my boaty riches. I'm not. Partly because I plausibly tell myself I've assembled this collection of interesting boats with an eye on the future; that in a few years' time, unless circumstances change, we shall be spending more time in England and will have more time to use them. And partly because it would be a shame to unload them since each is a gem. But I renew my promise to sell *Tinqua* and before leaving England put her on the market among Sharpie sailors. It would be a shame if someone bought her and didn't use her properly and the best way to avoid that is to be picky about potential buyers. To my knowledge there is, as yet, no legislation against discrimination in boat sales.

The prospect of spending the fall rebuilding yet more frames doesn't thrill me but it's got to be done. I toy with the idea of fixing every other one but reject it. I've finished with the cabin and can at least look at what I've done there knowing I have, to the best of my ability and with no expense spared, done it right.

Now I'm working in the cockpit lockers and am having a dreadful time. The problem is that I can't even think about fitting new frames here without first cleaning the bottom planks, which are impregnated with fifty years of leaking fuel and accumulated bilge water. The only remedy is to scrape them. The gunge comes off in great black rolls. Eventually, I get back to the wood. But I can't sand it because the heat simply grinds the muck that is left into a paste and impresses it in the wood, making things worse. I wonder what I'll find when I get to the engine bay.

The worm-eaten bottom plank.

One morning, drilling through a bottom plank and into the frame above for a new bolt, I am surprised when the drill shoots through the plank in less time than it takes me to say 'shit!' immediately afterwards. I cling to disbelief for a few seconds before admitting I am looking at a rotten plank. The thing is I can't understand why. The bottom surface of the plank is good. So is the top although I can't see what's under the frame. So how had it become hollow? How had I missed it when I spent hours scraping and sanding the bottom? Test borings with small drill bits confirms the worst. The plank has been hollowed out from the inside by (I learn later) a teredo worm that somehow penetrated it, presumably through the transom and ate its way through fifteen feet of white cedar. It must have been one fat worm.

———◆———

Mild panic. If this plank is bad what about the others? Maybe they're all hollow? Maybe the bottom's rotten and will eventually fall off! I hadn't signed up for this! Listen, stupid, you've (fortunately) drilled through every frame forward of here (the cockpit), and has that happened before? No. Then while its quite likely teredo worms have attacked other planks the problem is most likely to be in the stern and you'd better check there very carefully to find out. I seriously doubt the bottom is going to fall off.

Tap, tap, tap. Every inch of every plank. More test bores when in doubt. And yes, there are more echoes and yes, there have been more teredo worms and yes, they'd been hungry at the time and yes, they had probably sacrificed their lives to eat my boat and had died doing so. Which means *Mudlark* is a floating cemetery as well as a ghost ship.

———•———

I conclude that I have four bad bottom planks. The first is affected for about fifteen feet, the others for about twelve, eight and six respectively. They must obviously be removed, and until I get to the transom (where the bottom planks were fastened to the bottom board of the transom) they come off quite easily. Having removed them I have four sizeable gaps in the bottom of the boat but cannot fill them until I finish cleaning inside and repairing the frames. Meanwhile I have a convenient way of dropping things on the concrete floor. Fine for garbage and debris. Less so for sanders and other tools. Each time it happens I have to stop work, climb down the ladder, retrieve what I have dropped and climb back. The good news is that this is yet more exercise.

———•———

Even the central section of the bilge is filthy, and even though I'm not going to add frames there I decide to clean it while I'm at it because it will have to be done eventually. It takes forever. But as I move closer to the engine bay I realise it's time to get the engine out and up to New Jersey where Dave Van Ness is going to restore it.

Larry helps again with the forklift and the engine comes out without resistance. Larry sets it on wooden blocks and I rent a van for the journey to Ridgewood. Not having driven a vehicle containing such a huge and heavy object before I am a bit nervous but the trip goes smoothly. I find the address at the second attempt and find Dave inside a workshop crammed with elderly Graymarine engines, most bigger than mine.

We go over what he will do, beginning with an assessment of what must be replaced and rebuilt. I tell him there's no deadline. As far as I can see I'm not going to be using it for a long time to come. Next year would be fine.

I go back to the frames and find the engine bay about as I had expected. The frames are very strong here and have stood up better than elsewhere because the stern seems to have suffered less than the rest of the boat once the leaks in the bow made her bow-heavy. But there's the expected coating of grease and oil and it takes ages to clean the engine runners which must, if bad, be replaced, although, before degreasing, they look alright.

They are. But I decide to double all the frames they sit on just to be safe. I also sister the frames at the chine even though they are in much better shape than those further forward. Whilst I'm at it, why not? And whilst I'm at it I have a closer look at something that's not on the current agenda but will be in due course – and yet again I am shocked when I pry away at the joints where the oak bulkheads framing the engine bay are attached to the coamings and find some unwelcome surprises.

The engine bay with the engine removed.

The underside of the portside coaming abaft the forward bulkhead where Bob Crowder made a repair in 1993 is full of rot. The adjacent area of deck, which looks alright from above, has been hollowed out underneath. And the joint between the coaming and the bulkhead relies mainly on two lag screws into the end grain of the bulkhead. The situation is much the same on the starboard side of the forward bulkhead. And although there is no rot in the coaming, the deck or the bulkhead itself, the joint between the coaming and the rear bulkhead also relies on lag screws into end grain, which most people would say is an inherently weak arrangement.

I decide to deal with all that later, and get back to the frames in the steering cockpit, where only a couple are bad. Then into the lazarette, which is wide enough to lie in but less than two feet deep. To get in I have to lever my legs in and out with my hands. But the frames back here are the best in the boat and the bottom boards are pretty clean, and I decide I can get by with a few sisters. But I also decide the stern knee must be repaired because it is cracked and when I tap it a big chunk falls off.

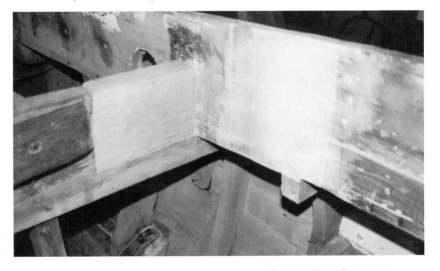

The repair to the rotten coaming.

Boarding school

The frames are a watershed because they mark the point where deconstruction meets reconstruction. From now on, as far as I know (I'm wrong), there will be nothing more to take to the dump. And it has taken me less than three years to reach this point!

It's finally time to close the gaps in the sides and the bottom. Before starting, I renew my acquaintance with the guys at Gougeon Brothers in Bay City, Michigan, where WEST is manufactured. They have always been extraordinarily helpful. No matter how many times I've called, no matter how stupid my questions (even when I ask the same question several times over to ensure I understand the answer) they are patience itself and convey a strong sense of knowing their stuff. Such a contrast with run-of-the-mill 'help desks', which often give me the impression that answers to my questions are being read off a computer screen by someone who doesn't understand them.

I want to check the sequence again. In particular, whether it will be best to begin by cutting, fitting and fastening the new side and bottom planks or to start by reaming the (mainly cotton) caulking from the seams between the old planks and filling them with epoxy.

The advice is to fit the new planks first, epoxy them in place (having removed any old caulking that could affect the bond between old and new planks), clean the other seams to expose new wood and fill them with epoxy prior to fairing and coating. Should I do the bottom or the side planks first? They say it's up to me and I decide to do the bottom first. For one thing I reckon it's easier to start there than on the sides, for another I'm fed up dropping stuff on the floor.

Bottom down …

The original bottom – the one built by Mr Smith – lasted only a couple of years. The second one has done nearly fifty. So I look for white cedar to replace the boards I took out. Question: Where do you find fifteen-foot lengths of $1^3/_4$" × 9" white cedar in Maryland? Answer: You don't.

I'm willing to travel (but not too far), so I try the Harbor Sales Company in Sudlersville and other places on the Western Shore of the Bay. Nobody has it. Smaller stuff yes, that size no. Then Chesapeake Woodworkers in Hurlock suggest yellow cypress. I look it up and ask about its habit of soaking up water like a sponge. But you're going to cover it with epoxy, aren't you? On the outside, yes … and a seed was sown that grew into a question: why shouldn't I epoxy the inside too? The question takes a while to mature. Meanwhile, seeing no real option, I decide to go with yellow cedar.

It's lovely wood. It looks good, smells good and works very easily. I measure carefully but because the bottom planks carry the same width from end to end the only challenges are to cut them exactly to length for a good fit fore and aft, and to bevel the sides carefully to match the slight curvature of the bottom. The rocker is not a problem because the longer boards are long enough to flex and the short one is in the flat end run to the transom. I bolt and epoxy the new boards in place, having first cleaned the adjacent sides of the old ones to expose new wood. I feel quite pleased when I finish. I don't then know the topside planking will be harder … much harder.

... Top up

It's curved-component time, and before moving to the topside planks I hit the books, most of which I've inherited from Ted Squier, a lifelong sailor who willed his maritime collection to me.

On Bob's advice I turn first to *How to Build a Wooden Boat* (McIntosh 1988). David ('Bud') McIntosh has been described by one of his readers as 'a master of his craft' and 'an exceedingly poor teacher' who 'buries critical theses in an avalanche of lyrical verbiage that achieves nothing other than obscuration of the point' (who's throwing stones in a greenhouse?). And by another as the author of 'one of the clearest explanations of building a traditional wooden boat ever presented' and of definitive answers 'on how to lay out curved components'.

I find McIntosh hard going but decide it's a function of his topic rather than his style. I read everything else of potential relevance on my shelves including *Planking and Fastening*, an excellent compilation of *WoodenBoat* articles edited by Peter Spectre and Maynard Bray (1996).

New side plank in place.

Reading is a useful precursor to measuring, spiling, bevelling, fitting and fastening, but it's time to get on with it. With beginner's luck and a serious commitment to take as much time as it takes to get it right, the first four planks prove easier than I expect. The last, a twelve-footer that finishes at the stem and has more twist than the others, proves much harder.

My first attempt fails because, in my efforts to get it to twist in to the stem I remove too much wood from the top edge and have to do it again. The second attempt passes Bob's inspection. A professional would doubtless have done better in less time but I am quietly thrilled to have done something I never dreamed I could do, something that is, I tell myself, the essence of traditional wooden boat repair. I move to the next task with more confidence.

The big gaps in the hull filled, it's time to fill the small ones. My main concerns are to ensure each seam is bevelled so it's wider at the front than the back; to ensure the seams are neither so wide that epoxy will ooze out the other side nor so narrow that it won't fill the seam; and that there's new wood on both sides to which epoxy will stick.

This task proves difficult. Some of the advice – including the Gougeon Brothers' very helpful manual (Gougeon Brothers 2000) – is to use a circular saw for the job. But even with battens as guidelines I find it hard to keep the saw in the seam. I also find the depth of cut varies, sometimes too deep, sometimes too shallow, partly because the thickness of the fifty-year-old planks is uneven and partly because I can't maintain even pressure.

As a result, a task that (according to others) should have taken a few hours

The seams reamed and filled.

takes more than two weeks and an arsenal of tools including a regular router, a router attachment for the Rotozip, metal picks and a variety of Fein tool attachments including a teak knife designed to remove caulking from deck seams, a carbide-tipped grout removal blade and the 'E' blades that have already proved invaluable in other applications. Once they're clean it's easier to use a standard ($7\frac{1}{2}$") circular saw set at a depth of 1" to expose new wood. But again my best results come from the Makita $3\frac{3}{8}$" circular saw.

I take a long time on the seams because the success of the project partly depends on ensuring the topside planks are well bonded. It's not perfect. There are larger gaps where my hand slipped, and even when I'm done I'm not sure I extracted every last bit of foreign material from the seams. But Bob says I've done an adequate job. And that, as usual, is all the assurance I need. The next task – filling the seams with thickened epoxy (105, 205, 403 and 406) – goes well. In some places the mixture seeps through bigger gaps than I had meant to make but I make a point of scurrying up the ladder to clean off residues on the inside before it sets hard.

With the planks in place the final job, prior to beginning what I expected to be the tedious process of fairing the topsides, was to fasten the new cutwater to the repaired stem. I took an inordinate amount of time getting the inner and outer curves right, the main difficulty being that the inner surface of the cutwater had to match the outer surface of the stem as closely as possible. I knew I could fill gaps with thickened epoxy but – having been critical of the gaps I had found there when I took the boat apart – I wanted to get it right.

And in the end it pretty much was. Certainly there was no daylight and whatever gaps remained were mercifully small. Cam had by now arrived to spend the Easter break in America and I asked him to hold the cutwater in place while I drilled through the stem and cutwater to fit the eye bolt for the bobstay. We set up carefully because I badly wanted the eyebolt in dead centre. I started drilling at a downward angle. And a muffled scream coincided with the moment I felt the bit break out the other side.

All things considered he was very decent about it. Easton Memorial patched him up efficiently and we went back to Oxford for the rest of the day. Naturally he felt sick. So did I. The one consolation was (as I told him a few days later when I thought it prudent) was that we had drilled a perfect hole. And before I clear-coated the cutwater I inscribed 'Cam's Hole' on the bloodstained mahogany.

Fair thee well

Another Christmas. Another New Year. Another agenda that is really another phase of the old one. The topsides are at last almost ready for new chineboards. Reframed, re-planked and refastened, each side is now in effect a single piece of wood, each plank joined by epoxy to the planks above and below. All that remains is to ensure the new chineboards lie flush against the lower planks, and that means I have to fair the sides.

Against all odds the hull has remained remarkably fair. Despite the bad frames, after fifty years none of the fastenings has failed, none of the planks has sprung and the hollows are no worse than you'd expect in almost any hull of that age. Mr Smith certainly did some things right, and as a result the job I'm about to do will be easier than it might have been.

Fairing a wood hull is reckoned to be one of the more tedious and tiring tasks in the book. It's difficult to use power sanders because they tend to leave grooves, swirls and hollows. Better, say the experts, to use long boards with special adhesive abrasives. So I shift to yet another new suite of tools I've never touched before. Short boards for fairing automobile panels from the auto supply store in Easton. And two longer fibreglass ones with different amounts of flexibility from Oceana in Annapolis.

Oceana seems to stock everything a professional boatbuilder might need and is mainly patronised by guys from boatyards who buy huge quantities of stuff. Every time I go there they ask for my account number and I explain I don't have one and they say that'll be retail then and I wonder how much the discount is and ask if I can have an account and they say 'are you a professional boatbuilder?' and I say no but I work like one and they smile and say sorry and I pay retail. It hurts because buying the best – which is all they sell – is a sure way to reduce your bank balance faster than you can wreck a cedar plank with a belt sander. Not that any of these professional guys would use a belt sander on a cedar plank – but if they did they wouldn't wreck it.

The longboarding motion is somewhat tiring but with the right abrasive quickly produces the fair surface it's meant to produce. Even the stiffer board works like a dream on my gently curved tumblehome-free topsides. Before using epoxy I clean

Fairing the topsides.

the dust off the hull (although some people say leave it on). I start with a single coat of unthickened 105 resin, using 205 hardener because it's cold outside. My initial aim is to saturate and seal the wood and to build up a hard surface. So I apply three coats, wet on wet, letting each dry to a tacky state before adding the next. I let the third harden overnight.

In the morning I wash it thoroughly using clean water from a spray bottle and frequently renewed Scotchbrite pads to get a clean surface. I then sand lightly to key the surface and start filling the voids with a mixture of WEST 105, 205, 407 and 406 to minimise runoff. Too much 406 and you're sanding rock-hard glass, which is very tedious. Too little and the mixture tends to sag. The thing is to use enough 407 to get a stiffish mixture in the first place though not so much it becomes unworkable. As with everything it's a matter of practice – although having done quite a lot of this before, my learning curve is less steep than usual. It's rather novel to know I know what I'm doing.

It still takes time, although my schedule is now partly controlled by Gougeon Brothers' chemistry. Fortunately, the shop is warm even on cold days and I am grateful to Georgie for letting me leave the heating on all night so the temperature remains constant throughout the critical period when the epoxy is curing. And even though I am very careful about pumping the right number of strokes of resin and hardener and stirring the mixture carefully before and after

The fairing done.

adding filler, the first thing I do each morning is to check yesterday's work to make sure it has gone off properly. I have made mistakes before.

January becomes February and I finally finish fairing the topsides. I'll wait to add additional clear coats until I have fitted the chineboards and epoxied the bottom.

Back to the bottom

There were two consolations to the prospect of spending the next several weeks manoeuvring around jackstands lying on my back: it was early February and not mid-June; and this time I would not be working on bottom paint. But working on your back is working on your back and yes I know my forebears did much worse things, but I'm not going to pretend it's fun.

Before starting, I clean the shop floor. That's not something I do every day, although I know I should. I tend instead to push the dirt into little unstable piles under the boat. But if that's where I am going to work I want it clean, otherwise the trolley will keep getting stuck in muck. So out comes the shop vac, one of the most useful power tools ever invented. But then, depending on my latest toy, I think that about many tools. A shop dustpan and big brush works well too.

The task ahead is the same as the one I've just finished. I'm going to remove

The bottom faired and coated, with battens over the seams.

everything between the bottom planks, expose new wood to which epoxy filler will stick, fill the seams and fair and clear-coat the bottom. Then – call this belt and braces if you will and I'm not sure I want people to know about it – I'm going to put battens on the seams. So it won't look good but who will see it except when she's hauled – or turns turtle (in which case I'll have other things to worry about).

Epoxy-coating the bottom and adding the battens takes eight weeks. Not full-time because I'm not there all the time. I travel twice to Europe and once to Canada to give speeches and between times lie on my back scraping, clawing, sawing, gouging, reaming. The seams eventually look good enough although some are wider than I'd intended. But there are no more bad planks. I fill the seams, sometimes from above, taping the undersides to stop the epoxy running through, again using a mix of 105, 205 (it's just not too warm), 403 and a bit more 406 to minimise sagging. I take particular care with the seams under the frames, cleaning the undersides of the old frames as best I can.

Fairing the bottom is harder than I thought it would be. Much harder than filling the seams and much harder than fairing the topsides. Partly because it's quite uneven, partly because it's difficult to work overhead and partly because I'm again dealing with clouds of dust, this time from cured epoxy. I know cured epoxy (unlike partially cured epoxy) is inert and will do me no more harm than other dust, and certainly less than the dust from copper heavy antifouling. But dust is dust and I'd rather keep it out of my lungs. This time my timing is not bad – it's not yet so hot I'm suffering in the half respirator and body armour – but it's still unpleasant.

I fasten the battens – ¹/₄" × 2" cypress over each seam – and regret the fact that when I sight along them from the bow some are not quite straight. I decide not to worry about that and declare victory in early May.

But this is where I came in!

Three years and four months after I started to replace the chineboards, and 34 months after I was supposed to finish, I was finally ready to get on with them. The frames and planking were probably stronger than the day *Mudlark* got her bottom wet for the first time. The topsides were probably as fair now as they were then, and as for the bottom, well it wasn't going to leak. I thought about not renewing the chineboards but discarded that idea when Bob pointed out there was still no proper chine log, that it would be foolish to subject the rebuilt hull to any stress that could be avoided, and that I should do what I had originally set out to do. Anyway I had been periodically moving half a dozen 4 × 8 sheets of ³/₈" marine plywood around the shop for the last three years and might as well use it for its intended purpose.

I worried about getting out the right shapes for the chineboards to fit the curvature of the hull but found that the top edge of the board conformed perfectly

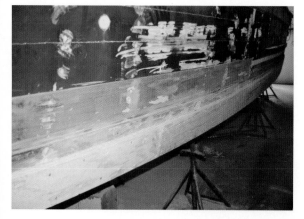

The new chineboards.

and that I could mark off the cutting line for the bottom edge from underneath. I decided against scarf joints in favour of butt joints for two reasons. One was that I was not sure about cutting good scarfs. The other was that I was going to laminate two layers of ply over staggered joints which meant the joints would be covered and would in any case be sealed with several layers of clear-coat epoxy.

Bob suggested I might fasten the chineboards with monel staples using an air-powered staple gun. I looked into it, wondered what possible use I might have for an air compressor once the job was done, considered the cost, and voted against. I bought one two years later to work on my house in Virginia.

Instead, I fastened the first layer of boards with 1¹/₄" square-drive stainless-steel screws using the Milwaukee right-angle drill, which had become a firm favourite – although by this stage it was coated with a mixture of hardened epoxy and dirt and looked disgusting (I sometimes wished I worked more cleanly). I scribed the curves for the underside pieces and left the outboard sides proud to be cut and bevelled later using the power planer and a small block plane. Having screwed them in place I used the finished curves to lay out the second underside layer and finally cut and dry-fitted the second side layer that lapped both underside layers. Once all four layers (two on the sides, two on the bottom) were epoxied and refastened, the last step was to cut a 45° bevel on the top edge of the side boards. I found the de Walt grinder with a sanding attachment much the best tool for the job and was delighted when the final edge had no dips or humps.

The starboard side done, the portside followed, and the job I had set out to do was finished. Too bad the prep work took a bit longer than expected.

———————❖———————

Before leaving for Norfolk again I made a return trip to New Jersey to collect the engine. Dave Van Ness had done a splendid job. It gleamed with new paint and new parts and, best of all, the bench test confirmed that with the new parts I couldn't see the engine ran as good as new, buttressing Dave's claim that a Graymarine was still 'the best engine for sailboats'.

Back at Easton I used the yard's hoist to lift the engine from the truck I had borrowed from Bob and set it on two wood blocks near the bow and wrapped and taped it in plastic sheets until I was ready to put it back in the boat. Then I went off for the summer to play with my English boats.

The rebuilt engine.

———————❖———————

Oxford, MD, 20 September 2003

● All things considered we got off lightly.

I finally got back here this afternoon, having left on Tuesday to batten down the hatches and ride out Hurricane Isabel in McLean. There, we worried about some of the trees behind the house – especially an 80-foot-tall dead one – but there was little rain because the storm moved very fast and blew right on by. We lost power for a day and a half but got it back yesterday and suffered very little compared with millions of people whose homes and lives have been wrecked by Isabel – one of the worst tropical cyclones to hit this area since the Chesapeake–Potomac Hurricane of 1933.

Before leaving Oxford I drove *Metalark* (the aluminium speedboat) up the river to Easton Point, hauled her with Larry's help and put her on blocks in the shop near *Mudlark*. I then drove the Jaguar XJS I had left standing outside the shop for a few days to an Easton workshop for service.

Meadowlark had to stay at the dock in Oxford because I had nowhere else to put her. I doubled and lengthened the lines (realising she might float above the dock) and hoped for the best (realising she might land on the dock or be smashed against a piling). She's not insured so I called BoatUS – they have the insurance on *Mudlark* – and asked if I could get cover. The woman laughed and asked if I'd heard there was a hurricane coming and said 'no way', which was what I expected. But it was nice to know people had a sense of humour at times like this. I dragged *Lesser Mudlark* behind the shed, put the scull and the canoe inside the house, had a word with the Devlins, who are staying, and left town.

Returning (I already knew from the Devlins that *Meadowlark* had survived undamaged) I found a high water mark about three feet from the back steps. The water had flowed under but not into the shed and I wondered if the rabbits that live under it survived. The fences had floated up and out of their holes and lay flat on the grass.

It was a different story just a little way down South Street. It's odd how you can live somewhere – on and off in our case – for several years without noticing things like relative heights, but there is actually a subtle hill on South Street and we are at the top! A few inches makes a huge difference. I understand parts of Oxford were flooded two or three feet deep but have not gone poking around. There's nothing I can do to help – a lot of official and unofficial help is already on hand – and gawping at other peoples' misfortune seems voyeuristic. The good news in town is that nobody was injured.

I'm going to the marina tomorrow. I'm sure it must have been hit, being so close to the water, but I don't want to get in the way this evening and will wait for daylight.

Easton, MD, 21 September 2003

● It's worse than I expected. Much worse for Georgie because the marina store was flooded more than two feet deep on Thursday night. Although she prepared for the worst she's lost some stock. It's also worse than expected for the boat owners whose boats were lifted off their stands or smashed into pilings at their slips, although none was sunk. And it's worse than expected for me, although – as in Oxford – it could have been worse. Suppose I'd left the XJS outside!

By far the most serious damage is to the engine. On Tuesday afternoon, after Larry had helped me store *Metalark* inside, we talked about using the hoist to lift the engine out of the potential reach of flood water but finally decided it would be OK on the floor. As it turned out it was submerged for roughly ten hours and will almost certainly have to go back to Dave Van Ness. That much exposure to salt water (even though in the mid-Bay the water is less saline than at the Atlantic entrance) has probably ruined the new pistons.

A second problem is that the band saw and table saw were both partially submerged. Both tools are on legs and both have sealed motors mounted quite high. They may be OK but I shan't know until they've dried out and I've tried to run them. Meanwhile I've lubricated them and am hoping for the best.

The other thing is that the deadwood on *Mudlark*'s stern, including the shaft hole and the bottom of the transom, was submerged. The deadwood had been epoxied and faired but the transom had not and the shaft hole was flooded. I don't think ten hours' submersion will have done any real harm; I'm just glad I'd finished coating the bottom because I would have otherwise had to wait for the moisture content to fall to less than 15% before resuming work – which could have taken several weeks.

The only other damage is to wood I had left on the shop floor. Fortunately I put almost everything I could lift out of harm's way on *Mudlark*'s decks. *Metalark* just floated off her blocks and as the water retreated settled on the shop floor. She is undamaged.

The shop was flooded because the surge tide that raced up the Bay and then into the rivers and creeks was far bigger than anyone anticipated. Including people who have lived here all their lives and have seen previous hurricanes, including Hugo in '89, the double whammy of Gloria and Juan in '85 and even the big one in '33 – which was before they started naming them. Isabel would have done more damage had she moved more slowly because then there would have been more rain, but she was only a category 2 storm by the time she reached Easton. It was the surge tide that did the damage.

———◆———

It took me a week to clean the muck from the shop but even that had a good side because it was an opportunity to chuck out stuff I had been meaning to chuck out for ages. There was also news from BoatUS that my insurance would cover the repair of the engine and other minor damage. They did a brilliant job, getting their assessors around very soon after the storm.

An event like Isabel, even if you get off lightly, gives you pause and (banalities be damned) puts things in perspective. Most of all it's a strong reminder of our vulnerability. Although we can now predict the size and timing of 'weather events' like hurricanes with amazing accuracy we shall never be able to control their outcomes.

Although it was our engine that suffered, our post-event thoughts were mainly about our house. In this game of inches it was clear that a foot or two of extra altitude made all the difference. But looking ahead and with vague notions of sea-level rise and forecasts of increased hurricane activity in the backs of our minds, we wondered – for the first time – about the long-term future of Oxford's fragile peninsula. What would it take to flood the whole town, including the hilly bits? An extra two or three feet – a metre in modern British usage? What would it take to wipe it off the map or at least do such devastating damage some people would not rebuild?

It also struck me for the first time that if a significant part of a settlement like Oxford, which has grown slowly and organically over several centuries (by American standards, Oxford is *rather ancient*) were destroyed, the settlement we know would be destroyed too because its shape, size and form would change.

It then struck me that Glynis and I had achieved a dubious double by choosing not one but two flood-prone homes, because our home in Norfolk, like our home in Oxford, stands on the water's edge. In Norfolk, the highest spring tides, especially when pushed by northerly winds, lap over the Quay. In 1953, when high tides coincided with a ferocious storm in the North Sea, the Granary was flooded to three feet. In 1978, when it was still being used as a granary, there had been two feet.

A 200-year flood would bring even more water and could do huge damage. So what if our three-level apartment is at the top of the building (we never say 'penthouse' because it would seem silly in Norfolk). Our back-to-back garages on the ground floor opening on to the Quay at one end would certainly get wet, even though there are flood boards inside the green doors. There's nothing new in any of that. The risks were there last year and will be there next year. Isabel has just sharpened our senses.

Back to work

Once cleaned up it was back to work, and by early October I had settled in to a process that would, I believed, reduce the risk that my efforts of the previous three and three-quarter years could end in frustration. The process was to epoxy the *inside* of the hull.

From the time I decided to coat the outside in WEST epoxy I had worried about what would happen when the inside got wet. It could hardly be avoided. Seas would come aboard and sit in the bilge. Rain would fall in the cockpits and sit in the bilge. A boat was meant to get wet. I could imagine nothing more absurd – not even neurotic obsessions with perfect brightwork, flawless paint or spotless decks – than a neurotic obsession about keeping the inside of a boat dry.

The problem was that assuming the boat *would* get wet inside (and with *Mudlark*'s flattish bilge the wet would spread around) what would happen if wood that was epoxy-sealed on the outside was only protected on the inside by conventional marine paints that allow wood to 'breathe' and are thus permeable? Surely moisture would be trapped inside the hull?

I knew boatbuilders who said wood does *not* have to breathe. I also knew Gougeon Brothers had told me each time I asked that if I was going to coat the exterior of the hull I should fill the seams, that if I was going to fill the seams I should coat the exterior, and that no matter what I did on the outside I should not even think of sealing the inside unless I could get at the underside as well as the top and side of every frame and every surface of every plank. It was all in their book (Gougeon Brothers 2000)

That wasn't guidance. That was dictat.

And when I asked about water that somehow got inside the uncoated hull they said I should make reasonable but not frantic efforts to keep it out (it is after all, a boat) but above all be sure I had good ventilation. If there was a little water in the bilge, not to worry: it would soon evaporate. I understood the argument. I accepted Gougeon Brothers as experts. Yet I was still uncomfortable with their advice. And that summer, in England, I had discussed my concerns with boatbuilding friends.

I talked first to Richard Cracknell, who had taken over the yard started by his son William, who had died in a tragic boating accident in December 1999. Richard showed me a carvel hull on which he had coated the inside planks and frames and had filleted the frames to prevent moisture penetrating beneath them. It was, he told me, a well-established technique in the restoration of old wooden boats and he knew of no case where, when properly done, it had failed.

James Case, who was in the midst of rebuilding yet another International 12 Square Metre Sharpie, said the same thing and reminded me that his own sharpie, *Rockabye*, had been encapsulated without stripping the planks to get at the undersides of the frames. He had, instead, very carefully sealed them with epoxy fillets. The result was, he said, a moisture-proof boat that needed very little maintenance apart from painting and varnishing. And because he had used two-part linear polyurethane paint on the topsides and bottom (sharpies being dry-sailed and therefore not antifouled) and two-part urethane varnish on the deck and spars, maintenance was far less onerous than it would have been with traditional finishes.

Both Richard and James told me they understood my problem but could not understand why Gougeon Brothers were so emphatic about not treating the inside like the outside. They also assured me that, in England, their practice was common practice. But both stressed it was very important to do the job right. If you didn't take the time to prepare the bonding surfaces or failed to fillet every nook you would have problems.

So it seemed I might, after all, have a choice. Back in Bay City, Michigan, there was advice I didn't like. Here, in Norfolk, was contradictory advice I did like. What to do?

I called the technical team at Wessex Resins in Hampshire, the UK manufacturers of WEST system products, explained my dilemma and told them what Richard and James and Gougeon Brothers had said. They emphatically confirmed what I had been told by Richard and James: that as long I filleted the frames I could encapsulate a wooden boat without taking it apart; that there were no shortcuts to sound preparation; and that there must be no gaps in the fillets. This meant if I was going to do it I would have to be completely sure I could get at every part of the hull; and that subject to those conditions it was not only what I could do, it was what I should do.

When I explained this was the exact opposite of what the guys at Bay City had told me, they suggested I call Bay City again, describe our conversation and ask if the reason they had given me different advice was that some (or many) people in America had tried to seal the insides of hulls, had not filleted frames properly (or had been unable to reach them) and had subsequently run into serious problems.

I did that. And this time Gougeon Brothers confirmed that was indeed what had happened and explained that was why they routinely and consistently advised strongly against inside coating. They also told me there had been a lively debate on exactly this issue between the Gougeon brothers themselves, and that one of them had sealed the inside as well as the outside of his boat and had filleted his frames.

Then they said that if I was sure I could do it I could go ahead on the inside, although they would continue to discourage others from doing that because their past experience had been so poor. I rather wished they had been more forthcoming before but appreciated that failed projects are in nobody's interest. So now I knew the way ahead. It's odd I was so exultant because it meant that when I got back to America I would have to do a lot more work than I would have had to do had I taken the Gougeon Brothers' original advice. On the other hand, having done so much already, a bit more would hardly matter.

Coating the inside of the hull.

When it actually came to doing it I choked on that idea. A fine entry is a very fine thing when you're looking at it from outside. When you're inside trying to remove paint from sharply converging planks you have other ideas. The saving grace, once again, was the shallow depth of the hull, which meant I only had to get the paint off five planks. And once I got out of the forepeak it was easier, and became even easier as I moved backwards from under the foredeck into the cabin and then to the cockpits and the engine compartment, although the lazarette was a predictable low point in more ways than one.

I wished very much I had decided to take this route before I repaired the frames. It would have been vastly more efficient to strip paint from the planking at the same time I stripped it from the frames. Now, where I had left smears (and in the forepeak some few gobs) of hardened epoxy in places where the fillets would have to go, the remnant smears and gobs had to be rigorously and vigorously washed, Scotchbrited and sanded to prepare the surfaces for fillets. Where I had been less careful (where frames were invisible) more than a few gobs of hardened epoxy meant even more work.

———◆———

By December 2003 *Mudlark* was encapsulated top to bottom, front to back, inside and out. I had a boat that was sealed forever against *ingress*. Because unless I or someone else (it wasn't going to be me) decided to remove the epoxy, get back to the wood, ream seams, roll cotton and hammer it in place, none of the thousands of board feet and the even more thousands of carefully chosen, measured, cut and shaped pieces of a dozen species of wood would ever get wet again. 'And if they do,' I told Larry as I laid on the last clear coat, 'I'm going to kill myself!' Seeing he looked a bit startled, I quickly added, 'Well no, not really – but I'd be very, very, very disappointed.'

The encapsulated transom.

So what did I have? Was this still a wooden boat? Was this mummified, plasticised, inert object still a plank-on-frame yacht? Would Mr Smith say it was still a wooden boat (after I'd explained to him what epoxy was)? Would LFH say it was still a wooden boat – or would he dismissively tell me it was a former wooden boat covered in frozen snot? Would Rich Gannon at the Martha's Vineyard Marine Railway, who according to Michael Ruhlman had said that strip-planked, cold-moulded, epoxy-encapsulated *White Wings* was 'not a wooden boat', also say that *Mudlark* was not a wooden boat?

And did I care? I knew the answer to that one. I did care about tradition, about heritage, about keeping faith with the past and about the wooden boat as an icon of continuity in a throwaway plastic world. But I cared more about preservation, about giving old things new life, about making them good for the next twenty or even fifty years – long enough anyway to last me and leave something for my successor. And if the price of preservation was the use of frozen snot, if the best or perhaps only way to extend the life of an old boat was to use state-of-the-art tools and materials that I could learn how to use, there was no doubt in my mind. I was glad I had done it.

Juno, Charlie Ward's marriage of English east coast tradition with the latest technology. Painting by Godfrey Sayers.

If anybody told me I had somehow violated a trust, denigrated traditional craftsmanship or broken the rules I would (probably) resist the impulse to tell him (or her) to get lost, and instead explain that I was unequivocally certain I had done the right thing the right way; that I was pleased and proud with what I'd done; that if I were to do it again (which I wouldn't because once is enough) I'd do it the same way except that, knowing what I knew now, I'd do it faster, better and more economically; and that – here's the punch line – if the old guys had had access to modern tools, materials and techniques they would have used them too.

In England, Charlie Ward's magnificent barge yacht *Juno* is a scaled-down (45-foot) version of a traditional sailing barge. Rigorously designed (by Andrew Wolstenholme) and expertly built (by Charlie), she perfectly captures the essence of the working barges that once thronged the east

Sailing Barge 'Juno'

Exploring the North Norfolk Coast

coast of England. She also incorporates the last word in technology because designer and builder passionately believe in the dictum that if the old builders had had it, they'd have used it! Of course they would.

Easton, January 2004

● I returned to the shop after Christmas to face the fact I have a hull but not a boat. A hull is, after all nothing more than a platform and a vessel. A platform for the oars, sculls, quants, sails and engines that make it go and make it a boat. And a vessel for containing people, cargo, possessions, gear, food, berths and amenities that make it a useful and enjoyable boat. Before I can say I have a useful, enjoyable boat I have a lot of work to do on the platform and the vessel.

Platform jobs

A hull can move even if there is nowhere to sleep, eat or be merry or miserable, while a fully equipped cabin on an immobile hull is simply a floating caravan. The highest priority was to make her go. This meant I had to:

- fit the new mizzenmast step I had made from the pattern of the old one (a 5"× 15"× 10" block with a cut-out for the mast, laminated from five 2" blocks of white oak) between the engine compartment bulkheads;

- fit the new mainmast step I had made from the pattern of the old one;

- fit the deck hardware and fittings, some of it old and refurbished (bronze main, genoa and leeboard winches, fairleads, sheet leads, cleats, boom gallows, jib boom track, deck plates, ventilators, flagstaff sockets), some of it new (traditional stainless navigation lights, stainless ventilators, bronze boat badges, a klaxon horn, a brass compass);

- reinstall the engine and the stern gear, made to measure by Kastel Brothers at St Michael's;

- replace the standing and running rigging;

- refinish and reinstall the masts;

- fit the refurbished leeboards.

Vessel jobs

To make the boat habitable I had to:

- fit the new stainless opening portlights (four oval ones from Hamilton Marine in Searsport, Maine, two round ones from a chandlery in Amsterdam);

- install the new main hatch I had built in odd moments over the previous several weeks, incorporating bronze hatch runners and a bronze-rimmed round prismatic decklight from Davey and Co. in Colchester, England;

- make and fit a new mahogany frame for the refurbished cabin door;

- make and fit new mahogany trim to go around the cabin roof and on top of the coamings;

- finish the deck by restoring the ancient windlass (a massive affair sitting at the inboard end of the bow platform) and the new fore hatch, incorporating another prismatic decklight from Davey;

- make and fit new lift-off marine-ply panels on top of the engine compartment at either side of the mizzenmast step;

- make and fit new fixed marine-ply panels on the engine compartment bulkheads incorporating (on the forward side) a pair of oak engine-access doors with seductively curved tops and handmade stainless hardware that had been made for but never used on an English boat (I had bought the doors at John Crook's chandlery in Wells, and carried them to America in my baggage);

- make and fit new sides and covers for the main cockpit lockers and new sliding doors for the lazarette;

- make and fit new sole boards for the main and steering cockpits;

- rebuild the galley, incorporating a new sink (keeping the Fynespray faucet I had bought in 1993), a new, recessed Origo alcohol stove to replace the surface-mounted Origo I had installed at the same time (I had taken it to England to put on *Moonfleet*) and storage for plates, cups, silverware and food in removable coolers;

- rebuild the head, installing a new self-contained toilet plumbed to a new holding tank in the port cockpit locker;

- rebuild the berths, using the existing framework, with storage bins underneath;

- paint and varnish every epoxied surface on the boat – inside and out.

Apart and together, the lists looked forbidding, but the items were specific and mostly small compared with the comparative vastness of the sides and bottom of the hull. Moreover, partly as a relief from endless sanding, fairing and filling, I had taken time out over many months to refinish the masts, make the new main and fore hatches and the mast steps, refurbish the leeboards, cabin doors and boom gallows, and clean and polish the deck and cockpit hardware. As a result, I had a (relatively) flying start because most of the preparation and repair work had already been done.

———◆———

There may be people who can sustain enthusiasm for projects like this without sagging. I had periodically sagged throughout but I was now enjoying it more than ever before. Not to the point of whistling, singing or even humming while I worked – I never do that anyway. But I was finally having fun.

First because, whereas working on the hull I had not known how long things would take because I was doing virtually everything for the first time, I was now on relatively familiar ground, having spent seven years messing about on deck, in the cockpits and on the masts and was therefore doing things I thought were within my compass.

Second because I was back in the realm of what one of my staff at the World Bank used to call 'pointoutables', meaning things you could see and touch that had a direct bearing on appearance as well as functionality and fitness for purpose.

The bounce in my step in the winter of 2003/04 as I worked through the lists was accentuated by rumours that Georgie was planning to sell the marina and with it the shop. That meant I had to finish with all deliberate speed or at least reach a point at which *Mudlark* could be safely moved if the business was sold.

Rumours didn't exactly whirl through the alternately crisp and soggy air of Easton Point about who was going to buy the marina or when it would happen, although in March they acquired a new specificity that suggested they might be true. Then, one day in April, Georgie told me she had agreed to sell to a local automobile dealer who kept a brace of charter fishing boats at the yard. He began to appear from time to time, a short, slight figure with a penchant for black shirts and pale ties, usually accompanied by his charter captains and a couple of other employees. He never introduced himself or even spoke to me. And after I said hello to him and he ignored me I ignored him back.

When he took over in May nothing changed except that Georgie, with whom I had got on very well for nearly five years, was no longer there. It was not long before Larry, who seemed uncomfortable with the changes, said he was leaving too. I agreed to pay the new owner the same amount I had been paying Georgie but the mood altered. A succession of men who didn't seem to know or care about boats came and went. One afternoon I went across to the store for supplies and had to translate almost every term I used. Not one of the new crowd spoke a word of boat: 'What's antifouling? What's a shackle pin?'

It was time for me to go too because I cared neither for these people nor for the new scene and could not imagine leaving *Mudlark* in their care while I went to England. I had no idea why the car dealer had bought the marina but suspected it might not be because he loved boats. The rumour said his aim was to get planning consent to turn a potentially prime development site into something other than a marina, although there seemed little chance Talbot County would relinquish the adjoining public launch ramp and parking area. But that was not my problem. My problem was to find *Mudlark* a new home.

I looked around for alternatives. The boat was fit to be moved. The hull and interior were ready to paint and provided the epoxy coatings were not exposed to sunlight she could, if necessary, be stored outside under wraps while I was in England for the summer. After everything I'd done it would be worse than dreadful if ultraviolet rays were to destroy the epoxy I had so painfully faired and glazed.

It would of course be better to leave her inside, preferably somewhere I could paint her and do the final jobs before putting her back in the water in the fall. But this time I struck out. There was no available inside storage within striking distance. So she would have to stay outside. Oxford seemed the best option. I called Tommy Campbell to ask if he had room. He did, but only until October, when his boats would be hauled and he'd need the space back. But at least the problem was resolved for now.

———◆———

Jack's Point Boatyard, Oxford, MD, 15 June 2004

● We agreed to put her here rather than at Town Creek Boatyard, which is a stone's throw away, because there is more space at what used to be called Bates Yacht Basin but was recently renamed Jack's Point Boatyard when Tommy took over. It really makes no difference to me as long as she's safe for the summer.

I asked another Jack (Jack Morrison, who runs Gateway Marina, where I spent a year and a half rebuilding *Meadowlark*'s main bulkhead) to bring her down from Easton because he's one of the few people around with a hydraulic trailer to get *Mudlark* out of the shop (which was how she got in). It spat with rain on the way down but cleared up in the afternoon and I spent three hours wrapping her in new heavy-duty green tarps as though my life depended on it (which in a way it did).

———◆———

When I returned I briefly considered painting and varnishing *Mudlark* at Jack's Point but decided it would be harder working in the open than under cover, not least because it would be a great pain to keep covering and uncovering her. But I couldn't find anywhere inside. Then someone said that Jack Morrison might have space. Jack said I could put *Mudlark* in the ferry boat that sits at the edge of his yard at Trappe across the Choptank River from Cambridge, and that he'd truck her over from Jack's Point when I'm ready.

———————

Trappe, MD, September 2004

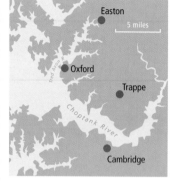

● I'm extremely relieved to have found inside storage within easy reach of Oxford, although I can't honestly say I prefer Trappe to Easton. And I certainly don't prefer Cambridge to Oxford. Not because of the English associations – which these days make me lean towards Oxford because I'm spending a lot of time organising the Emerging Markets Forum which will be held next year at Templeton College. But because, well, Cambridge is just less attractive.

By road, it's about 17 miles or half an hour from one to the other. By water, it depends on your boat. In May 2003 it took me about six hours to sail *Meadowlark* to Oxford from Cambridge because the winds were light and flukey and the old Seagull outboard refused to run in the well. With a good breeze it might have taken half that time. A fast motor boat could do it in under an hour.

The cultural distance between Oxford and Cambridge is much greater than the linear distance. It's true that the two places share some common history and that both have traditionally lived on and from the water. But whereas modern Cambridge is a rather shabby place with a struggling economy, Oxford is small, quiet and prosperous.

Oxford people often say the best thing about Oxford is that it's not St Michael's, meaning that unlike St Michael's – a larger town on the next peninsula – it's not full of shops with hand-carved, gilt-encrusted signs selling things people want but don't need; that unlike St Michael's it's not full of yuppies and muppies strutting their weekend stuff; that unlike St Michael's it's not full of flashy cars; and that unlike St Michael's it's not full of gawping tourists looking at the shops, yuppies, muppies and cars.

Meadowlark – our Columbia 21 fibreglass day sailer.

But the odd thing is, people in Oxford hardly ever mention Cambridge – and I imagine people in Cambridge might have little to say about Oxford.

I've agreed with Jack I'll rent space on what was the ferry's car deck from now through next spring. There, I'll paint the boat, install the engine (it's just sitting in the boat at the moment) and stern gear and then launch her and bring her down to Oxford.

Cam has signed up to help with the next phase. He was in at the beginning, has been back on the job from time to time, and it's fitting he should be here for what I hope will be the final phase. I'm really glad he's had a share in the project.

Before we can start painting we have a few other things to do. I have told Cam they won't take long. The hull is ready for paint but we still have to do some prep work on the cabintop and decks, prepare the transom for varnish and make good the rubbing strake (which I've decided to paint). I'd originally intended to re-varnish it but have decided it's too banged up and has too much filler, and that I can't correct the different profiles either side of the stern (it's faired to the stem at the bow). But the main problem is that the wood was never intended to be varnished. True, Bob varnished it – against his better judgment – during the initial refit in '93 and is against painting it now because he thinks it gives her more character. I'm going to paint it anyway.

There's also the matter of the waterline.

I knew *Mudlark* must be considerably lighter than when she went up to Easton Point in December 1999, partly because I'd removed the huge, heavy monel tanks (eventually offloading them to a scrap-metal dealer near Cambridge for much less than I'd expected, having persuaded myself monel was valuable) and partly because the once-saturated hull had dried out. True, I had used more than 100 gallons of cured epoxy and hardeners on the hull (minus what I had sanded off) thereby adding back some of the lost weight. But since the engine weighed the same as it had before it was rebuilt I was sure the net weight of the hull was lower than before restoration.

I was less sure how the changes would affect fore and aft balance. In the old days she had been bow-heavy because of all that water. But it seemed to me the net effect of removing the water and leaving the weight of the engine unchanged would be to reverse the balance, making her relatively stern-heavy. But by how much? And how would it affect the waterline?

The question wasn't new. Indeed, before stripping the hull I had carefully marked the scumline at stem and stern to provide reference points, ignoring the slightly wobbly painted waterline. From time to time since then I had used the reference points in casual efforts to join the marks with level lines. But what had been an occasional diversion in the Easton shop was now an urgent, practical issue because I was about to spend time and money on antifouling and topside paint and both had to begin and end somewhere.

A naval architect could have told me where to put the new waterline but it did not occur to me to ask one. Instead, I decided to use the old reference marks and to make a more serious effort to join them, realising the line would probably be too high (which meant there might be a lot of antifouling above the true waterline) and might go downhill from bow to stern (because of the new distribution of weight), and that I'd have to do it again after the boat had been floated and loaded.

The adjustable jackstands made it easy to get the reference marks equidistant from the shop floor at bow and stern. I wondered how I would have done that with the crude shims and props used in England.

To get the waterline I first tried Maynard Bray's technique of sighting along taut strings attached to sawhorses at either end of the boat (Spectre 1995), but not being sure I had a straight line, used a second (bucket and hose) method to check it with slightly different results. So I decided to use a remarkably cheap ($30) but perfectly good laser level from Sears for a third impression. Because the red laser line wasn't very bright this meant waiting until it was nearly dark inside the ferry, but I got what seemed to be a perfectly straight line and marked it with tape. *Moonfleet* has an incised waterline that was put there when she was built. Bob has told me how to do it and I've read several articles on it but I've found it impossible to control the hacksaw blade recommended for the job. Perhaps the problem is trying to score a line in hardened epoxy?

———————

Trappe, MD, December 2004

● Bob came by today to see how we're doing in our new quarters and told us he had known this old ferry boat when he was in the Navy and used to cross the Bay on her from Hampton Roads to the Eastern Shore. He says she was hauled out here

The old ferry boat at Trappe.

about ten years ago and was used as a bar and an antiques store before Jack bought her last year. It's a slightly funky place, quite dark inside with lots of broken glass and old furniture and fittings lying around. But it's not for long and she's far better off here than outside.

Well, I've finished painting and varnishing, and if I do say so myself she looks good. But these next-to-last steps – the last ones will be to install the engine and stern gear and rig the masts – have been unexpectedly painful.

You know how some people sometimes spend vast amounts of time over very long periods considering decisions they know they'll have to make and then the moment comes and they're still not sure what to do? I know people who spent many hours over nine or more months (some people start early) debating this or that name for an expected child and then their baby arrived and someone asked 'Name?' and they were still thinking about it.

———————

I've spent far more time than I should have – although I enjoyed it – thinking about colour schemes for *Mudlark*. Strangely, there seems little written on the subject of colour schemes for boats. Lots of good things on how to paint and varnish (e.g. Wittman 1990) But not much on which colours to use. I found an article by Maynard Bray (in Spectre 1995) but the schemes seemed too subtle and in some cases too complicated for my purposes. Even the scheme for a sharpie was less helpful than I'd hoped.

As far as I can tell, there's no software for simulating boat colour schemes. I know there is software for simulating car colours because I've spent hours playing with it. Surely it wouldn't be difficult to design something similar for boats, even if the hull forms were generic? Am I overestimating the potential market? Or could it be that some people are not very interested in colour schemes for boats? The disproportionate numbers of white plastic hulls in both the US and the UK suggest that may be so.

When I bought *Mudlark* she was white all over but I wanted a dark green hull with a red bottom, tan deck and off-white trim. Later, I would have painted *Moonfleet* (also sort-of-white all over when I bought her) in the same colours, but people in north Norfolk never paint boats green because they think it's unlucky. Not being superstitious I can't say that bothered me, but I didn't want to offend anyone and painted her topsides dark blue instead, and liked the result.

Having encapsulated the hull I decided, after hours of consultation with paint manufacturers, to use brushable two-part polyurethane paints. That meant the spray-only brands of polyurethane like Sterling and Awlgrip were out because I was not about to buy or hire spray equipment and in any case didn't like what I heard about icocyanates. So I decided to use Epifanes because they have better colours and more variety than Interlux and because while it would have been a

The first version of the paint job.

classic case of 'penny wise, pound foolish' to try to save money having spent so much already, Epifanes was significantly cheaper and I got an excellent deal at Hamilton Marine in Searsport.

There was actually another reason too because whereas Epifanes' technical people in Thomaston, Maine were extremely helpful, the Interlux people in New Jersey were condescending, even abrasive. Not just once but several times. Why, they asked, had I not used Interlux epoxy instead of WEST? And then as good as said I had made the wrong choice and that if I used Interlux paint over WEST and it didn't work out it would be my fault for having the wrong substrate!

Tempted as I was by Epifanes' very dark green polyurethanes – especially the one that was almost black from some angles (descriptively called 'Black Green') I knew Gougeon Brothers strongly advised against dark colours over epoxy and settled on 'Gray Tone' with 'Green' on the sheerstrake and waterline.

It was a failure because, even after all my efforts at simulation (using crude computer drawings and paper and coloured pencils) the grey was too cold while the green looked right on the sheerstrake but not (with grey above it) on the waterline. So I did it again in Epifanes cream polyurethane, which looked warmer and went better with the sheerstrake. Having epoxied the cabin sides and coamings I used cream polyurethane there too (having tried white and not liked it) and left the waterline green because it went well with cream topsides.

That left the deck and cabin top. In the pre-restoration era, when I spent so much time and money painting and repainting *Mudlark* as an alternative to doing something useful, I could not find the colour I wanted for the deck until I learned that Hamilton Marine in Searsport, Maine had done a deal with the Dutch paint manufacturer Epifanes to produce two old favourite colours that used to be made by Interlux. One was 'Miami Tan' – described by Peter Spectre (1999) as a 'noble colour'. The other was 'Oregon Buff'. And 'Miami Tan' had been exactly what I wanted for my deck. A few gallons of it were wasted on the abortive paint job in 1999 but the eventual result was good

Now I was doing it again I knew 'Miami Tan' (now renamed 'Downeast Tan' – 'Oregon Buff' had become 'Classic Buff') was a bit dark but I loved the colour and it had held up well when I used it before. Having been impressed by Peter Spectre's comments on the traditional marine paints made by the Kirby firm in New Bedford, Massachusetts, a subsequent conversation with Mr Kirby himself and the transparent honesty of the website declaration that online colour reproductions were 'inexact', I was tempted to use one of Kirby's 'topside and deck' paints. But none of the available colours was quite what I wanted and I eventually opted to stay with 'Downeast Tan' on the deck and used 'Classic Buff' on the cabin top, engine compartment covers, cockpit seats and cockpit soles – figuring that if I didn't like the effect I could always ask Mr Kirby for custom colours at a later stage.

I clear-coated the mahogany trim on the cabin and coamings, which had to be done from scratch, using WEST 207 special hardener, which is designed for this purpose, and finished with Epifanes two-part Polyurethane Clear Gloss over the hardened epoxy. I was pleased with the immediate result but also nervous, having learned from experience that time is the only real test of brightwork. But I had also learned it pays to add extra coats and laid on four rather than the minimum recommended two.

Without having set out to do so I thus ended up with an all-Epifanes boat. Not because I had a prior attachment to their products (I had tried their varnishes but other than that had only used Miami Tan) but because they had what I wanted.

Having previously epoxied the masts and spars I decided not to strip them again to bare wood. Instead I removed the remaining varnish and then recoated with three wet-on-wet layers of epoxy and finished with three coats of two-part Epifanes clear polyurethane.

Then it was time for Christmas in England.

January to July 2005

This should have been the final episode, ending with a triumphant splash as *Mudlark* returned to her natural habitat and arrived a few hours later at Town Creek after an absence of five and a half years. It didn't work out like that, because a house and another car rally intervened.

The house was our home of 27 years in McLean, Virginia, in which, like many couples at our age and stage, we had been rattling around since Cameron had gone to St Andrew's four years earlier, our three daughters having already shipped out to British boarding schools and universities.

It had been many years since all the bedrooms had been used simultaneously. The exercise room was clean but unvisited. The garden was a scene of neglect and betrayal. True, all the other rooms in the house, including both studies, were used, but we truly didn't need all that space and with all our children and three grandchildren in Britain and more likely than not to stay there, it was time for us to move on.

Inertia prevailed until we were invited to join a group of friends in an overland drive from London to Sydney in the fall of 2005. That prompted three decisions. One, we would go. Two, Glynis would retire from the Washington International School. Three, since we would no longer need to live in Washington we would sell the house.

We had not sold a house in the USA since our first home in McLean had been sold in our absence in South America in 1978. So we had never been through the process that began in January 2005 – for which, despite having listened to friends talk about what they had been through, we were quite unprepared.

Soon after we returned to McLean after Christmas a realtor called to assess the value of our property, tell us how to plan for the sale and explain that if we wanted to sell it well – we had a very saleable house in what realtors (and English estate agents) like to describe as a 'sought-after area' – we would be well advised to take her advice.

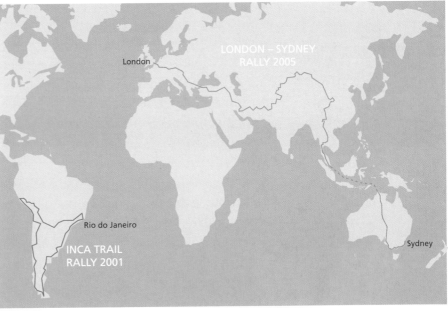

The routes of the 2001 Inca Trail and the 2005 London – Sydney rallies, each of which played a part in interrupting work on *Mudlark*.

I tend to bridle at strong-arm sales talk and my initial thought was to suggest the realtor get lost. But something told me I had better listen carefully because she knew her business and had an impressive record. So we listened. And once the initial shock wore off – it never quite left us until we handed over the keys in June – settled in to a mammoth restoration programme that in less than three months saw every inch of the house, inside and out, repainted, every room recarpeted, every bathroom rebuilt, the kitchen renewed and the plumbing, lighting and landscape redone.

It was a horrendous experience – far worse than restoring *Mudlark* – and by

the time our rollercoaster ride on the Washington real-estate market was over we were exhausted. Virtually all the work was done by professionals. My initial boasts ('I'll take care of that', 'I'll do the plumbing', 'Leave the painting to me') crumbled in the face of humiliating reality that peaked when some work I had done myself on the deck in the back yard had to be professionally re-done after it failed a state inspection because I had not realised the building code had changed. But I did a reasonable job as project manager; the painters and decorators, plumbers, electricians and landscapers did excellent work; and the realtor did a brilliant sales job. Most important, the house was ready in time for the big spring sales event when Washington houses, surrounded by azaleas and daffodils, look their best. It sold in one day for more than the asking price.

Why am I telling you this? Because it explains why *Mudlark* and I were not very intimate in the spring of 2005. We saw each other occasionally when I got down to Oxford on weekends and odd days. But it's hard to sustain a relationship when you don't see each other much and there's a significant distance between you.

Despite this I could have made some progress, but the original plan of a spring launch was knocked firmly on the head as we came to terms with the fact it was not just a matter of selling the family house. There were other questions: could we fit the contents of our family house into the Oxford house in addition to what was already there? No. Should we sell the Oxford house and buy a bigger one? No (we liked Oxford, there were very few other suitable houses in town, we didn't want to move to another village, and we didn't want a house up a creek). So should we expand the Oxford house? Yes. And meanwhile put our stuff in storage, get permission to expand the house as much as possible within the strict laws that govern the Oxford Historic District, and arrange to have the work done while we were travelling to Australia.

So in the spring of 2005 we were busy selling one house, preparing to expand another and getting ready for the rally, and it all took time that would otherwise have been spent on *Mudlark*. Once we had put most of our belongings in storage and moved ourselves to Maryland in June there were just a few weeks before we were off to England and another magical mystery tour. The final tasks of reinstalling the masts and rigging and stern gear, re-launching at Gateway and powering down the Choptank to the Tred Avon and Town Creek would have to wait until the following spring.

August to December 2005

It would in any case have been silly to leave *Mudlark* at our dock while we drove to Sydney by way of Europe, Turkey, Iran, Pakistan, China, the Malay Peninsula and Singapore. So she spent the rest of 2005 patiently waiting for me where I left her in a dry, protected, gloomy car deck, perhaps a bit chilly – although it was an unusually mild winter – and quite safe.

Meanwhile the rally – fifteen vehicles including twelve pre-1970 classics (the oldest a 1957 Jaguar XK140) and three 4×4s (including our Hyundai) – left London on 14 August and reached Sydney three and a half months later. Considering what might have gone wrong, nothing did; nobody was injured, all but one of the cars (a last-day smash) made it to the end and the potential risks – political violence, common banditry, landslides – came to naught – well, almost naught.

We met again briefly in December when we passed through Oxford on our way to England from Australia. All was well, as it was when we checked again on our next visit in January. In the following weeks, as I sat writing this book at the end of my gantry overlooking Wells Harbour, I picked up the phone from time to time to call Gateway and ask if she was alright. They always guessed she was – what, after all, could have happened to her? The ferry wasn't going anywhere.

Last act

We returned to Oxford on 21 April 2006 and spent the next four months settling in to what was in effect a new house and getting *Mudlark* ready to launch. The main tasks on the boat were to install new wiring and reinstall the cooling and fuel systems for the engine. That took far more time and effort and induced far more frustration than I had anticipated but it eventually got done.

But having confirmed our previous experience that Norfolk in winter is a good time and place to write, walk, eat and drink (and think about boats), it was while thinking about boats that I decided I must take care of just one more thing – lee helm.

Among my many imaginary conversations with *Mudlark*'s Ghosts, the most taxing ones had been conversations with Fenwick Williams about why, at Horvath's request, he had changed Meadow Lark's sail plan but had left the hull, including the position of the leeboards, exactly as LFH had drawn it – and them.

I had the advantage of knowing that with Williams's rig and LFH's leeboards, *Mudlark* carried lee helm and that in anything less than a good breeze or under a small headsail she would not reliably go through the wind. I found it hard to believe Williams had not realised that the significant gap between the CE and the CLR would result in lee helm or that his (apparent) solution of a club-footed jib to go upwind and a genoa to go downwind was, at best, awkward. As things stood I was planning to re-launch *Mudlark* without curing the problem, and I had a nagging feeling that would be a mistake. The question was, could I correct it?

I had already raked the masts as far aft as I could. I knew I didn't want to cure the problem by restricting sailing to days with relatively strong breezes when *Mudlark*'s tendency to miss stays was less pronounced. I knew that getting everyone on board to move aft when going about was, at best, inconvenient. I knew that pirouetting on the trailing edge of the leeboard while hanging on to the leeward shroud to kick the board down and forward (thus moving the CLR in the direction of the CE) was a crude, even suicidal, approach. I knew that running

lines from the leading edges of the leeboards through toerail blocks to the cockpit didn't work unless it was done very quickly because the leeward (working) board immediately came under so much lateral pressure it was harder to move it that way than by jumping on it.

In short I saw no solution, and was resigned to living with lee helm as I had done until now and as my predecessors had done through the forty years they had owned her.

Then one morning in February I drove to the Broads village of Coltishall for a conversation with naval architect Andrew Wolstenholme, the designer of Charlie Ward's *Juno*. He looked at the original and modified construction plans and sail plans. He agreed with my assessment of the lee-helm problem and shared my perplexity about why Williams had had not anticipated it or, if he had anticipated it, had sought to resolve it by relying on alternating headsails. But then he said, 'You know you could get rid of lee helm by moving the leeboards.'

As we talked, Andrew said the next most extraordinary thing after the really extraordinary thing (that Williams had designed lee helm into the boat) was that nobody had thought of moving the leeboards before. When structural deformities are discovered in human beings – usually in childhood – then, at least in wealthy countries, corrective surgeries are routinely undertaken to cure them. Most such surgeries are far more complicated and have less certain outcomes than the corrective surgery needed in this case.

He said the changes he had in mind involved new oak supports to take the weight of the leeboards, new holes through the sheerstrake for the leeboard bolts, new bushings, and re-reeving the leeboard tackle. He also said the efficiency of the hydrofoil sectioned leeboards would improve because their new positions would yield a slightly improved angle of attack and would thus give improved lift.

So there was a way forward. The only issue was whether I should make the changes before re-launching *Mudlark* or wait until the next time I hauled her. In the end I decided to wait because once I was back in Maryland I realised it would take me some time to do a good job (I work slowly) of fashioning the oak supports that would be critical to the success of the repositioning project, and that it would be a job best done the following winter.

———————————◆———————————

Oxford, MD, 31 August 2006

● *Mudlark* was launched today at Gateway but I didn't take her back to Oxford because I am returning to Norfolk tomorrow and have decided it's safer to leave her at the yard until I can sail round with Glynis and Cameron and Pete Dunbar when we get back at the end of September. But she sparkled in the new paint, which saw strong light for the first time yesterday when she was pulled out of the old ferry – and if I do say so myself she looked quite good.

The Ghosts were there, of course, probably wondering what had taken me so long – or perhaps why I had bothered to spend so much time and not a little money fixing what is, when all is said and done, still an old – indeed older – boat. But there were no harsh words from them or me, and I think we have at last come to terms with each other. Although I have, at times over the last six years, cursed each of them roundly, I now think of them as good guys – and good ghosts.

Although *Mudlark* is finished she will forever be a work in progress because there will always be something to improve. I already know that over the winter I shall be making the oak supports that will allow me to move the leeboards forward as Andrew Wolstenholme suggested. And I know that once I've done that there will be other things.

The launch.

But the joyful prospect is that, six years after I began what turned out to be a very different project than I expected, Glynis and I now have a well-found, simple boat that is fit for our purposes. After some shakedown cruises we plan to circumnavigate the Delmarva Peninsula and then explore the Intracoastal Waterway. A cruising boat is after all a means to an end. Our ends are some modest voyages.

Some technical terms

Butt block

Wooden block used as backing for butt joints in hull planking.

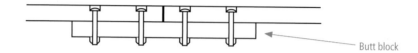

Butt block

Butt joint

Method of joining planks end-to-end (inherently weak without butt block).

Chine

The angle between planks – typically the sides and the bottom – in a boat whose cross-section is angular. When the angle is sharp, it is a 'hard chine'.

Chine log

Chine log

Chineboard

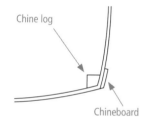

Longitudinal piece of wood, usually notched in to frames, to which the outboard bottom plank and lowest side plank are fastened in a hard-chine hull.

Chineboard

External wooden plank sometimes used (e.g. on *Mudlark*) to reinforce the bottom/side joint in a hard-chine hull (in the case of *Mudlark* originally used only on the side of the hull but during restoration modified to include overlapping bottom and side sections).

Cross-keelson

Cross-keelson

Keelson

Keel

Bottom boards

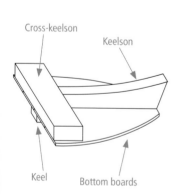

Crosswise timber above the keelson, giving strength near the bow of a boat.

Deadwood

On *Mudlark* the deadwood is a wooden keel extending aft of the lead keel.

Flare

Concave outboard curve of hull below deck level.

Frames

The 'ribs' of a boat, to which the hull planking is fastened.

Hood end

End of plank where joined to stem and transom.

Keelson

In general, a keelson is a strong longitudinal timber on the centreline fastened to the central bottom plank directly above the weighted keel, which is usually lead or iron. The Meadow Lark design has only a partial keelson in the bow section.

Leeboards

Boards attached to each side of boat. They may be wood or metal, usually pivoting on a universal joint (allowing the leeboards to swing sideways as well as up and down) from a point near or forward of midships. They serve the same function as a centreboard or daggerboard but are on the side of the boat. Except when close tacking only the leeward board is lowered to provide lateral resistance to the water and thus reduce sideways drift.

Quant

Long pole, usually with a ball-shaped end (to reduce the chance of getting it stuck in muddy bottoms), traditionally used on the Norfolk Broads to move wherries when the wind fails. Also used on traditional Dutch sailing craft, including *Matilda*.

Rocker

Fore-and-aft curvature of hull bottom.

Scarf joint

Method of joining boards by mating surfaces at acute complementary angles to increase surface area for glue/fastenings.

Strake

Longitudinal plank in hull. The 'sheerstrake' is the topmost plank, defining visual sheer of hull.

Stringer

Longitudinal light strip of wood let in to frames to help maintain alignment and rigidity of hull.

Trunnel

Wooden peg used to fasten planking to frames (derived from 'tree nail').

Tumblehome

Hull form in which maximum beam (usually in stern section) is below deck level.

Bibliography

Baldwin, James. *The Wonder Book of Horses*. Century, 1905.

Bolger, Philip C. L Francis Herreshoff. *WoodenBoat* 55 (Nov/Dec 1983); 56 (Jan/Feb 1984).

Chappelle, Howard I. *American Sailing Craft*. Crown, 1939.

Chappelle, Howard I. *Boatbuilding*. Norton, 1941.

Gougeon Brothers. *Wooden Boat Restoration and Repair*. Gougeon Brothers, 2000

Herreshoff, L Francis *Capt. Nat Herreshoff: The Wizard of Bristol*. Sheridan House, 1953.

Herreshoff, L Francis. *The Compleat Cruiser*. Sheridan House, 1956.

Herreshoff, L Francis. *Sensible Cruising Designs*. International Marine, 1973.

Hounshell, David A. Ford Eagle Boats and mass production during World War I. In M R Smith (ed.), *Military Enterprise and Technological Change*. MIT Press, 1987.

McClave, Ed. A close look at wood screws, part II. *WoodenBoat* 53 (Nov/Dec 1983).

McGuane, Thomas. A bird for thin water. *WoodenBoat* 38 (Jan/Feb 1981).

McIntosh, David. *How to Build a Wooden Boat*. WoodenBoat Books, 1988.

Nakashima, George. *The Soul of a Tree*. Kodansha America, 1981.

Parker, Reuel. *The Sharpie Book*. International Marine, 1993.

Peterson, Bill and Bauer, Fred. Fenwick Cushing Williams, naval architect. *WoodenBoat* 56 (Jan/Feb 1984).

Pye, David. *The Nature and Art of Workmanship*. Cambridge University Press, 1968.

Ruhlman, Michael. *Wooden Boats*. Penguin, 2001.

Scott, Ian. The Sharpie: Olympic class. *Classic Boat*, April 1999.

Spectre, Peter (ed.). *Painting and Varnishing*. WoodenBoat Books, 1995.

Spectre, Peter (ed.). *Frame, Stem and Keel Repair*. WoodenBoat Books, 1996.

Spectre, Peter. On the waterfront. *WoodenBoat* 150 (Sept/Oct 1999).

Spectre, Peter and Bray, Maynard (eds.). *Planking and Fastening.* WoodenBoat Books, 1996.

Starr, William J. Thomas Clapham: an appreciation. *Yachting*, December 1915.

Taylor, Roger. Introduction to *Sensible Cruising Designs*, L Francis Herreshoff. International Marine, 1973.

Thoreau, Henry David. *Walden: or A life in the Woods.* Ticknor and Fields, 1854.

Trefethen, Jim. *Wooden Boat Renovation: New Life for Old Boats Using Modern Methods.* International Marine, 1993.

Wittman, Rebecca. *Brightwork: the Art of Finishing Wood.* International Marine, 1990.

Ian Scott

Ian Scott retired as a Director of the World Bank in 1996 and now divides his time between academia, consulting, long-distance driving and messing about in (mostly) wooden boats. He has written three previous books and edited another, has contributed chapters to three more and has written numerous articles, columns and reports on economic development, urbanisation, management, organisation, knowledge, classic boats and American politics. He lives on the north Norfolk coast in England and on the Chesapeake Bay in the USA.

JOSEPH CONRAD: MASTER MARINER

PETER VILLIERS

Before he published his first novel in 1895, Joseph Conrad spent 20 years in the merchant navy, eventually obtaining his master's ticket and commanding the barque

Otago. This book, superbly illustrated with paintings by Mark Myers, traces his sea-career and shows how Konrad Korzeniowski, master mariner, became Joseph Conrad, master novelist. Alan Villiers, world-renowned author and master mariner under sail, was uniquely qualified to comment on Conrad's life at sea, and the study he began has been completed by his son, Peter Villiers.

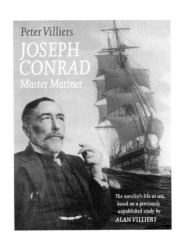

'A book that finally does justice to Conrad's time at sea'
Traditional Boats and Tall Ships

Illustrated with 12 paintings in full colour by Mark Myers RSMA F/ASMA

UK ISBN 0-9547062-9-3   USA ISBN 1-57409-244-8

CRUISE OF THE CONRAD

A Journal of a Voyage round the World, undertaken and carried out in the Ship JOSEPH CONRAD, 212 Tons, in the Years 1934, 1935, and 1936 by way of Good Hope, the South Seas, the East Indies, and Cape Horn

ALAN VILLIERS

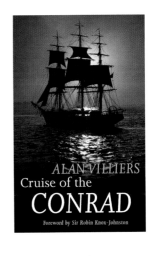

In 1934 the Australian sailor and writer Alan Villiers set out to fulfil his life's ambition – to obtain, equip and sail a full-rigged ship around the world, and enthuse others with his own love of sail before the opportunity was lost for ever. He was successful. His record of that extraordinary journey, more odyssey than voyage, was first published in 1937. In this new edition, complete with a short biography of Alan Villiers and richly illustrated with his own photographs, it will inspire a new generation of sailors and sea-enthusiasts.

'No other book like this will ever be written'
The Sunday Times

With a foreword by Sir Robin Knox-Johnston • Illustrated with photographs

UK ISBN 0-9547062-8-5   USA ISBN 1-57409-241-3

THE MARINER'S BOOK OF DAYS

PETER H SPECTRE

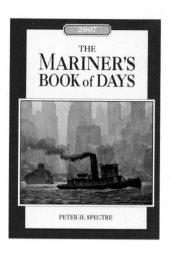

Published annually since 1991, *The Mariner's Book of Days* is an ever-growing encyclopedia of nautical fact, fiction, and folklore, and has been hailed as the best, most entertaining nautical desk diary and calendar to see print. An invaluable reference, each annual edition is completely different from its predecessors, and all have become collector's items. On every right-hand page is a week of days, with the nautical significance of each explored in brief by the author. On each left-hand page is a collection of nautical miscellany evoking the rich traditions of the sea. Entertaining and informative, illustrated with a variety of lovely etchings, engravings, sketches, and watercolors, *The Mariner's Book of Days* takes readers on a 365-day voyage through history.

'A keeper well after the year is over and done'

> *Sailing* Magazine

2007 edition: ISBN 1-57409-226-x

A MARINER'S MISCELLANY

PETER H SPECTRE

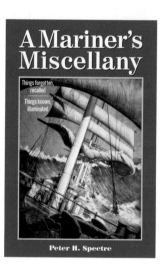

A wonderful amalgam of practical information about boats, anchors, rope, and ballast, cheek by jowl with poetry, legend, lore, superstitions, language of the sea, art, thoughts about literature, and more. Spectre's unique reverence for boats and literature of the sea, and his many years as an editor of *WoodenBoat* Magazine, make this book a rich collection of maritime knowledge, and an intriguing reference work of sailor's lore. Spectre is more than the editor of this book; he writes with deep knowledge about the topics covered, and presents many worthwhile facts about clipper ships, rowing boats, seasick remedies, superstitions, navigational lore, and much more. The book is intended to pay homage to the writers and editors that have inspired Spectre over the years, in the hope that its contents will carry new sailors and readers to what William McFee calls 'harbors of memory,' and C G Davis calls 'the ways of the sea'.

'To read this book is akin to opening a box of treasures. There is at once an instant recall, memories rekindled, expressions and words long forgotten, poems, ditties, flag signals, nautical advice, even the smells of long forgotten meals. They are all there and so much more ... Highly recommended.'

> *Sea Breezes* Magazine

Illustrated

UK ISBN 0-9542762-1-8   USA ISBN 1-57409-195-6

THE WAPPING GROUP OF ARTISTS

Sixty years of painting by the Thames

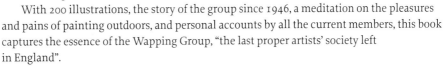

For sixty years, members of the Wapping Group have met to paint by the River Thames en plein air. Outdoors and undaunted in all weathers, come rain or shine, they have set up their easels from the broad tideways of the estuary to the willow-fringed backwaters up-river – taking in the whole of riverside London in between.

With 200 illustrations, the story of the group since 1946, a meditation on the pleasures and pains of painting outdoors, and personal accounts by all the current members, this book captures the essence of the Wapping Group, "the last proper artists' society left in England".

'... a delight to the senses and an essential new addition for any bookshelf'

E14 Magazine

'Sixty years after it was created, the Wapping Group is still flourishing and has won itself a secure niche in the artistic life of the capital ...'

Classic Boat

UK ISBN 0-9547062-5-0   USA ISBN 1-57409-218-9

WITH A PINCH OF SALT

A collection of nautical expressions and other stories

as interpreted by

CAPTAIN NICK BATES

Are you **clewed-up** about all those expressions that so enrich the language of sailors – not to mention the landlubbers who have **Shanghaied** their vocabulary? Do you know **Captain Setab's Second Law of Dynamics**, or why **timbers shiver**, even in **horse latitudes**, where a **brass monkey** has nothing to fear? This little book, **chock-a-block** with the wit and wisdom of a Captain who **came up through the hawse pipe** to command one of the most famous vessels afloat, gives you **the whole nine yards**.

'... a nice piece of work ... remember it when Christmas comes'
    Telegraph [NUMAST magazine]

UK ISBN 0-9547062-3-4   USA ISBN 1-57409-227-8

ROUGH PASSAGE
COMMANDER R D GRAHAM

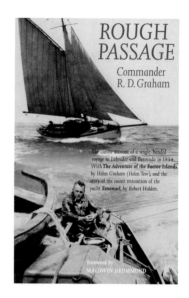

In 1934 Commander R D Graham sailed alone in his 30-foot yacht *Emanuel* from England to Newfoundland, cruised on the coast of Labrador, fell ill, sailed to Bermuda in November ('twenty-three days of uninterrupted misery'), wintered there, and finally brought his little vessel back across the Atlantic to her old moorings in Poole Harbour.

Also included is *The Adventure of the Faeroe Islands*, an account of *Emanuel*'s 1929 voyage by R D Graham's daughter Helen (later Helen Tew).

Illustrated with original photographs, this new edition of the seafaring classic is brought up to date by Robert Holden's account of the recent restoration of *Emanuel*, allowing R D Graham's 'little yacht' to take her rightful place as part of Britain's maritime heritage.

A must-read for anyone with the slightest interest in the sea, or in human nature.

'One of the most remarkable small-boat adventures of this or any other time'
> *Arthur Ransome*

One of the 'great cruising accounts' listed in Peter Spectre's *A Mariner's Miscellany*

UK ISBN 0-9547062-4-2   USA ISBN 1-57409-212-x

LAST VOYAGE OF THE *LUCETTE*
DOUGLAS ROBERTSON

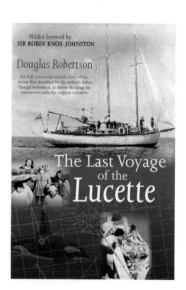

On board their 43-foot schooner *Lucette*, the Robertson family set sail from the south of England in January 1971. Eighteen months out, in the middle of the Pacific, *Lucette* was holed by killer whales and sank. Four adults and two children survived the next 38 days adrift, first in a rubber life raft, then crammed into a 9-foot fibreglass dinghy, before being rescued by a passing Japanese fishing vessel.

This is a vivid and candid account of how they survived, but also of the delights, hardships, dangers and the emotional highs and lows they experienced, both before and after the shipwreck.

Douglas Robertson has taken his father's classic book, *Survive the Savage Sea*, as his starting point, but drawn upon his own memories of a life-changing experience.

With a foreword by Sir Robin Knox-Johnston.

'You'll be spellbound ...'
> *The Ensign*

'A fantastic read and thoroughly recommended'
> *The Nautical Magazine*

UK ISBN 0-9542750-8-x   USA ISBN 1-57409-206-5